Hieroglyphs and the Afterlife in Ancient Egypt

Detail from the funerary papyrus of a man named Nebqed, showing him offering to the god of the dead, Osiris. Early to mid–18th Dynasty, *c.*1400 BC.

Hieroglyphs and the Afterlife in Ancient Egypt

WERNER FORMAN and STEPHEN QUIRKE

UNIVERSITY OF OKLAHOMA PRESS

Norman

Photographs © 1996 Werner Forman
Text © 1996 Stephen G. J. Quirke
© 1996 Opus Publishing Limited

Published by the University of Oklahoma Press, Norman,
Publishing Division of the University, by special arrangement with
Opus Publishing Limited, London, England.

1 2 3 4 5 6 7 8 9 10

Library of Congress Cataloging-in-Publication Data

Forman, Werner, 1921–
   Hieroglyphs and the afterlife in ancient Egypt / Werner Forman
     and Stephen Quirke
       p.   cm.
   Includes bibliographical references and index
   ISBN 0–8061–2751–1 (alk. paper)
   1. Egyptian literature—History and criticism. 2. Funeral rites
and ceremonies—Egypt. 3. Egyptian language—Writing,
Hieroglyphic. 4. Future life.
   I. Quirke, Stephen. II. Title.
PJ1487.F67 1996
893′.1—dc20   95–45424
                                       CIP

This book was designed and produced by
OPUS PUBLISHING LIMITED
36 Camden Square, London NW1 9XA

Filmset in Bembo by SX Composing Limited, Rayleigh, Essex
Illustration films by Radstock Reproductions Limited, Midsomer Norton, Somerset
Printed by Jarrold Book Printing Limited, Thetford, Norfolk

Page 1   Glassy faience inlay in the shape of the hieroglyph for
the 'horizon', showing the sun rising between two mountains.
Ptolemaic or early Roman, *c.* 3rd century BC–1st century AD.

Contents

CHAPTER 1

Hieroglyphic Script and Art

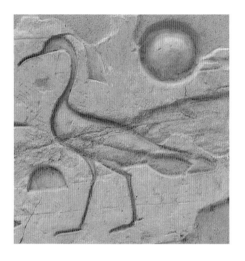

Left   The god Thoth, patron of writing and scribal wisdom, is shown here as striding man with ibis head. Wooden figure with traces of gilt and resinous coating; head bronze. Late Period, *c.*600 BC

Above   The hieroglyph depicting the crested ibis was used to write words derived from the root *akh*, uniting the concepts of light and power. Luxor, 19th Dynasty, *c.*1250 BC.

THE accidents of survival have privileged one particular family of texts from ancient Egypt, those placed in the dry tombs and chapels of the cemeteries along the Saharan desert edge of the Nile Valley. Hundreds of papyri, hundreds more chapels and burial chambers preserve the words with which the ancient Egyptian elite aspired to live forever. The full forms of Egyptian hieroglyphs were never intended for daily usage, where cursive shorthands evolved for the vast archives of law, accountancy and for the libraries of literature which have all but entirely disappeared in the history of Egyptian towns or the damper soil of the Valley and Delta. Instead they aim invariably at the horizon of eternity, preferably using the most durable materials, stone and gold, obtained from the same deserts that would preserve the bodies of the dead. The terrain of the hieroglyph can only be a sacred terrain; they are confined to tomb and temple, with the rare exception of ceremonial doorways or pillars in the grandest houses of the living. Every hieroglyph belongs to an everlasting world, but some texts form an inner core in which the endeavour to outlast eternity reaches its most self-conscious. This inner core spells out the precise phrasing by which a dead person could be made into an eternally rejuvenated being. Today we call these ancient texts funerary literature, but this technical term does them little justice; these are texts to transfigure the dead, to make human beings into immortal gods.

The ancient Egyptians themselves often used the term *sakhu*, meaning recitations that would turn a person after death into an *akh* a 'transfigured spirit'. The only alternative was to die and remain *mut* 'dead'. These opposites of *akh* and *mut* are roughly equivalent to the European contrast between the blessed dead and the damned. As in European tradition, paradise is envisaged in terms of light, and the word *akh* itself is one of a group in which the idea of light and radiance is paramount, such as the Egyptian for 'horizon', *akhet*, the home of light. Faced with the alternative, the Egyptians concentrated all their resources into securing this eternal

radiance. They found in the natural world two dominant patterns offering hope of surviving death alive, the daily rebirth of the sun, and the annual renewal of plant life in the earth. Both find expression in a series of episodes relating the stories of Ra the sun-god and Osiris the god of the blessed dead, known to us largely from the texts of transfiguration of the dead.

In the beginning the Egyptian world was a void called Nun, an expanse as undefined and undifferentiated as the waters. The germ of life within the void took shape out of the void, just as young plant life grew every year on the silt that rose from the sinking floodwaters of the Nile in summer, and birds appeared perched on the first solid earth above the flood. Life and Goodness were the twin spirits of this first life, which was identified by the Egyptians as the natural source of energy, light and warmth, the sun, in Egyptian *ra*. Out of this original matter, also called Atum 'the all' or 'undifferentiated', a first fissioning produced as if 'son' and 'daughter' of the sun a male and female principle, the male being Shu, the dry air, and the female being Tefnet, the moist. This first couple then produced a second, the earth-god Geb and the sky-goddess Nut. These were

The daily birth of the sun is depicted on this Late Period sarcophagus as a scarab beetle lifting up the solar disk out of the horizon of night, with primeval forces of nothingness on either side, here the male and female forms of non-solidity (the watery Nun and Nunet) and of unlimitedness (Heh and Hehet), without special attributes but identified by their names. 30th Dynasty, *c*.350 BC.

kept apart by Shu, the air, but won through Thoth, god of wisdom, time to unite and yield a fourth generation of two gods, the good Osiris and the anarchic Seth, and two goddesses, Isis as sister-wife to Osiris and Nephthys as sister-wife to Seth. After rebellion by humankind, the creator Ra withdrew to heaven, and the kingship on earth passed from Shu to Geb to the perfect Osiris. In jealousy Seth slew his brother, but Isis revived him through her healing power to bear a son Horus. Mirroring the move of Ra, Osiris descended to the underworld to rule the dead, while Isis nurtured Horus until old enough to challenge Seth and win back the kingship.

Every one of these episodes comes to life in the fate of each person after death. Egyptian religion is largely a solar religion, and the daily rebirth of the sun offered each man and woman the promise of merging with the sun, joining his retinue, and being swept into an eternal cycle of resurrection. When the dead body was split open for the necessary removal of soft organs in mummification, the action was equated with the blow struck Osiris by Seth, and the Greek historians relate that the man who had to cut the body open was then ritually chased away by the other embalmers who pelted him with stones. In the same rites the survival of Osiris gave the hope that even the most horrific death might be overcome, and each deceased person came to take the name Osiris before his or her name, not merely to affirm their piety but to assert the achievement of immortality. The triumph of Horus, declared 'true of voice' in his legal battle with Seth, became similarly the hallmark of a triumph over death, whereby the name of each deceased man and woman was followed by the phrase 'true of voice', 'justified', specifically declared by the tribunal to be free from evil.

Coffins and papyri of the tenth century and later depict the world as a group of deities, with Nut arched as the sky over the body of Geb, the earth. Above the sun-god is depicted circuiting his creation with three hieroglyphs *nefer* 'good' to denote divine harmony. 21st Dynasty, *c*.950 BC.

In the fight for life the Egyptian gods and goddesses become intimately involved in the fate of the deceased and join the array of resources at his or her disposal. Ra, Osiris and Horus stand with, and for, the deceased, in their complex strategy to become a transfigured spirit. Alongside these divine persons a no less prominent place belongs to one of the most remarkable inventions of ancient Egypt, the hieroglyphs, a perfect fusion of art and language.

The Egyptian term for hieroglyphs is 'words of god', a phrase that insists upon the unity of speech and script, of the words that we write with the words that we speak, and implicitly with the objects that those words denote. In the Egyptian view, words do much more than represent a meaning agreed upon by the community. They embody the essence of their object. For example, the word 'hippopotamus' does not merely identify an animal species; rather, it reveals the very essence of 'hippopotamus' as a god-given object within the divine order of creation. Each word carries a profound knowledge of its object, and a measure of power over it.

The Egyptian equivalent of the encyclopaedia contains no definitions of words in some alphabetic order, but a list of names grouped according to type. Surviving examples, mainly of the eleventh to eighth centuries BC, extend over cosmic divisions and types of divine and human beings to names of cities, fauna, flora, foodstuffs and, in at least one case, clothing, pottery and other man-made products. The headings to these namelists promise to confer upon the reader a comprehensive knowledge of his world. Words bestow a knowledge that in turn implies power, and this sacred and potent domain falls under the patronage of Thoth, embracing all compendia of wisdom from texts of healing to mathematical handbooks. By the same view of the world, knowledge is received, not invented, and not all knowledge can be acquired by human beings, or even by gods, for all knowledge would amount to the universal power that is the Lord of creation.

This god-given immutable order so perfectly expressed in Egyptian art and texts did arise in a specific time and place, the thirty-second century BC in the Egyptian Nile valley. The mystery of the emergence of hieroglyphic writing in Egypt is as intriguing as its beauty and, a point often overlooked, its efficiency in conveying the ancient Egyptian language.

Late fourth millennium BC pottery includes a range of buff-coloured ware decorated in deep purple with motifs of men, animals, birds, boats and mountains. These echoes of a prehistoric civilization survive for us in burials; the towns and so the society that created them appear to have been obliterated from the record, leaving the tombs alone to provide a partial view. Among the motifs on tomb pottery we encounter several that anticipate hieroglyphs on the later Pharaonic monuments. Around the boats river waters may be depicted as zigzag lines, resembling the zigzag hieroglyph used to write *n* (from Nun 'the primeval waters' or a related

This Early Dynastic stone vessel already encapsulates the purpose of hieroglyphs in sustaining cult. The arms outstretched to receive food form the hieroglyph *ka* 'spirit of sustenance', and embrace the bowl where the food would be placed for the dead, itself in the shape of the looped cross, the hieroglyph *ankh* 'life'.

Right The goddess Seshat, personification of 'Writing', shown in the act of inscribing the palmleaf rib which denotes the word *renpet* 'year' in the hieroglyphic script. Luxor, 19th Dynasty, *c.*1250 BC.

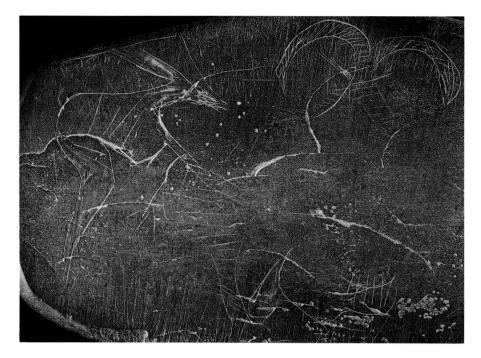

word) or in triplicate to write *mu* 'water'. Above appear rows of triangles joined together like the rounder forms of the double hump hieroglyph *dju* 'mountain' or the triple hump hieroglyph for *khaset* 'desert hills' and the foreign lands beyond the mountainous Saharan horizon of the Nile valley. These occasional motifs occur disconnected as figurative elements in pictorial compositions.

Without warning, the use of signs changes. This happens at the same time that a separate lifestyle in parts of the Nile Delta to the north disappears under the ceramic and material traditions of the Nile valley to the south. The disjointed symbols of prehistoric pottery now suddenly fall out of their figural compositions into a new framework where sound achieves equal status with sight, where the meaning and hearing of words finds articulate expression. The idea for such a system, for a script, develops apparently a little earlier in Mesopotamia, although there too the record of this fourth millennium revolution remains confined to an extremely small body of evidence.

Although Mesopotamian writing probably appeared earlier than Egyptian hieroglyphs, the differences between the two scripts make a direct link unlikely. If the Egyptians adopted anything, it seems to be the idea that signs could convey specific sounds and words. Possibly small objects such as seals reached Egypt indirectly from the Syrian and Arabian land and sea trading routes, and these introduced artistic motifs such as niched facades and men overpowering paired animals, as well as the idea of writing. Whatever the origin of the script, it stands distinct from Mesopotamian writing in its most characteristic feature; it retained the pictorial forms with which it was born.

On combs of the fourth millennium BC figures of animals (*above*) and birds are captured in schematic outline, that allows no more than a general identification as quadruped or winged creature. A palette of the same age (*above left*) presents wildlife in still more cursive form, in assured strokes that tend beyond figurative art toward abstraction.

Right On the ivory comb from Abydos we find the first evidence for two uses of the falcon to depict a deity. One falcon rests on the sign of the palace, enclosing the name of the king, Djet of the First Dynasty, while the other sails across the wings of the sky on a boat, natural means of transport in the civilization of the Nile. Throughout ancient Egyptian history the dual motif persists of falcon-god in the heavens, from the Fourth Dynasty the sun-god Ra, and falcon-god on earth, in myth Horus and in historical time the king as incarnation of both Ra and Horus. The comb unites the earliest examples of that double vision with early forms of the hieroglyphic script developed at the same time, and destined to survive as long.

Script and pictorial composition belong together in Egypt, because the signs are themselves small pictures. This does not mean that the signs can only represent exactly what they portray. Hieroglyphic writing in Egypt combines two uses of pictures, one to denote what they are (the depiction of a door-bolt denotes 'door-bolt', that of a mountain denotes 'mountain') and the second to denote the sound of the Egyptian word (the depiction of a door-bolt, in Egyptian *se*, denotes the sound *s*, and the depiction of a mountain, in Egyptian *dju*, denotes the sound *dju*).

This enables the script to write words which cannot be represented by a simple picture, such as beauty, sorrow, evil, happiness. The sound is conveyed by signs to represent sound, and the type of word is determined by signs to represent objects, the so-called 'determinatives'. Thus the bolt *s* with the picture of a seated man writes the Egyptian word *se* "man". The bolt *s* with the loaf *t* (*te* is the Egyptian word for bread) and the picture of a seated woman writes the Egyptian word *set* "woman".

There is no limit to the number of possible hieroglyphs, because any object can be written simply as a small drawing of that object. Yet the number of signs widely used in texts before the Ptolemaic Period (c.300 BC) would probably not exceed five hundred, and some Eighteenth Dynasty temple buildings bear texts using less than two hundred signs. The system functioned efficiently in particular because it did not use many determinatives to indicate type of object. Less than a hundred such signs were in common use, and most of them are instantly recognisable, such as man for men or their names, woman for women or their names, crossed circle (perhaps a settlement plan) for towns and their names, rectangle with a gap on one side (a house plan) for houses and estates, man wielding a stick for words of action or aggression, walking legs for words of movement, and so forth.

The sound-signs too, although potentially limitless, tend to present two or, more rarely, three consonants, with supporting sound-signs denoting one consonant. The single consonant signs served the useful purpose of dispelling ambiguity, either where one sign carries more than one phonetic reading, or where two signs look so alike that they might be mistaken for one another. The chisel sign was used to represent two different pairs of consonants *m* + *r* or *3* (the glottal stop, as before vowels at the start of English words) + *b*. It is not known why this single sign could be read in two different ways; perhaps two different words were suggested by the sign, either two separate tools of similar appearance, or one specific and one general word for 'tool'. Whatever the reason, any ambiguity in reading is removed by the addition of sound-signs for a single consonant, the owl *m* and mouth *r* in the first case, or the leg *b* in the second. In many cases sound-signs for two or three consonants do not involve this ambiguity, but nevertheless a sound-sign for one of the consonants is added, redundant in reading but essential to the aesthetic appearance of the

Painted pottery from the late fourth millennium BC includes pictorial features such as boats, here with masts, sails and crew. Alongside occur features later echoed in the hieroglyphic script, notably the mountain ranges and water lines. Yet, unlike the later signs, on pottery these elements remain part of the scene.

sequence of signs as an artistic unit. The designer of a hieroglyphic text always took care to arrange the signs of each word in a neat group such that the words follow one another in distinct blocks. This principle of block writing confirms the unity of art and script in Pharaonic Egypt.

In the Egyptian language, as in Arabic and Hebrew, many if not most words are built on a skeleton or 'stem' of three consonants, with many words from the same stem. In speech different words from the same group were probably distinguished by their vowels or accent. The script distinguishes words of the same sound not by giving the vowels, but by adding the determinative to the sound-signs denoting consonants of the stem. If this makes it difficult for us to know how words were pronounced exactly, because we have no direct information on the vowels, it leaves us with the advantage of a script which is extremely easy to read, once we accept the combined usage of sound-signs and picture-signs. The difficulty for beginners comes not so much with learning the hieroglyphic script as with learning the Egyptian language, now dead.

Indeed, Egyptian hieroglyphic texts are much easier to read than the early alphabetic texts of Greek and Latin, because ancient texts provide no spaces between words. In a Greek or Latin text it can be difficult to be sure

The canonical image of the lion as King in defence of order takes form in the remarkable pottery sculpture from Nekhen, focal city of southern Upper Egypt in the period leading toward unification.

14

The lion provided the Egyptians, like other peoples, with a perfect expression of majestic power. An example from the late predynastic period, on the eve of unification, is the Battlefield Palette (*above*), upon which the lion presents the power of the king destroying his enemies. However, another votive palette of the same date (*right*) presents a lion as enemy, shot down with arrows.

where one word ends and the next begins, whereas Egyptian words are usually clearly ended in hieroglyphic texts with one of the common 'type-of-word' signs. When the Egyptians began to write their language with the signs of the Greek alphabet, with a few additions, forming the Coptic script, they did so for religious reasons. In the fourth century AD, Christianity became the state religion, and the new sacred texts could not be written in hieroglyphs, because those were identified along with Pharaonic art as idolatrous images of false gods. The new alphabet of the Greeks saved the early Christian fathers from the Pharaonic tradition, but, in a language where many words sound similar, it made their texts much more difficult to read, a reminder of the efficiency of the hieroglyphic script.

Although the script may have been relatively easy to learn, at least for a native speaker, this does not mean that everyone in ancient Egypt learnt hieroglyphs. Writing remained until modern times the preserve of a more or less restricted minority. The men who could read and write ran Egypt. However, in this respect ancient Egypt is no different from Roman, or even Victorian, Britain.

Literacy rates do not relate to the ease or difficulty of mastering a script. The labourers and farmers were no less excluded from literacy and power when Alexander the Great brought the Greek alphabet to Egypt in 332 BC, or when Christianity adapted that alphabet to write the Egyptian language with the Coptic script, or when the Arabs conquered Egypt in AD 640, introducing their script which is used today. Equally the examples of modern China and Japan demonstrate that high literacy rates can be achieved in some societies even where the script is considerably harder to learn than hieroglyphs. In short, the extent of literacy against illiteracy depends not on the type of script but on the cast of the particular society. In ancient times the script, like the Greek and Latin alphabets, was restricted to a tiny minority, because that minority controlled and administered its society.

The writer in Egypt was not a servile member of staff at the beck and call of everyone around, but a participant in rule, because he wrote for the Pharaoh and his administration. This explains why the statue of the secretary belongs not to the lower stratum of officialdom but to the finest works of art produced in royal workshops. The scribal statues of Amenhotep son of Hapu brilliantly exemplify this quality. The scribal craft belongs to Thoth, and its practitioner here, Amenhotep son of Hapu, is appropriately not some humble clerk but the most powerful man in court at one of the highest peaks of Egyptian civilization, the dazzling reign of Amenhotep III. The statue illustrates the procedure and tools of writing in its most immediate form, reed upon papyrus rather than chisel upon stone. Amenhotep holds his reed brush in one hand poised to continue a text already begun and legible upon the roll of papyrus drooping over his

Left The tomb-chapel of the Third Dynasty official Hesyra included a group of wooden panels with depictions of the deceased and his name and titles with prayers for offerings in hieroglyphs. Hesyra appears with his scribal equipment of palette, waterpot, and reeds; the artist has taken as much care with the hieroglyphs as with the full-scale figures, as can be seen in the two details.

Above The output of less accomplished workshops reminds us how rare and difficult an achievement fine hieroglyphic art remained at all times. Crude versions of hieroglyphic texts were produced by local, inadequately trained craftsmen at all periods. This stela exemplifies the efforts of unskilled Middle Kingdom artists at Abydos to obtain eternal offerings for their clients by means of hieroglyphic texts and canonical depictions. Late Middle Kingdom, *c.*1800 BC.

right leg. His crouched position on the ground, probably on a reed mat, can be paralleled from tomb chapel scenes of scribes in accountancy or secretarial work, and reminds us of the general absence of chairs in African and Middle Eastern tradition.

Papyrus paper was made from the pith of the papyrus reed, cut in strips laid in two layers at right angles and then beaten together to produce a slightly corrugated but generally smooth ivory-white surface ideal for writing. This simple but effective procedure stands out as the most brilliant Egyptian invention, outlasting the Pharaohs, their art and its gods, to die out only when oriental cloth paper replaced it in the eighth to ninth centuries after four thousand years of use by the Egyptian, Greek, Latin and then Islamic worlds. The principal pigments were soot black and, for the equivalent of underlinings and headings, red ochre. Red was used to highlight phrases for special attention, such as the totals in accounts or the dates at the start of a text, but, as a dangerous symbol of fire and blood, had to be avoided for certain words, notably names of gods and kings and the phrase 'year of reign'. As may be seen on the lap of Amenhotep son of Hapu, texts were written from right to left, a feature of most scripts to which the Greek and Latin traditions of Europe form the exception. Thus the start of the roll on this statue, already bearing columns of hieroglyphs, lies at the right end over the right leg of the scribe.

The main difference between the statue of Amenhotep and the daily routine of scribal practice lies in the form of the script. The statue presents the carefully retained full pictorial forms of the hieroglyphs, more or less as they were developed in the thirty-first century BC. By contrast, the daily task of writing letters, accounts and legal texts required more rapid movement of the brush, producing a simplified script which we call hieratic. Hieratic could be written calligraphically for literary manuscripts and important state documents, or more rapidly for less formal letters and accounts. In the first millennium BC calligraphic hieratic became reserved almost exclusively for religious texts such as temple library rolls or funerary papyri, while the shorthand of business affairs and letters evolved in the seventh century BC into a new, still more cursive, standard form, which we call the demotic script. All three scripts were in use when Greek writers visited Egypt, and these foreign travellers gave us the Greek terms *hieroglyphs* 'sacred carved signs', *hieratic* 'priestly' and *demotic* 'popular', convenient labels even if they refer strictly to the three divisions of writing after 700 BC; there is nothing priestly about a business letter in the twentieth or tenth century BC, but hieratic has become our name for the script that is less cursive than demotic.

If the evolution of cursive forms seems to our empiricist eyes quite a logical tendency, then the hieroglyphs defy our reasoning because they arrest the pictorial stage for permanent and eternal use, remaining the anchor even for the 'practical' shorthand hieratic script, in which each sign

Left The image of the scribe signified status second only to the king and gods whose order the scribal secretary served, and accordingly could be used to depict the most powerful in the land. Here the scribe is the influential minister of king Amenhotep III, a man named Amenhotep son of Hapu. The text on the base assures the reader that Amenhotep will intercede for him with the gods for any petition.

Below The Ptolemaic Book of the Dead of a man named Khahep demonstrates the use of red to highlight parts of a text such as a heading to a section, in this case the title to each formula. The rest of this hieratic text is written in carbon black, which could also be used within headings to avoid the dangerous association of red with blood. In the vignette, the serpent and hieroglyph of ribs, denoting 'slaughter', are drawn in red to emphasise their hostile nature. The text accompanying the vignette is entitled 'formula for repelling the swallower of the ass', a reference to a demon who would devour the 'ass' and by implication all impurity. Only the blessed dead, pure of wrongdoing, could repel such a demon.

19

can be 'read' or transcribed into its underlying hieroglyphic form. This privileged position for hieroglyphs is particularly striking when we consider that most scribes never learnt hieroglyphs because hieratic sufficed for their daily needs. Only a select core of the elite of literate men continued beyond their training in hieratic to take on a knowledge of reading and copying the sacred originals of the script, the hieroglyphs.

Whereas Chinese and Mesopotamian, not to mention the alphabetic scripts of the Middle East and Europe, shed their overt pictorial forms, Egyptian hieroglyphs themselves endure as a microcosm of art. Each sign may be considered a miniature image, and each large-scale image in a pictorial composition functions as a hieroglyphic sign writ large. The early church in Egypt demonstrated a thoroughly Pharaonic attitude when it discarded both ancient writing and art at once, implicitly acknowledging that they belong inextricably together.

The rules for depiction apply equally to the small scale of hieroglyphs as to the largest scenes on temple walls. For ease of recognition, each object is considered from its most characteristic aspect, if necessary broken down first into separate elements. This approach reveals more than a decision on how best to depict the world for the sake of conveying information to an-

Egyptian artists used specific conventions to avoid ambiguity, as for example between statues and moving persons. In front of the first pylon at Luxor temple (*above*) stood six statues of Ramses II. These face out with their backs to the pylon, but the contemporary relief from the first

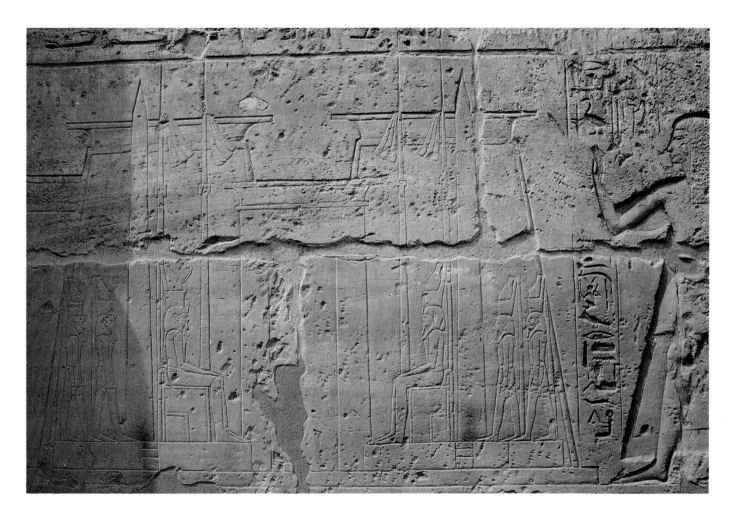

court of the temple (*above*) depicts them in pure profile. In this way the Ramesside artist distinguishes the stone statues of the king from moving persons such as the king's eldest son, to the right. The body of the prince appears as a composite union of parts seen from their most easily recognised viewpoint, thus the head and legs in profile, the eye and shoulders full frontal.

Left Fragment of Middle Kingdom relief in which the name of a city is written with the cat hieroglyph repeated three times; the Egyptian word for cat is the onomatopoeic *miu*, and that must have been the name of this otherwise unattested settlement. The cat hieroglyph is a small version of a depiction of a cat according to the rules of canonical Egyptian art.

other human being. The aspective art of the Egyptian royal workshops aims to install its subjects in eternity with all the power of creation. Artistic creation ceases to see itself as technical output and becomes a religious event on the same level as a birth, whether the birth of a child or the origin of matter.

In Egyptian art the figures must live if they are to serve their purpose of securing eternal order, in the temple, or eternal life, for a tomb-owner. Each statue, each coffin in human shape, each principal image received a rite of consecration, the opening of the mouth, in which its mouth was touched by special ritual blades to enable it to breathe and to receive offerings. Once consecrated in this manner, the image could sustain life, opening a channel between this world and the world of the gods; the mummified body in the coffin, the cult image of the god, the statue of king or dead nobleman, all were inanimate objects which the Opening of the Mouth transformed into living forces, or, more accurately, receptacles for that invisible, intangible force which we call life. The sculptor himself could be called *sankh* 'the one who brings to life', vivifier. The power of bringing to life was Heka, and one of the ritual blades in the Opening of the Mouth was itself named Werhekau 'great in *heka*-power', a name we meet again in the feminine form Werethekau as the cobra on the brow of the king. As power of creation Heka takes visible form in the art itself, following a canon of rules handed down through the ages as carefully as hieroglyphs. The principles of this art can best be illustrated from original examples, most appropriately here from an image of Werethekau herself.

Consider the image first from a description in English: a serpent with the head and breasts of a woman suckles a human child. The first reaction of a modern reader may be incomprehension, if she or he tends to compose pictures as a photograph would present them. There is little room in naive literal mindedness for hybrid forms or self-contradictory scenes such as a snake larger than a man, or beast with human head. For us, monsters are banished to the marginal domain of fable, and difficult groupings of objects can be contained within a safely unreal world of imagination. Look now at the Egyptian depiction of this unimaginable scene. The ancient artist, working without the prejudice of the literal mind, has been able to create a seductively persuasive composition without monstrosity. The serpent denotes power from within the earth, and the rising cobra with swollen hood, poised to strike, presents that power in action, defending order against chaos. Here it nurtures a boy identified by his crown and regalia as the king, child of the gods and himself the earthly champion of their order. In order to depict the serpent suckling the human male, the artist gives it the head and breast of a woman, without compromising either the metaphor of the cobra or the harmony of the scene. The artist has taken each part of the body separately, rendering it from its most instantly recognisable angle, and reunites the separate elements into a unity.

Different traditions throughout history have used the procedure of dissecting and reassembling to produce an effect of monstrosity. In Egyptian art the combination of superficially disjointed elements yields instead a seamless harmony. By keeping constantly in mind the overall composition, presenting each element as a perfect unit, and keeping to the established proportions between each element, the ancient Egyptian artist avoids the discord that might be expected in joining features that are separate in nature.

The line of hieroglyphs on the pendant identifies both figures: 'the perfect god Tutankhamun, beloved of the goddess Werethekau'. The famous boy-king reigned only a decade and died at no more than seventeen years of age, an historical detail that lends especial poignancy to the scene. The goddess embodies the vision of power at the heart of the Pharaonic manner of seeing and recreating the world. Werethekau appears as a separate goddess rather than a name for other goddesses, principally on the walls of temples constructed at Thebes in the fourteenth and thirteenth centuries BC, one of two periods from which temple building on a massive scale survives in Egypt. These scenes show the goddess with the body of a human female, enabling her to hold sceptres, with the head of a lioness, to identify

The goddess Werethekau with the body of a serpent suckling the child king Tutankhamun. The goddess is wearing a double-feathered crown with cow's horns in this pendant of sheet gold attached to a string of beads.

her with the force of a lion, ideal symbol of power over enemies. In texts Werethekau occurs already a thousand years earlier as one of the names for the force protecting the king, presented graphically as a cobra rearing up on his brow. This cobra might be cast as a diadem, and was most aptly named in Egyptian *iaret* 'the rising serpent-goddess'. In Egyptology *iaret* is usually rendered 'uraeus', from the Greek version of a treatise on hieroglyphs written by a fourth century AD Egyptian named Horapollo. Other Greek texts translate the *iaret* simply as *basiliskos* 'royal crown'.

Of all the names for the cobra diadem Werethekau presents the most concentrated phrase, so compact that it can only be half-translated as 'goddess great in *heka*-power'. The word *heka* denotes the assertive power by which creation originally unfurled and ever since has reinforced its existence. In the Egyptian presentation of the journey by the sun-god on his Nile barge around the skies of heaven and underworld, the sun Ra receives an escort commonly featuring three gods, Sia 'perception', Hu 'pronouncement', and Heka. Whereas the first two may be more readily understood as divine seeing and divine command, Heka transfers less comfortably into the language of our time and so requires more conscious effort at understanding.

Heka is often translated as 'magic', but our word implies a rift between official and forbidden religious practice, and no such rift can be detected in ancient Egypt. The English word magic can mean wonder or enchantment, but it also carries the negative connotations of superstition and of practices condemned by society. The very word was devised by the ancient Greeks to denote foreign and suspect beliefs and rites, said to be practised by the Magi who were vaguely thought to live somewhere in the direction of Persia, arch enemy of classical Greece. Today 'magic' remains for the most part relegated to a secondary role of opposition, whether to religion or to science. By contrast the ancient Egyptian world knew no such concept for a marginal area of belief and practice. Our 'magic' equates with *heka* only in the sense that it evokes astonishment and awe. It singularly fails to convey the role of *heka* in Pharaonic texts and images. There, far from being exiled to the margins of society, *heka* expresses a creative and protective power, a precondition for all life. Such a force might be channelled abusively to suit evil or anti-social ends, but the Egyptians had no special word for that abuse, in the way that the Greek and Judaeo-Christian tradition used the word 'magic'. The primary meaning of *heka* remained the creative urge, a power beyond good and evil.

Heka accompanies the sun-god on his journey over the skies, and the same power rears up as Werethekau on the brow of the king championing the order of the same god on earth. Individual human beings too could find a defender in *heka*-power, as we read in one Middle Kingdom literary text, the *Instruction for king Merykara*, where the good deeds of god for humankind are recalled: 'He made for them *heka* as a weapon to ward off the blow of events'. The use of *heka* by individuals is confirmed by a number of papyrus scrolls, the books of the ancients, containing words of *heka*-power to be recited to retain or regain good health. Modern prejudice finds it most difficult to resist labelling these texts as 'magical', disengaging them from more 'medical' passages, but the distinction violates an ancient unity. Originally recitations formed with prescriptions and instructions for treatment the three dimensions of healing. From our distance we cannot easily assess how well any one tactic worked, but we can at least appreciate the need for each of the three branches of healing: medicaments, physical treatment, spoken word accompanying treatment. These words were denoted *heka*.

Another word often translated as 'magic' is *akhu*, power connected with the concept *akh*. Like the *akh* 'transfigured spirit' or blessed dead, and the *sakhu* 'texts for transfiguration', this word locks into the underlying concept of 'light' as the precondition of life and one of the least tangible powers in the world. The idea of light includes a sense of usefulness, and *akh* could be used to speak of the son who acted piously for his father, or by extension the person, above all the king, who acted for the good of the gods. This web of ideas fills the name of Akhenaten 'he who is *akh* for the sun-disk'. In texts for healing and defence of health, *akhu* 'power of light' or 'of transfiguration' often stands parallel to *heka*, the central word for the force of creation.

In the fight against danger and disease Egyptian healers used images as well as words. In the fourth century BC in particular they interwove text and image through the practice of inscribing their incantations on standing stones ('stelae') bearing a depiction of the god Horus as a child or on statues of the healer himself. The supreme example of the Horus stelae is the Metternich stela, named after the celebrated nineteenth century Austrian diplomat to whom Mohammed Ali, governor of Egypt, gave the monument in 1828. The stela dates to the reign of the last native king of all Egypt, Nakhthorhebyt (360-342 BC), and presents an unusually extensive series of incantations and images of deities and forces to be controlled.

Among healing statues the outstanding example is that known as Djedher the saviour. The fourth century official and sage Djedher commissioned an image of himself as a faithful temple guard squatting on the ground, a type found as early as the Middle Kingdom and which we call the block statue. The image of Djedher sits upon a solid pedestal containing a basin at the feet of the statue. Every available space on surface of both statue and pedestal is covered in hieroglyphic texts giving the incantations to be recited by healer over the patient. Each text of healing, or *heka*-text, protected Djedher in life and after death against danger throughout eternity, but also played a wider social role. Any living person could seek defence against disease and danger by drinking water that had been poured over the image and collected in the basin at its feet.

The statue of Djedher-the-saviour presents him squatting on the ground, with his arms resting on a 'Horus-stela', in front of a basin to collect water poured over the statue and stela. The entire work of sculpture is covered in hieroglyphic texts of incantations against scorpion sting, snake bite and other ailments, intended to imbue the water poured over the surface with healing properties. From Athribis, *c.*350 BC.

The quality of workmanship on both Metternich stela and statue of Djedher proclaims their status. These are not products of superstition at the margins of a society, but meticulously calculated creations from which the highest officials of the day sought to harness the forces of the world to the defence of good against evil. The statue of Djedher fuses art and script into a fountainhead into this world for the waters of life. Even if the rhythm and metre of the incantations seem lost now except to our imagination, this sculpture offers a glimpse of an ancient marriage between sight and sound, art and poetry.

The immortality of these statues and texts belonged in the first instance to the gods, and to obtain eternal life the individual must join them after death. The Egyptians adopted various strategies to this end, seeking union with the daily resurrection of the sun as the creator sun-god Ra, and with the annual resurrection of plant life in the earth with the god of the mummified dead Osiris. They also took the specific analogy of food for sustenance, recognising that human life depends in this world on food for energy, and set out to sustain the body after death with food offerings, just as they presented offerings to the images of gods. This sustenance might

The scene of Nefretiabet at her table of offerings displays the uses to which hieroglyphs could be put, to convey either sound or image or both. To the left a line of signs gives her name and title 'king's daughter'. The rectangular compartments above the table contain signs combining phonetic renderings of specific commodities, such as oils and incense, with images of them or their containers. Around the table offerings are identified directly with a picture of the offering, such as a haunch of meat or loaf of bread; here the only specific sound is the lotus *kha* denoting *kha* 'a thousand' to emphasise the eternal supply. The right-hand section consists of a highly detailed list of types of linen, peculiar to the early Old Kingdom.

On a pillar of the White Chapel of Senusret I, *c*.1900 BC, the king directs with the staff *kherep*, itself the hieroglyph for 'direction', a table of offerings to the god Amun-Ra in ithyphallic form as god of male fertility. Behind the king his *ka* or spirit of sustenance holds a standard in one hand, and embraces the king with his other arm. Upon the head of this figure the Horus name of the king is written between the two arms of the *ka* hieroglyph. The divine nature of the Horus name is expressed in the long beard of gods which the figure wears.

be supplied by the family for a dead person, or an officiant might be paid to maintain the necessary daily cult. Yet the Egyptians were fully aware of the weakness of the flesh, of the uncompromising truth that all family lines eventually come to an end, even if they managed to keep their interest in offering to their dead longer than three or four generations.

Hieroglyphs and canonical art fill the abysmal gap by providing a ritual guarantee of eternal sustenance, the texts and images creating directly and perfectly the necessary food and drink for the dead forever. The principle of sustenance throughout eternity receives expression in the Egyptian word *ka*, sometimes used simply for 'food', but most often in the innumerable hieroglyphic inscriptions appealing for offerings from king to gods to be handed on to the *ka* of a named individual. Since kingship must endure forever, there would always be a king offering to the gods, giving a perpetual source of sustenance, if only the person could secure a share in it for his own life after death.

Yet the *ka* was not simply a ghost to be conjured after death. It expresses the very essence, we might say loosely spirit, of living. In the concept of *ka* that energy so mundanely present as calories in a diet rises to a level

Above The stela of King Djet of the First Dynasty was freestanding at the tomb of the king at Abydos, and presents a neat border, rounded at the top, within which the falcon rests upon an upright rectangle. The lower part of the rectangle is inscribed with the niched facade generally identified as the royal palace; the upper part contains the Horus name of the king in the hieroglyphic script, in this case the single sign of the cobra (denoting the consonant 'dj').

Right The wooden statue of king Auibra Hor of the Thirteenth Dynasty, with gilt collar and inlaid eyes. The figure stands naked and bears upon its head the *ka* hieroglyph, a pair of outstretched arms. As on the White Chapel of Senusret I, this *ka* figure of a king wears the long beard indicating divine status.

which we consider abstract and spiritual. Our analytical thinking imposes insistently binary models on the world with pairings such as body and soul, physical and spiritual. The *ka* defies modern habits of thought, presenting at once 'physical' food and 'spiritual' energy, and thereby preserves the unity of our earthly existence, in much the same way that *heka* denies us our habitual recourse to paired opposites such as 'magic' and 'science' or 'rational' and 'irrational'.

In Egypt the first instance of divinity on earth comes in kingship, and the *ka* of the king presents an extreme illustration of the force with which this word must always have been invested in Pharaonic times. The *ka* or sustaining energy of kingship is the very god of kingship, Horus, expressed as the celestial falcon so majestically dominant over its skies of flight. The first surviving hieroglyphs are the names of kings written within a rectangle depicting the Early Dynastic enclosure-wall, with a niched brick facade, surmounted by a falcon identified from later texts as Horus. 'Horus' is the Latin adaptation of the Egyptian name Hor, originally Heru, meaning 'the distant god', and this celestial power manifested itself on earth in the palace as the king. The Horus name cast each new king of Egypt as a new and unique form of the god, and its use survived exactly as long as Egyptian kingship, lasting from the emergence of the nation-state in the First Dynasty until the erosion of a distinctively Egyptian kingship under the Roman emperors ruling Egypt thirty-five centuries later.

In scenes of kingship a small figure often shadows the king, bearing on his head the Horus name between the arms of the *ka*-hieroglyph. The figure graphically proclaims that Horus is the *ka*, that vital sustaining energy, of kingship and of each individual king in turn. One image above all conveys the view that the king through his *ka* is divine, the wooden figure of an ephemeral monarch, Auibra Hor of the Thirteenth Dynasty. It may be no accident that this unique statue of the *ka* of kingship was found in the burial of a king whose own birth name was Hor, expressing identity with the god Horus on two levels. Outstanding among the few goods of this burial, the *ka* statue proclaims the divinity of the king sustained by the god with whom he shared both kingship and name. Although no other major monument of king Hor survives, this image of a naked man crowned with *ka*-hieroglyph captures all the brilliance of the royal workshops of the classic Twelfth Dynasty. The king stands before us here not as the mortal frame of a short-lived monarch but as an immortal god. Kingship can claim in the *ka*-statue of Hor to embody perfectly the force that sustains all life.

If the king walked on earth already as a god, his subjects aspired to the same immortal status after death. During the Old Kingdom kingship reserved to itself the special trappings of its particular form of divinity. These included the royal headcloth, an angular false beard, an array of

29

Right The purpose of reliefs on tomb-chapel walls was to produce offerings to sustain the life of the tomb-owner. In this scene from a chapel of the late Old Kingdom the hieroglyphs between two groups of butchers identify the action, with the exhortation from the butcher on the left to the other to 'take hold'. The line of text above reads from right to left and specifies the occasions at which offerings would be given, in this case 'every festival day forever'.

Left The false door of Idu of the late Old Kingdom presents not only the space for offerings, here graphically in the shape of the hieroglyph *hetep* 'offering' (a loaf on an offering mat), but more strikingly the tomb-owner himself emerging out of the burial chamber below, with arms outstretched in the emphatic gesture of the hieroglyph *ka* 'spirit of sustenance', with hands upturned in expectation of food and drink to sustain his existence beyond death.

sceptres, and the *uraeus*. Another feature of divinity attributed to the king cannot be so tangibly encapsulated in words or images; this is another aspect of eternal life, the *ba* or power of movement.

The *ba* appears in Egyptian art as a swallow in flight, a metaphor for freedom that cannot be bettered. Usually the bird is given a human head, the body expressing the attribute (here freedom to move) and the head expressing identity (here the human man or woman whose *ba* is depicted). The *ba* appears outside texts of kingship and in art only after the Old Kingdom, when kingship had evolved a new panoply of distinguishing features and no longer prevented its subjects from adopting, strictly for survival after death only, certain royal motifs such as regalia and expression as *ba*.

In Old Kingdom tomb-chapels the hieroglyphic monuments of the elite restricted themselves to securing the eternal sustenance required for the *ka*. Yet this still implied a certain mobility because the deceased had to cross in some manner that small but crucial gap from his or her body to the offerings themselves. This passage from the world of the dead to the world in which food and drink were still being prepared, ideally, for the deceased takes the instantly recognisable form of a door, cut into eternal stone, to be passed only by the deceased for the sustenance of eternal life, that is of the *ka*.

These 'false doors' evolved in the Old Kingdom but continued in prominent use in offering-chapels for king and subjects alike in the succeeding Middle and New Kingdoms.

No two offering chapels contain precisely the same edition of scenes and texts, testifying to the fertile imagination of Egyptian craftsmen. The variety can be all too easily overlooked by a modern casual observer who might see in the unfamiliar canon of Egyptian art constant repetition. For

The jewellery worn by Pharaoh afforded amuletic protection, making full use of the pictorial appearance of hieroglyphs as well as images of attack such as vulture and cobra. On a pylon-shaped pendant from the tomb of Tutankhamun, the kneeling figure of Heh 'eternity' raises the *shen*-ring of eternity between two cobras, each on a basket; an Egyptian word for basket was *neb*, and the sign was therefore used for other words with the same sound *neb* but meaning 'lord' and 'all'. One cobra wears the white crown, the other the red crown. The group can be read as a cryptogram, that is a hidden writing, of the throne-name of the king, Nebkheperura 'Ra is lord of forms', with the *shen*-ring evoking the sun Ra, the three gods as the 'forms', and the basket on each side as *neb* 'lord'. Such hidden writings recur in the jewellery of Tutankhamun. The string upon which the pendant is hung comprises the hieroglyphs of cloth loops *sa* 'protection' and *ankh* 'life', the sceptre *was* 'power', and the basket *neb* 'all'.

all the haste of most modern visitors, some variations in tomb chapel decoration cannot fail to capture our attention. One such image appears in the tomb-chapel of Idu at Giza, built in the shadow of those mightiest pyramids, then already three hundred years old. The false door in this chapel presents the owner not discreetly melding into the background of reliefs and texts, but violently disrupting the barrier between burial below and offerings above. He emerges as a sculpture out of the very earth with arms outstretched and hands upturned, a graphic rewriting of the *ka*-hieroglyph, to ensure that he will receive food and drink for eternity. The scene echoes the 'appeal to the living' inscribed in hieroglyphs upon offering chapel walls, asking passers-by to utter the words of the formulaic prayer for a share in the offerings made by the king to the gods. In return the appeal promises that the owner of the tomb will act on their behalf in the tribunal of the afterlife, to oppose any disease or danger that might strike the living on earth. Idu appeals with equal force in an image of disturbing directness, symptom of a continual Egyptian insistence that human community includes the dead along with their living relatives.

In front of the stone door would be placed a table for offerings and basin for libations, and texts would specify the name of the person to whom all this sustenance was directed. Again, on the walls of the wealthier tomb-chapels scenes in painting or the far more durable stone relief carving would cast in eternal mould the materials for good living and the means of their production. These texts and images were not devised for the purpose of recording a past lifestyle, even if that recording is one of the most beneficial accidents for us. Their function is not to represent, but to create life. For that reason they carefully edit out of existence any elements of disorder, decay or disease, and thus purify eternal life of any obstacles or noxious features in the world of our experience. All people appear eternally and ideally youthful, all creation abundant and flawless.

Although the Old Kingdom tomb-chapels include none of the texts spoken at burial among their scenes for eternal sustenance, they sometimes show the moment of recitation. Beside the officiant, ideally the eldest son, who performs the ritual for uniting the dead with his offerings, stands a second no less important figure holding a papyrus-roll. Hieroglyphs label the scene as 'the reading of *sakhu*', returning us to the concept of *akh*, the transfigured dead.

The efficiency of all monuments in both image and text flowed from the consecrating ritual of 'Opening the Mouth'. In the late Old Kingdom miniature kits for the ritual were included in elite burials as a means of reinforcing this life-conferring process throughout eternity. Once the mouth of an image had been touched, that image could function as vessel for the *ka*, and become an anchor for the *ba*, in other words become as secure a framework for eternal life as the body had been for the short span of mortal existence.

Each image is most alive when it bears a hieroglyphic text, for there its identity, the essence of its object, is articulated in the name, that special home of power. The horizon of eternity explains why the mouth of the coffin too should be opened. As much care was lavished on creating the perfect face for the eternal coffin, 'chest of life' in the Egyptian phrase, as on relief, statue or painting. From the Twelfth Dynasty to the Roman Period, the classic shape of coffins became mummiform, showing a body wrapped in linen bandages but the head left free, precisely as in images of the gods Osiris and Ptah. Here, as in the image of the *ba*, the body conveys an attribute, here the divine status of the mummified dead, while the head identifies as male or female human being. A text would complete this ideal picture with the addition of the name.

In the ritual of opening the mouth, the most important actor can too easily be overlooked as we observe the rite of passage through which mortal human is transformed into eternal life. On the scenes of 'Opening the Mouth' the 'holder of the ritual-book' bears aloft a partly unrolled papyrus manuscript from which he reads out every step of the procedure. In this man and manuscript we meet the kernel of the civilization, the power to infuse an image, generation after generation, with form and content of hieroglyphic harmony. That harmony can be seen in the finest products of Pharaonic artists, but it lies equally present, only more hidden to us, in the texts which we call funerary literature, the *sakhu* 'transfigurations' which aim to secure eternal life for the deceased. These surfaced first inside the royal pyramids of the late Old Kingdom, then on the coffins of Middle Kingdom nobility, and the tradition continued in the New Kingdom tombs of kings and, most famously, on papyri, the so-called Books of the Dead. This book is devoted to the intricate history of these series of texts across the two and a half thousand years of their use.

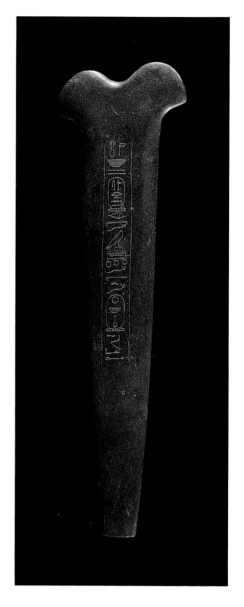

The most distinctive implement in the ceremony of Opening the Mouth, the *peseshkaf* was one of the blades used to touch the mouth of an inanimate object to enable it to channel offerings to a spirit, in other words the ability to sustain life. This example is inscribed in hieroglyphs with a dedication from Senusret I in favour of an earlier king.

CHAPTER 2

Pyramids, Mute and Voiced

The valley temple of Khafra abuts onto an additional, unique feature, the great sphinx with its own temple. This is the earliest known colossus using the body of a lion, to express royal and divine force, together with the head of a human, wearing the *nemes* headcloth to show that this is the king of Egypt. The impact of this vast statue, on the scale typical of the Giza monuments, led New Kingdom and later rulers to address the sphinx as a form of the sun-god, Horemakhet 'Horus in the horizon', sometimes in the guise of a Western Asiatic deity, Hauron. In the Eighteenth Dynasty, king Amenhotep II had a stela inscribed with an account of his visits to the site when he practised his skills at chariot riding in the desert. His son Thutmes IV set up a stela in his turn, recording a dream in which the god promised him the throne if he would clear the sphinx of sand.

WHEN we refer to the tomb in Egypt, there are two distinctly different spaces involved, burial chamber and offering chapel. Each of these gradually became home to its own set of texts and images. As sacred places, both chapel and burial are set aside in darkness from the profane world. However, the chapel is designed to be entered by torch-bearing relatives or officiants bringing offerings to sustain the dead, and would be lit by the sun at least when its doors were opened by them. By contrast the burial chamber remained more firmly closed to the light, protecting the body from being disturbed after the funeral. The distinction is marked by a simple but telling difference in approach: the chapel is on the same level as the ground, that is the world outside, while the burial chamber lies usually below ground level and can be penetrated only by clambering down a steep corridor or rough stairway. We cross a threshold horizontally to the chapel to communicate with the dead, but must climb down vertically into the burial chamber if we want to enter their world.

This single point, so obvious that it can easily be overlooked, reveals a great gulf but also the link between the two parts of the Egyptian tomb complex. The body must be kept safe, placed inaccessibly within the depths of the earth, but it must also be fed, requiring a space which can be reached by those providing the food. From one period to another the precise arrangements for burial and offering vary. Some centuries dispense with offering chapels altogether, while others might add a second offering chapel at great distance, in another town, particularly from the Middle Kingdom on at Abydos as town of Osiris, god of the dead. The construction of a chapel and the cutting of a burial chamber in the rock both involved considerable expense, and were never affordable to other than the wealthiest in the land. Each time that we consider a tomb complex with chambers for burial and offerings, we face the peaks of achievement of Egyptian civilization.

Although the two sectors of the Egyptian tomb serve the same end, to

secure eternal life for the owner, the offering chapel received texts and images long before they appeared also in the burial chamber. Already in the First Dynasty monumental standing stones ('stelae') immortalised the name and titles of the king and his courtiers at their tombs. The only texts below ground are the labels identifying names, quantities and dates of the objects buried with the deceased for his eternal sustenance. Over the next three centuries the texts on the stelae expanded to add to the name and title the offerings which the dead wished to receive. Meanwhile the space around the body below ground remained devoid of text, with one startling and unique exception in that unparalleled creation, the Step Pyramid of king Netjerkhet, the king Djoser of later tradition.

The Step Pyramid of Netjerkhet stands as Janus in the record of Egyptian civilization, symbolising at once the end of its formative years and the beginning of its three classic millennia. The ancient Egyptians themselves recognised its genius when in the Late Period they came to treat the leading official of Netjerkhet, Imhotep, as a god of healing and

Right The statue of king Netjerkhet from the chapel on the north side of the Step Pyramid presents the king wearing the long squared false beard, and the *nemes* headcloth. The inlaid eyes were prised out in ancient times, but the image remains one of the earliest and most powerful among surviving royal sculpture.

Below The pedestal of another lifesize statue of the king shows the nine bows, traditional designation of the enemies of Egypt, trodden beneath his feet, with three lapwings to the front providing a hieroglyphic writing of the word *rekhyt* 'populace'.

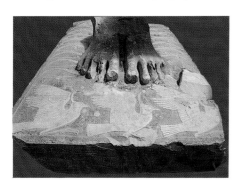

wisdom. For the first time a king used stone on a massive scale to replace the mud brick of the tomb superstructure in his bid for immortality. The sheer quantity of sculpting brought a new level of knowledge of stone, stimulating the royal workshops to a quality and form that was maintained until, three thousand years later, the land lost its distinctive workshops under the late Roman Empire. In the underground galleries of this first pyramid, walls of blue-green faience tiles conjured in relief the impression of reed matting with upper borders in patterns of repeated *djed*-pillars, the sign for stable life. The west wall of one gallery is broken at three points by niches framed by the name and titles of the king; at the back of each niche the king appears performing ceremonies known from earlier and later depictions of the *sed* or festival for the renewal of kingship.

The proportions of both hieroglyphs and large scale figures in these scenes have already attained the perfect vision of classic Pharaonic art, attending equally to the part and the whole. By contrast the surviving royal and private sculpture from the reign of Netjerkhet displays the same concentration on a single element, such as the head, that we find in the aftermath of Pharaonic art in Coptic Egypt. We do not need to disparage those different systems of expression – personal taste would be the object of a separate study – to recognise that Pharaonic art aims at and achieves its own separate agenda of harmony. The reliefs beneath the Step Pyramid find precedents in isolated works of the First and Second Dynasties, but introduce us to what was to be henceforth a virtually uninterrupted history of Egyptian art in royal workshops. It is all the more curious that the precise layout and individual features of this monument, such as the underground reliefs, find no parallel in the great succession of royal tomb complexes of the Old Kingdom. For Netjerkhet, the tomb becomes an eternal *sed* festival, rejuvenating rather than just preserving the body of the king. Then, after this brief outburst of colour, the burial chambers sink back into a mute darkness for three centuries.

The Step Pyramid would have been just one of a series of vast funerary

The surviving chambers of the chapel of Meresankh, a Fourth Dynasty queen, give the impression of an underground tomb, because they are cut from the rock. However they belonged to the space above ground, where family and funerary priests of the deceased were expected to enter to offer food and drink to sustain the dead. At Giza the outcrops of rock enabled architects to design offering chapels partly cut in rock and partly constructed in stone blocks, but both forming a rectangular mass of stone for offerings above the site of the burial chamber.

enclosures at Saqqara if the other kings of the Third Dynasty had carried their projects through to completion. To the southwest king Sekhemkhet had laid out an area still greater than that of Netjerkhet, 500 by 200 metres. The name Imhotep was found written in ink at the northern enclosure wall, a sign that the same man supervised both constructions. Yet the building was left unfinished, and only that one wall received its covering of fine Tura limestone. The underground galleries were also unfinished, and we do not know whether they were ever intended to be decorated. In the centre lay a chamber with a calcite sarcophagus, discovered intact with its original seals and garlands of flowers, but mysteriously empty when opened. In 1967 Jean-Philippe Lauer found a second underground chamber beneath a squared mound or 'mastaba' at the southern end of the Sekhemkhet complex. This small chamber housed a gilt wooden coffin containing the body of a child. In our almost complete ignorance of the Third Dynasty kings, we cannot be sure that these are the mortal remains of Sekhemkhet himself, but an early death would explain the unfinished condition of the funerary complex.

There remain to be explored and explained a third great complex at Saqqara and two unfinished royal tombs at Zawiyet el-Aryan, all of which may belong in the Third Dynasty. According to the later Pharaonic king-lists, the dynasty ended with the reign of a king named Huni, whose tomb has not been identified. For his cult a stepped pyramid was set up on the island of Elephantine at the southern end of the kingdom, and from that site comes the first instance of the oval ring of sovereignty enclosing the name of Huni. Other stepped pyramids along the Nile valley may date to the same reign, forming a network of support for a central tomb that is itself ironically lost to us.

It is often stated that the ruined pyramid at Meidum should be ascribed to Huni, but ancient texts name the place Djed-Sneferu after the first king of the Fourth Dynasty, Sneferu. If this evidence has been overlooked, the error reflects a genuine embarrassment of riches in tombs for this king, for another two full-size pyramids and at least one in a series of small step pyramids all belong to the royal funerary cult of this reign. Following the gap in the surviving monuments after the Step Pyramid it seems virtually incredible that a single king could have presided over the construction of not just the first, but the first three true pyramids. Here we should remember that the monuments of the Third Dynasty extend beyond the experience of building the Step Pyramid of Netjerkhet, and that the architects of Sneferu could build upon the expertise gained from work on even unfinished monuments. Whatever the breaks in the surviving record, the royal workshops of the Fourth Dynasty operated in an unbroken tradition already five hundred years old, reaching back to the first monolithic use of granite in the burial chamber of king Den of the First Dynasty. And yet the birth of the Pyramid Age in the monuments of Sneferu still strikes us

Among the foretastes of classic Pharaonic art in the Step Pyramid complex, the engaged columns with open lotus capitals appear perhaps the most characteristically Egyptian to a modern eye. This section of wall has been restored using ancient blocks.

Left The shallow depression running from the Meidum pyramid down to the edge of the fields marks the causeway from valley temple to the offering chapel at the foot of the pyramid. This complex is the earliest surviving example of a scheme simultaneously separating and joining the different elements of burial-place, place of offering, and place of arrival from the world of the living.

Below The pyramid-complex at Meidum includes a chapel on the western side, where the causeway from the edge of the cultivation ended. At the very foot of the pyramid stand two stelae marking the open court of offering in the presence of the sun-god, father of the king. After death the king would be reunited with the sun, and the offerings for his cult would cement that union.

with the force of its novelty and its sheer scale. Power has never before or since been so massively concentrated or so physically expressed as in the pyramids of the Fourth Dynasty. The three great pyramids of Sneferu contain more stone and imply greater manpower than even the Great Pyramid of Giza from the reign of Khufu, his son and successor. Without dated inscriptions it is not now easy to determine which monument was established first, but it seems possible that all were planned together as the points of the royal cult. The smaller step pyramid at Seila in the Fayum would provide a local echo of the same colossal central directive.

The pyramid at Meidum presents among the most dramatic visions of the past if only for the power revealed in its ruin. The collapse of the outer layers seems to have occurred not less than a thousand years after the reign of Sneferu, for visitors in the fifteenth century BC left pious graffiti recording their visit to the chapel, which was buried under the rubble when the pyramid collapsed. The loss of this casing helps us to reconstruct the development of the pyramid, a copybook study in the birth of a new artistic form. An original core of two or three steps was built up into a step pyramid in Third Dynasty style, comprising seven steps or layers, to which an

Above The view from the desert side of the pyramid at Meidum best represents the massive bulk of the core ruin. The original angle of incline has been estimated at 51 degrees 52′, giving a maximum height of 92 metres. The rubble around the base has not been fully investigated, but it might, if methodically examined, provide valuable clues to construction methods as well as the reasons for the collapse of the monument. Above the mound of rubble rises the inner 'Step Pyramid' of stone buttresses around the central tower.

eighth step was added in the first amendment to the building plans. Then came the decisive stroke of imagination. The stairway to heaven was changed into a smooth-sided mountain taking the same outline as sunrays through the clouds.

No texts survive to spell out to us the change in thought or faith that accompanied this momentous technical feat. Both Step Pyramid and true (smooth-sided) pyramid look up to the heavens, to the new cult of the sun. Netjerkhet had a freestanding stone shrine carved at Iunu, known to the Greeks as Heliopolis 'the city of the sun', and in his reign a courtier bore the name Hesyra 'praised by the sun-god', the first secure evidence that the sun (in Egyptian *ra*) had become Ra, the sun-god. The form of the true pyramid brings an unsurpassed geometric perfection to this new faith in the power of the sun with its daily rebirth. The reigns of Huni and Sneferu saw another solar innovation, the ring around the name of the king, a ring christened cartouche by early Egyptologists. Middle and New Kingdom texts of kingship speak of the rule of the king over all that the sun encircles, underlining the solar imagery of this and all successive Pharaonic ages. If a later monarch, Amenhotep III of the 18th Dynasty, might be

called the sun-king of ancient Egypt, Huni and Sneferu can be credited with the original idea.

Another innovation of the reign, at least in the surviving material, is the naming of estates throughout the country after the king. Reliefs from the funerary temple of Sneferu include scenes of women personifying lands in various parts of Egypt supporting the cult of the king for eternity. If the practice goes back to the First Dynasty, only now does it achieve such great prominence. Still today one town in southern Upper Egypt bears the name Asfun, derived from the term *hut-Sneferu* 'domain of Sneferu', making it one of the oldest known placenames in the world. It is difficult to gauge the significance of this new feature, because we still know so little about the ancient Egyptian economy, but it can scarcely be an accident that the change in the texts occurs precisely when the pyramids appear. Perhaps the new cult complexes simply included more space for reliefs and texts of this kind, or the workshops expanded their artistic repertory at that moment to respond to the challenge of a new architecture. Yet the

Among the most famous examples of Egyptian art are the remnants of the offering-chapel for Nefermaat at Meidum. The register of painting with geese and plants (*right*) stood under a larger scene of hunting, and gives the classic Egyptian vision of a harmony that would last forever. From the same offering-chapel, a scene of men catching wild birds and another of a child at play with domesticated baboons and a crane (*left*) employ an experimental technique of neither painting on plaster, nor relief carving in stone, but a combination of the two; the artist cut out the body area of his figures and filled it with solid pigment. This method of 'inset painting' was never used again.

Right   The curtain box from the burial of queen Hetepheres illustrates the new expression of kingship in the reign of her husband king Sneferu. Against the gold background the name of the king is highlighted in white within a new feature of the period, the name-ring expressing rule over all that the sun encircles. To left and right the vulture-goddess Nekhbet, for the south, and the cobra-goddess Wadjyt, for the north, offer the *shen*-ring to the king, symbolising the gift of sovereignty.

change also hints at a deeper effect on the land as a whole, as the country geared itself to express kingship as the universal dominion of the sun-god on earth.

The other pyramids of Sneferu stand at Dahshur, the southern fringe of the range of royal cemeteries that centre on Saqqara. No other king of the Old Kingdom would stray as far as Meidum again, south toward the entrance to the Fayum, a rich province around the shores of a lake fed from the Bahr Yussef, a branch of the Nile, as it drains west into the Saharan desert. Possibly the location at Meidum itself acknowledges the input of the fertile provinces of Egypt into maintaining the eternal cult of the king. The two pyramids of Sneferu at Dahshur each present a different form to the steep slope of Meidum. One changes angle midway, earning it the modern nickname of the Bent Pyramid, evoking the squat obelisks of the Fifth Dynasty that gradually came to take the elegant Middle and New Kingdom form so familiar to us today. The other is known today as the Red Pyramid after the gold-red hue of the local limestone at Dahshur

Sunlight through cloud at the
pyramids of Giza.

44

North. It takes a gentle slope, at 43 degrees 36′ compared with the 54 degrees 31′ changing to 43 degrees 21′ of the Bent Pyramid. In all three great monuments a central chamber, the real or ideal burial place for the body and spirit of the king, stands no longer buried in the rock but placed at or just above ground level, a further subtle shift in religious planning for which we have no clarifying texts contemporary with the monuments themselves.

The Egyptians called the Bent Pyramid at Dahshur South and the Red Pyramid at Dahshur North Kha-Sneferu ('Sneferu rises') south and north respectively, evidence that they were understood together as complementary parts of a single effort to immortalise the king. The final resting place of Sneferu may perhaps be identified as the Red Pyramid, where clearance of the burial chamber in 1950 revealed remnants of a rudimentarily mummified body.

Armed with his multiple centres of cult Sneferu might well hope to enter immortal life unimpeded. He did achieve memory in the literature of the Middle Kingdom as a king who enjoyed himself without harming others, rather ironically when one reflects upon the likely human cost of his building projects. The great enterprise of the Fourth Dynasty most probably rested on national service or 'corvée' labour, not on slavery. In Egypt slaves were an expensive and somewhat irrelevant luxury, because

At the southeastern corner of the Great Pyramid stands an offering-chapel of the Sixth Dynasty, some three centuries later than the monuments of Khufu. The entrance to the chapel has been restored to give an idea of the original combination of architecture and sculpture. The chapel was built for an official named Seshemnefer, with additions to the west by his son, a doctor named Ptahhotep. Such private monuments are overshadowed by the royal cult complex behind.

The general absence of inscriptions deprive us of the identity of the most spectacular find from the Giza plateau, a cedarwood barge that has now been reassembled and continues its precarious existence in a modern glass and concrete hall at the side of the Great Pyramid of Khufu, where it was discovered in 1954.

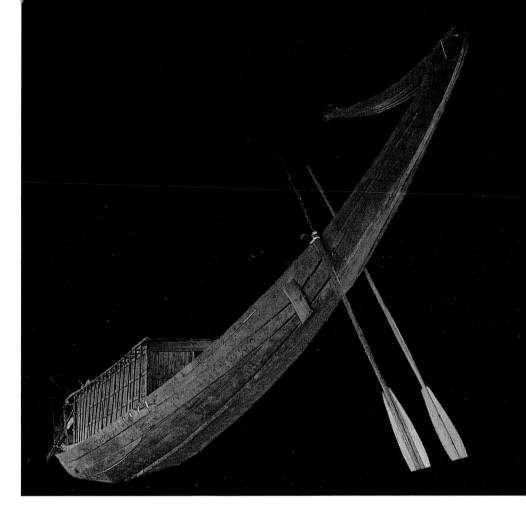

the Nile valley supported such a large population. Every year the annual flood covered the fields for three months, providing in theory an unlimited reservoir of workers, and periodically the irrigation dykes and canals would need to be repaired for the benefit of the whole local community, instilling a practice of local community service. These two factors, the size of the population and the local system of irrigation, must have helped the momentum of royal building projects as they veered vertiginously toward their peak under Sneferu and Khufu. Despite the generous attitude of posterity toward king Sneferu, the crushing magnitude of pyramid building can scarcely have escaped a cost in human life, any more than the great building projects of our own time.

For all the greater tonnage of stone in his monuments, Sneferu failed to achieve the single overwhelming impact of the burial place of his son Khufu. By concentrating the equivalent of the Meidum and Dahshur pyramids into one manmade mountain at Giza, Khufu left posterity a unique image of unrivalled scope, synonymous at once with an inhuman scale of power and a superhuman if not divine level of technical accomplishment. All the most bizarre theories of master races and extraterrestrial origins for these supreme Egyptian creations act in their way as a tribute to the Fourth Dynasty, simply by expressing a natural incredulity that man could organise and carry through so colossal a task. The Great Pyramid bore the Egyptian name Akhet-Khufu 'horizon of Khufu', the place where

the king would rise as certainly as the sun rises over the eastern desert mountains every morning. King and sun-god are now one, with an assurance never again expressed with such streamlined clarity. Giza has become today an unplanned outpost of the metropolitan sprawl of Cairo, greatest of the cities of Africa and the Middle East, and the monuments on its desert plateau can lose their impact under the levelling midday sun. Yet, in the silence of moonlight, or at dawn and sunset the Great Pyramid still conquers time. When the Greek historian Herodotus wrote of Egypt in the fifth century BC, the name of Khufu, already then dead for over two thousand years, signified tyrannical cruelty. It seemed impossible to the Greeks in their slave-made economy that so vast a monument could have been built without enslaving an entire people. The insult may be born of ignorance but it can also be taken as a compliment, a token of astonishment at what our eyes see but our mind cannot grasp.

The first successor of Khufu, his son Radjedef, did not attempt to match the scale of Giza, and turned ten kilometres farther north to Abu Roash where his tomb echoes in layout one of the two funerary complexes of apparently earlier date at Zawiyet el-Aryan. At least the lower courses of the monument were cased in the resplendent but costly red granite that had to be transported from the southern edge of the country at Aswan, but much of this has been removed over the centuries, leaving the unfinished complex still more battered. Another son and second successor of Khufu was Khafra, who returned to Giza to emulate his father with a pyramid complex named Wer-Khafra 'Khafra is mighty'. He had constructed a very slightly smaller pyramid on very slightly higher ground, and by an irony of destiny the summit of his pyramid retains its white Tura limestone casing, giving the impression that it rather than the Great Pyramid is the preeminent structure on the Giza plateau. It stands slightly set back from the valley, to ensure that the Great Pyramid would not block its view of the northern stars. The funerary complex of Khafra included the Valley Temple of monolithic granite columns, where the magnificent diorite statues of the king enthroned were discovered. Alongside, an outcrop of rock was sculpted into an image of the king as leonine master of the world, shown with the body of a lion, the body denoting the attribute, and the head of the king, the head conveying identity. This the first and greatest colossal sphinx demonstrates again the vitality of the age. Here classic form finds original outlets, and the Egyptians did not abandon the strength of these motifs until they embraced Christianity in the fourth century.

The third and last tomb of a king at Giza is the smallest in scale, and farthest back on the plateau, and scarred by the efforts of a twelfth century ruler of Egypt to destroy it, efforts abandoned only when the expenses soared, not least in human life as dislodged stones tumbled down on to their removers. This third pyramid is Netjer-Menkaura 'Menkaura is divine', built for Menkaura, the son and successor of Khafra. Despite its smaller size, it is cased in granite up to a height of sixteen courses, and its internal corridors also had granite walls, with massive granite blocks covering the burial chamber, here below ground as in the Third Dynasty and the tomb of Radjedef at Abu Roash. This and limited internal decoration with palace-facade relief point to a change in emphasis from towering exterior to fineness of detail, for which the skilled organisation of vast hordes of labourers gave way to greater numbers of skilled craftsmen from the royal workshops. Although hastily finished, the Valley Temple of the Menkaura pyramid complex yielded images of the king which now rank among the masterpieces of Egyptian art.

With Menkaura the experiment and achievement of sheer mass in perfect form comes to an end. His own monuments belong perhaps already more with the royal art of his successors than with the world of the pyramids of Sneferu, Khufu and Khafra. Words do not capture the impact of those first pyramids, but today onlookers might reflect that even in the century of modernism the Great Pyramid remains the most perfect geometric architecture conceived and realised by man. The modern reaches back in this case beyond forty-five centuries.

Above left The pyramid of Khafra retains part of the original fine limestone casing at its tip, giving it a distinctive appearance even from a great distance. Here it is seen behind the great sphinx.

Left The name of the king's cult complex can be read in this Sixth Dynasty hieroglyphic inscription. His name Khafra in a cartouche, the swallow *wer* 'great', and the pyramid sign name the pyramid complex 'Khafra is Great'.

Above In this sculpture the king Menkaura stands between the goddess Hathor, shown wearing the horned sun-disk, and a female personification of the district of Dendera as a source of foodstuffs for the king's cult offerings.

During the next two hundred years the tombs of the kings continue to confine text and image to the cult chambers of Valley Temple, Pyramid Temple and causeway between, keeping the burial chamber and underground galleries silent. The monuments of this age centre on Abusir, where kings Sahura, Neferirkara, Raneferef and Niuserra had pyramid complexes constructed with an impressive array of materials contrasting the darker and brighter sides of the night and day journey of the sun-god. Golden quartzite, red granite, bright white Tura limestone and pitch black basalt arrived from quarries in north and south to conjure this solar eternity for the king. The same sovereigns added to their quest for eternity a sun-temple, with an open court backed by a massive squat stone obelisk. Like the pyramid itself this may evoke the sacred *benben* stone at Iunu, the manifestation of the first ground upon which the creation of the sun-god could rest amid the primeval waters of nothingness. Although this squat shape seems far removed from the elegant monolithic obelisks of later periods, we may more easily recognise the classic qualities of the superb reliefs from corridors and chambers of both sun-temples and pyramid complexes. The passageway leading up to the obelisk and sun-court of king Niuserra at Abu Ghurab is known today as the Chamber of the Seasons for its lyrical depiction of nature and natural birth and growth. While the texts in these complexes continue to be restricted to dedication texts and offering formulae, the images grant us a vision, a 'reason why', behind the building of the pyramids. It remained only to record for eternity the articulation of that vision in the words uttered at the funeral of the king and in his cult at the temple.

The pyramids of the Fifth and Sixth Dynasties were built of small blocks and did not aim at the overpowering scale of Giza, as the emphasis of the royal cult shifted to relief decoration of walls in the complex. Robbed of their casing they revert to the rougher outline of a natural hill (*below*), although several survive as recognisable pyramid forms.

Left Sahura's pyramid from the ruins of the king's temple.

The break happens in the reign of Unas, an otherwise little known king who succeeded the much better attested innovator Isesi. Isesi had ended the practice of constructing sun-temples, and established his funerary complex back in the southern part of Saqqara. Unas followed him with a classic pyramid, temples and causeway just south of the Step Pyramid of Netjerkhet. We can only speculate whether or not the novelty of the reign of Unas was a concept born under his predecessor. For the first time the walls within the pyramids speak, covered in finely carved columns of incised hieroglyphs inlaid in blue pigment to stand out against the clear white limestone. The texts are the Pyramid Texts, for which no ancient title is known, a corpus of arcane formulae designed to procure eternal life for the king through the motifs of Ra the sun-god and Osiris the god who is king of the dead. With these texts we move into new realms of understanding as we look at the pyramid complexes of the Old Kingdom.

It would be a mistake to try already to read out of the texts for Unas and his successors of the Sixth Dynasty an original account of the Step Pyramid or the Great Pyramid at Giza. The study of the syntax may help to distinguish older from newer compositions, but remains at an early stage,

The spectacular drop in scale of royal monuments is amply compensated by the quality of exquisite relief scenes from the walls of Fifth Dynasty royal cult complexes. This fragment comes from the pillared court beside the pyramid of Userkaf at Saqqara, and presents a cluster of wild birds in a papyrus marsh.

particularly since such texts often assume an archaising mantle by using language as far from the vernacular as possible to increase the sacred aura of the spoken and written word. We must take the texts as they have come down to us, from the burial of the king in the specific reigns of Unas, Teti, Pepy I, Merenra, Pepy II and the ephemeral Ibi. In addition to these six monarchs of the twenty-fourth to twenty-second centuries BC, Pyramid Texts have been found in the burial chambers of queens of Pepy II, as the practice of inscribing text to secure immortality spread from the core of kingship to an innermost circle of royal favour. The texts have not been fully collected and published, and most of the chambers are more or less

The groundplan of the Unas cult complex follows the classic model of pyramid with temple, connected by a causeway across the desert to the valley temple at the edge of the cultivation. Surviving fragments of decoration from the causeway and temples illustrate the quality of Fifth Dynasty work, as in this scene of the king being suckled by a goddess, whose name is lost.

blighted by damage, complicating any attempt to study the original layout of the words around the underground chambers of the pyramid complex. In the single case of the oldest example, the Pyramid Texts of Unas, the tomb walls have survived all but intact, allowing us to recover a meaning from the arrangement of the different formulae around the space of burial. In the wake of pioneering research by Maspero, Sethe, Piankoff, Altenmüller and most recently Jürgen Osing, we can hope to look beyond the individual texts to rediscover the grand scheme or schemes that intended to grant king Unas eternal life.

In the Pyramid Texts we meet three lives of text simultaneously. Many

Left There is no explanation for the sudden decision to inscribe the walls of the burial chamber and antechamber with texts securing eternal life for the king. They appear in the pyramid of Unas, in a programmatic sequence, placing formulae against serpents and other aggressors at the extremities, points of possible entry, and covering the entire northern wall of the burial chamber with a tabulated 'menu' of offerings to sustain the body in the sarcophagus.

Right From the antechamber doorway, now jaggedly broken above, the burial chamber of Unas reveals the massive basalt sarcophagus in which the king had been supposed to rest forever, its lid heaved on to the floor of the chamber. The ceiling is a vault of stars, while the wall area immediately around the sarcophagus presents the protective device of an ornamental niched facade, the same motif that defended the exterior of First Dynasty enclosures as well as the Third Dynasty Step Pyramid complex. The triangular space above the western niched facade bears texts against harmful creatures, the right (northern) wall contains the great list of offerings, and the left (southern) wall bears a series of formulae for the resurrection of the king.

passages belonged in a first life to a variety of different contexts. Some were spoken to keep danger, particularly dangerous animals and insects, away from the living. Others were hymns to the gods, sometimes as litanies in which the speaker unites a whole series of individual names in a single act of worship. Litanies along with some texts spoken at the presentation of food offerings could be embedded within the daily ritual or special rites for particular feastdays. In their second life these same texts, with others devised for the task, were spoken in the course of the burial of the king as Osiris by his successor as Horus. Now the fragments of text united in a single stream of singular purpose, reinforcing each moment of the complex procedures of mummification and the delicate operation by which the body was taken from the Nile Valley up to the desert plateau and then down into the underground chambers of the pyramid. These stages must have been present in burials of rulers since the first burial of a man claiming kingship, back in the unrecorded centuries of the fourth millennium BC, but they survive in words only from the reign of Unas, thanks to the third life of these texts, their inscription upon the walls of the chambers beneath the pyramid.

The final arrangement over the two-dimensional space of the chamber walls brings changes to the linear, one-dimensional flow of texts spoken in series across the period of time of the burial. Although the texts read in a certain sequence, they must also obey the dictates of spatial area. The texts to preserve the body against harmful creatures belong, regardless of their place in the rites of burial, at the doorway and the west and east ends of the text area, to act as sentinels posted at points where intruders might try to force entry. Similar reasoning demanded that the wall closest to the final resting-place of the dead king be inscribed with those texts in which each part of his body was assured eternal life by being equated with that of a god or goddess. Again, this moves them out of the sequence of time into a new order dictated by the space in which they are written. Also without relation to the moment of ritual at which the words were uttered, the northern wall of the burial chamber is covered with a vast tabulation depicting and recording every item of food, drink and clothing which the dead king was to enjoy for eternity.

The great offering list, spread out like a pictorial menu behind the head of the deceased, spells out the first preoccupation of the Egyptians, to secure sustenance for the body after death. The first offering would have taken place at the burial itself, and should then be repeated by the family or their substitutes the priests for the cult of the dead every day. The fragmentary archives of the Fifth Dynasty found at Abusir confirm in meticulous records the survival of the royal cult for at least a century or so after the death of the king for whom it was initiated, but even the cult of a king began to lose its support grounded in the interest of the successors on the throne and, essential for the supplies of food, in the maintenance of in-

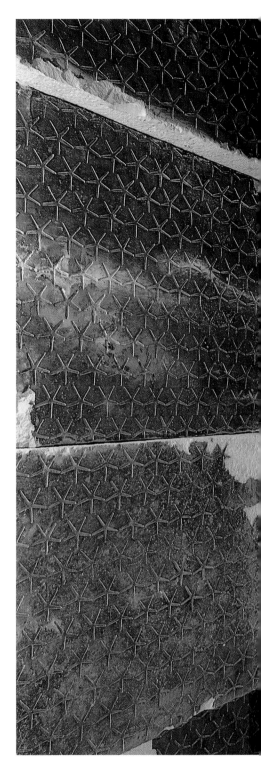

The successors of Unas followed his example in inscribing some underground chambers of their pyramids with hieroglyphic texts to reinforce their eternal existence, but the stock of texts never ceased to evolve, and no two pyramids

contain the same selection or sequence of formulae. The burial chamber of king Teti displays the continuity in principle, with the ceiling again adorned with stars, set at a particular tilt, creating almost an impression of motion.

alienable estates dotted through Egypt. The dead king would then depend entirely on the supernatural provision of security and sustenance, on the images and texts carved in his pyramid temple. It may be coincidence, but the earliest Pyramid Texts, those of Unas, date to about two centuries after the construction of the mightiest complexes for a cult of the dead king, the Giza pyramids. Perhaps the experience of witnessing the decline of even the most substantial cult complexes provided one among the many factors that led to the new practice of recording funerary texts for eternity. It is not solely speculation that the period of Unas saw an awareness of the need to reinforce the cults of dead kings; most of the Abusir archives for the cult of Neferirkara seem to date precisely to the reign of Isesi, energetic predecessor of Unas.

Aside from the texts for the body, its physical safety and sustenance, the great bulk of texts are distributed over the walls of the central chamber below the pyramid, where the descending corridor from the outside world descends to the lowest point of the darkness. From this chamber one doorway turns right (west) to the burial chamber, while a doorway opposite leads to a triple shrine for the images of the deceased. The eastern and southern walls of the burial chamber also contain part of this great series where they are not already taken for the deification of parts of the body or accompanying texts to the menu of offerings. According to New Kingdom monuments a thousand years later, the sky-goddess Nut rested her feet to the southeast, and therefore the daily birth of the sun-god from her womb would take effect in that corner of the sky. If we overlook, as in Egypt we so often can, the intervening thousand years, we would find a further spatial reason for the layout of these texts, as their physical place on the walls of the burial chamber would reinforce the eternal rebirth of the king by the daily resurrection of his father the sun-god.

The texts spell out the exact way in which the king could raise himself to immortality with the sun and stars. Any mortal misdeeds are left behind as he is embraced by the gods:

> There is no word against Unas on earth among men,
> there is no misdeed against Unas in the sky among gods.
> Unas has removed the word against himself, he has erased it,
>   in order to rise up to the sky.
> Wepwawet (the 'opener of ways') has let Unas fly to the sky
>   among his brothers the gods.
> Unas has moved his arms as a goose, has beaten his wings
>   as a kite,
> and flies up, the flyer, O men ! Unas flies up away from you.
>   (PT 302, north wall of the central chamber).

His ascension into heaven is greeted by the gods, in particular here by the gods of the most ancient centres of kingship, Pe at the northern end of the

57

kingdom (Buto of the Greek texts), and Nekhen at its southern end (the Hieraconpolis of the Greek texts):

> They come towards him, the gods, the powers of Pe,
> they come towards him, the gods, the powers of Nekhen,
> they come towards him, the gods of the sky,
> they come towards him, the gods of the earth.
> They raise Unas on their arms.
> You go forward, O Unas, to the sky,
> you climb it in this its name of Ladder.
> Let the sky be given to Unas, let the earth be given to him.
> So says Atum.   (from PT 306)

This passage is one of the many in which the motion of the original moments of the burial can most strongly be felt. The powers of Pe and Nekhen, advancing to raise up the king so that he can achieve eternal life, follow the same movement as the men who moved forward once in history to lift up the coffin containing the mortal remains of king Unas, to bring him from the valley up to the pyramid where he intended to live for ever. At one or two points the Pyramid Texts even preserve some of the 'stage directions' for the officiants in the ritual or those charged with carrying the coffin, such as 'place on the ground'. Every human action becomes the action of gods in this ritual, as many references to the gods in these texts applied directly to the men involved in the physical act of burial. Egypt is already, as in the gnostic texts of the late Roman period, the mirror of heaven.

In the quest for life after death, the obstacles both physical and in reason are legion, and the deceased must always fight to overcome them. A common strategy in Egyptian texts is to identify not the deceased but his destiny with that of the gods:

> If Unas is bewitched, Atum will be bewitched.
> If Unas is opposed, Atum will be opposed.
> If Unas is struck down, Atum will be struck down.
> If Unas is impeded, Atum will be impeded.
> Unas is Horus, Unas has come after his father,
>   Unas has come after Osiris.
> O you, Face-in-front-face-behind, bring this to Unas !
> 'Which ferry shall I bring you ?'
> Bring Unas the one which flies up, the one which alights.
>   (PT 310)

The end of this text expresses movement across long distances as journey by boat, taken automatically in Egypt from the daily experience of sailing on the Nile. Numerous texts for an afterlife in Egypt involve the boat of the sun-god, to sail the heavens for ever, or a ferryboat and ferryman, to

Despite differences in scale and theme, the cult for the king and those for his subjects overlap in certain respects, above all in their common dependence upon fields in the Nile Valley and Delta for offerings to sustain the spirit through eternity. The female personification of fertile estates for the cult of Sahura wears a green dress, denoting not the colour of a fabric, since fabrics could not be dyed green at this date, but the role of the goddess as an embodiment of green and flourishing plant life. Her arms proffer, at a slight but significant angle, the loaf on a mat, the hieroglyphic sign for *hetep* 'offering' and 'contentment', with three *ankh* cords hanging down, denoting the plural life to be gained.

leave the world below and reach the shores of the world of the heavens. Ferryboats embody in Egyptian style the rite of passage, the mechanisms by which all societies guide a person into a new status.

The Pyramid Texts provide the earliest connected information about the unfolding of creation. In the beginning existed only the undefined expanse, Nun, expressed as water, and the sum of all future matter, Atum, meaning 'All'. Creation unfurled when Atum appeared as Ra, the sun-god, out of the waters. This appearance was recounted with the help of a variety of metaphors, among which a prominent place is given to the embodiment of the first solid land as the *benben*-stone, an untranslatable word connected to the root *weben* 'to shine'. Creation continued when Atum/Ra produced from himself the god Shu, meaning 'dry', and the goddess Tefnet, meaning 'moist' or 'corrosive', two opposing principles of life. Again the 'birth' of this divine pair could be expressed in various ways, as spitting, sneezing or masturbation. All these terms, including the use of family relations, are metaphors to convey mysteries of creation.

With his mortal remains secure in the earth, equipped with the food and transport necessary for a good afterlife, the dead king had become a divine being on a par with the most powerful deities, above all the sun-god, the creator. Accordingly he appears on the west wall of the entrance from the sloping corridor into the central chamber as a force simultaneously physical and supernatural. On the model of numerous deities, his enhanced power is expressed through the metaphors of the animal world, such as the perception of divinity in voraciousness, embodied in the crocodile and given a name in Egyptian as the god Sobek.

> Unas emerged today from the flooding of the primeval waters.
> Unas is Sobek of the green feather, face on guard, brow uplifted.
>
> (PT 317)

The texts are unambiguous. The king is sustained by the eternal offerings, flies or sails past all obstacles to the sky, thrives as surely as the creator and his creation thrive, in other words becomes immortal as a god. Thanks to the hieroglyphs the moment of utterance of each formula at the burial of the king is transported onto an eternal plane, cast in stone to repeat the words automatically as long as the stone itself endures. The very hieroglyphs with which these texts are written embody the same confidence in clean-cut blue silhouettes against the bright white walls, beneath a ceiling adorned with stars. The star as much as the sun stands out as the dominant symbol of afterlife in the Pyramid Texts, and this may explain to some extent why they continued to be used by Egyptians of later periods as much as two and a half thousand years after the death of Unas. None of the later funerary literature contains such a celestial vision of the guarantee of life after death. The only comparable stock of imagery comes in the star charts on some Middle Kingdom coffins and, infinitely more

Above ground the pyramid complex of Teti provides a spectacle of devastation. Its pyramid temple rises barely to the first courses, giving no more than a general idea of the space where the formulae of the Pyramid Texts would have been recited for the immortalisation of the king. The pyramid itself became reduced to a hill of rubble centuries if not millennia ago. In the background the Fifth Dynasty pyramid of Userkaf has suffered a similar fate, overshadowed by the Step Pyramid of Netjerkhet.

spectacular, the astronomical ceilings of tomb chambers in the New Kingdom, those of Senenmut, first minister of Hatshepsut, and kings of the Ramesside period. Those pictorial accounts of the skies evidently did not satisfy the Egyptian fascination with the stars entirely; throughout the Middle Kingdom and later, the Pyramid Texts survived in the ritual of burial and of Osiris, god of the dead, to provide the voice of a specific belief, that the dead might stay alive just as the circumpolar stars never sink beneath the horizon of the night sky. The circumpolar star, called 'the star that cannot perish', can be regarded as a sign from nature that some matter is imperishable, a sign of hope precisely in the darkness of the night.

The contemporary monuments of the successors of Unas tell us little of their reigns. Conventional history, following the third century BC writer Manetho, make Unas the last king of the Fifth Dynasty of Egypt, and Teti first king of the Sixth. However this change of dynasty may derive from a simple misunderstanding, since Teti is placed at the top of a new column in one tabulated list of kings and their reigns; possibly Manetho or one of his sources took the new column to signify a substantial change, when it might merely be required by the spacing of the particular kinglist which they were consulting. Manetho also records that Teti was murdered, but again we do not know his sources for this apparent evidence of political

trouble. We can only state that the kings after Unas continued to build pyramids, of unimpressive scale, with Pyramid Texts in the underground chambers as well as fine reliefs over the walls of the pyramid temples above ground. The kinglists name a king Userkara as successor of Teti, but his burial place has not been located and the only signs that he existed are some sealings and an hieroglyphic inscription of dubious authenticity.

The next king in the lists is more securely attested, Meryra Pepy, or Pepy I, followed by Merenra Nemtyemsaf and Neferkara Pepy, or Pepy II. The order and number of kings is not entirely certain, as we depend almost entirely on the discovery of a royal burial-place to confirm the existence and date of an Old Kingdom king, but these are the kings for whom pyramids with Pyramid Texts are known today. In the reign of Pepy II, the Pyramid Texts are used for the first time for persons other than the reigning king, albeit for the person closest to the throne, the queen. The formulae themselves remain embedded in the ideology and imagery of the sun; the deceased requires the apparel of kingship, and will fly up to heaven to join the sun-god. The texts are adopted without modification to ensure the afterlife of a mortal woman, the queen of Egypt. Pyramid Texts are found in the underground chambers of the pyramids of three queens of Pepy II: Neit, Wedjebten and Iput.

The adoption of kingly texts flows naturally from the preeminence of kingship. As centrepoint of the Egyptian world, the king would be the first person for whom texts would be devised to secure eternal life. Any formula guaranteeing the eternal life of the king must stand automatically as the most powerful means of resurrection for all mortals. While the texts were spoken at burials but not inscribed for perpetual action, they may have fastened more tightly onto the specific burial of the king. However,

once they were written on the walls, and stood at one remove from the recitation at the funeral of the king, they may have become more open to reuse in the burial chambers of not just the king but also his subjects.

The stock of texts inscribed on the walls of each pyramid shows how fluid the tradition remained, despite the new custom of inscribing texts for eternity. No two pyramids contain the same stock of texts, and many texts found in earlier pyramids were not reused in the later ones. The themes do not change, but they allowed for continual reworking and new formulations, giving rise in each new generation to a fresh body of texts. However much it may seem to the uninitiated a land of repetition, Egypt never froze its religious literature as a Scripture. Either the content or the context underwent change at every stage of the life of a text. Individual passages among the Pyramid Texts occur at later periods in new sequences, with some additions, in temple rituals or non-royal burials. These lived on alongside a new stock of formulae for eternal life, generated by the Pyramid Texts but separate from them. Unlike the Pyramid Texts in the Old Kingdom, the new texts were not for the king or his queen, but for the wider circle of subjects of the king, and were written on the walls of their burial chamber or, more frequently, their coffins, from which their modern name Coffin Texts is taken. With the Coffin Texts the union of the king with the gods suddenly becomes a permissible model for any man or woman who could afford the luxury of a burial with texts.

The two traditions, royal and elite, find a single enigmatic link, discovered only in 1978, in a most unexpected corner of Egyptian dominion, the oases of the western desert. The French excavations at Balat uncovered the burial of a man named Medunefer, apparently governor of Dakhla oasis in the reign of Pepy II. Although the wooden coffin had not survived intact, the remnants bore fragments of text which Alessandro Roccati has been able to decipher and from which he could identify several parallels to Coffin Texts. The excavation director Michel Valloggia made the interesting suggestion that the signs now legible on the wooden coffin were imprints left by a shroud that had perished. Whether shroud or coffin was the original surface bearing the text, the most striking discovery is the presence of this type of text already before the end of the Old Kingdom. From the diminutive pyramid and single underground chamber of a king Ibi we know that Pyramid Texts continued to be devised and inscribed for the ephemeral kings who lost control over Egypt after the long reign of Pepy II. The texts of Medunefer, out on the fringes of Egyptian rule in the western desert, demonstrate that a new tradition had been developed while the line of Memphite kings still, at least nominally, commanded Residence workshops.

The location of the new texts, at the farthest limits of the realm, might indicate the milieu in which the elite first found it possible to use similar texts for eternal life to those used by the king. However it might be no more than an accident of survival; Coffin Texts or Pyramid Texts may await us in unexcavated elite burials of the late Old Kingdom at Saqqara. Indeed Pyramid Texts are inscribed on the shattered fragments of wall-decoration from the tomb of a man named Ankhenmeryra (meaning 'may he live for Meryra'), a name suggesting a date not long after king Meryra Pepy I. The aspiration to cross the sky with the sun-god is voiced in at least one late Old Kingdom tomb-chapel, indicating that the elite expected an immortality modelled on that of the king, even if we do not have the texts from those non-royal burials.

It remains difficult to date precisely material from periods of weak kingship. In Egypt there was no fixed dating point like the Christian BC-AD; instead years were reckoned by the reigning king, and the sequence of kings was crucial to calculating the passage of years. In periods of strong central power, many elite burials or offering chapels mention the reigning king, allowing us to fix the burial in time with a high degree of accuracy. When the kingship weakened, those burials had less motive to refer to the king, and without the name of a king it is that much more difficult to date a burial and the objects, and texts, in it relative to other burials, objects and texts. Recent years have witnessed considerable advances in dating by indirect means, by style or by changes in forms of material, or, in the case of texts, of signs and the spellings of words. Nevertheless dating of individual coffins and tombs remains a subject of hot debate, and never more so than in the period of the critical transition from Pyramid Texts of kings, and then of queens, to Coffin Texts of their wealthiest subjects.

Dating is complicated by the striking continuity in burial customs from three bands of political history, late Old Kingdom, First Intermediate Period, and early Middle Kingdom. The late Old Kingdom, the period of

During the First Intermediate Period, while the scarab-form was coming into circulation, the flat disk or 'button-seal' enjoyed a brief vogue. This example in gold has a ring for suspension above a tiny crouching male figure, with a motif on the base including two stylised animals. Despite its quality, it documents the breakdown in the hieroglyphic tradition of art at the end of the Old Kingdom.

the royal Pyramid Texts, witnessed a decline in central power, although a single line of kings still resided at Memphis and, in theory, still ruled all Egypt. In the First Intermediate Period, the line of Memphite kings was replaced in the north by kings from Henensu (Heracleopolis), and in the south by the governors of Thebes. The latter claimed kingship and gradually, in part by military conflict with the north, reunified Egypt under their control. The new period of unity under the Theban kings is the Middle Kingdom. Despite the momentous changes at national level, local burial traditions ignored any interruptions to a remarkable degree. If a provincial coffin of the late Old Kingdom is placed beside one of the early Middle Kingdom, it takes a specialist to explain the subtle differences, and, in the case of some cemeteries and for poorer burials, they cannot convincingly be distinguished.

Perhaps then it will be some years before we can recount in detail the history of the origin of Coffin Texts, and the place and time in which they split away from the original core of Pyramid Texts. Yet we can appreciate the scale of the change even in the stark outline of a new phenomenon: where there were texts for the afterlife of the king, suddenly the scope of the written text has spread out to a wider plane, below the king. In the Old Kingdom members of the royal court clearly expected a perfect afterlife, as expressed in the painted reliefs of their offering-chapels. Yet there the wording of the afterlife is never made explicit. With the Coffin Texts the chances of afterlife as a divine being, with the gods, are offered to the human subjects of the god-king, on the model of the original royal texts for an eternal life. This one dramatic turning-point ushers in a new history, two thousand years in which first Coffin Texts, then the Book of the Dead give voice to the way in which a human being may defeat death.

CHAPTER 3

Human Made Divine:
The Coffin Texts

In the finest surviving set of models the nobleman Meketra equipped his eternity with his place of leisure, a walled garden with central pool and a columned portico, exactly like gardens in the largest mansions at the late Middle Kingdom town excavated near Lahun. The need for water and shade is a recurrent motif in the funerary texts: 'to build a domain among the waters . . . this domain of mine is founded among the waters, among the domains (of the gods); their pools are dug, their sycamores planted'.

When the dust settled on the conflict of the First Intermediate Period, and Egypt had again a single ruler, Nebhepetra Mentuhotep from Thebes, we find the burial chamber of the king once more devoid of text, as it had been before Unas, while two distinct groups of texts are found side by side in the burial chambers of the elite. One of these consists of Pyramid Texts, and they follow more or less faithfully the wording but not the sequence of formulae found in pyramids of the Old Kingdom. The second group develops a new set of themes parallel to the preoccupations of the Pyramid Texts, and contains new texts as well as variants of the old. Most of these new texts occur on coffins, and for that reason the entire group has received the modern name Coffin Texts. Less often the texts are found on other types of object, from tomb chamber walls to statues and stelae (standing stones) placed in offering chapels.

At Thebes some of the courtiers of king Mentuhotep and his successors were buried in limestone chambers with walls constructed of separate monolithic slabs, each inscribed with the same texts and images that cover the walls of the contemporary wooden coffins. In the Delta, too, burial chambers of the Twelfth Dynasty were inscribed with Coffin Texts, as was the sarcophagus found at Lisht and belonging to a high official of the early Twelfth Dynasty named Mentuhotep. The massive cult chapel halls of Djefahapy at Asyut and Djehutyhotep at Bersha, two further high officials of the Twelfth Dynasty, contain examples of the same corpus on their walls and ceilings. Yet in all cases the coffin seems to be the kernel of the new tradition. The surfaces of the stone chambers seem to emulate the layout of a wooden coffin, and even the granite sarcophagus of the high official Mentuhotep, instead of baring its magnificent and costly stone surface, is plastered and painted within in exact imitation of the wooden coffin. At first sight this primacy of the coffin may seem surprising, but a reason may be found in the early history of this second strand of texts for an afterlife. The new texts began to take shape during the late Old

Kingdom and First Intermediate Period, when the country lost not only its unity but also much of its wealth. In these relatively impoverished conditions, the words securing eternal life were no longer spread over the stone expanse of tomb-chapel walls, but had to be confined instead to the wooden coffin. The birthplace of the new texts justifies their modern name Coffin Texts.

Some of the images on the coffins begin to appear in the late Old Kingdom, when the first decorated rectangular coffins were produced. These include the typically Egyptian motif of the pair of eyes with the markings of a falcon, presenting the power, above all the power of sight, of that bird of prey. This pair of eyes was set on the outer face of the long side of the coffin at the point where the head of the mummified person lay inside. The eyes conferred on the deceased the far-sightedness of the gods of creation and power, Ra and Horus, each of whom were evoked by the symbol of the human eye with the surrounding markings of a falcon's head.

The principal bands of text along the upper edge of the coffin, inside and out, also stem directly from Old Kingdom prototypes, and contain the most exquisitely detailed painted hieroglyphs of this and perhaps any period. Here the artist realises the full potential of his script, and transforms each sign, whatever its content, into a living creation. Even the record of a single consonant receives meticulous care in attention to outline and details, such as the wing of an owl (the owl denotes the sound *m*) or the body of a viper (*f*). Again it is the late Old Kingdom coffins that included tabulated lists of offerings, echoing the great pictorial menus on earlier Old Kingdom tomb-chapel walls and in the burial chambers of the late Old Kingdom kings amid the Pyramid Texts.

The upper bands on the inside walls of the coffins also began to bear friezes of objects, presenting items enumerated in the rites of equipping the deceased at burial. A small number of stone burial chambers from the Old Kingdom are inscribed with the first examples of such friezes of objects, but the motif only became widespread in the early Middle Kingdom with the transfer of texts and images from the burial chamber walls to the immediate surround of the body, the wooden coffin. Each item in the frieze belonged to a group with a particular place in the layout of the coffin decoration. Sometimes the layout obeys quite straightforward rules, such as the position of sandals at the foot end of the coffin, and headgear and anointing oils at the head end. Other items are less easy to fathom, such as unidentified emblems wrapped in linen. The name of each object is often written beside it in hieratic, the cursive form of the script, fixing still more specifically its presence in the service of the deceased.

A number of the items in the object ritual, as presented in the friezes, belong to the sphere of kingship, and would never be allowed in the hands of mere subjects of the king during their lifetime. At death, those same subjects are seeking eternity, a goal that implies a new, supernatural status

The remnants of walls from the temple of Nebhepetra Mentuhotep include fragments such as fallen Asiatics, identified by their yellow skin and beards, as well as the king among the gods, embraced by both the Theban falcon-headed god Mont and a goddess. The upper part of a register shows a vulture with wings outstretched to protect the king, beneath a star-filled sky-hieroglyph and, mostly lost, the *kheker*-frieze.

Below The temple of Nebhepetra Mentuhotep marks in monumental form the reunification of Egypt, and is the main surviving monument of the Middle Kingdom at Thebes.

as divine beings. Only in the grave, with this quest, can mortal men and women take up symbols of kingship as tokens of supernatural power. The crowns and sceptres of the object ritual do not detract from the power of the king; on the contrary they confirm kingship as the model for all aspirations of divinity, and their restriction to life after death underlines the royal prerogative.

The bulk of the Coffin Texts and Pyramid Texts were written in cursive hieroglyphs in the columns below the principal bands inside the coffins. It is difficult today to compare the burials of king and subjects in the case of these texts, because none have been found in any king's burial chamber of the Eleventh or Twelfth Dynasties. Possibly those chambers were entirely textless, in the new confidence of central power, harking back to the days before the Pyramid Texts. It is also possible that new texts had been inscribed on papyri or other perishable and moveable objects, and that these have simply not survived the destruction of the royal cemeteries. Even

In relief, the king is often followed by his *ka* either in the form of a human male or as a banner with arms to hold defensive weapons, but always with the name of the king surmounted by the falcon, his 'Horus' name. By combining the imagery the Egyptian artist spells out the religious message that the god Horus, god of kingly power, is himself the *ka* or sustaining spirit of kingship. This example comes from the White Chapel of king Senusret I at Karnak.

above ground, comparison between the cult of the king and that of his subjects is thwarted by the devastation of royal cult temples. Only fragments survive from the reliefs of the Theban terraced temple of Nebhepetra Mentuhotep, and the northern pyramid complexes of the Twelfth Dynasty.

King Amenemhat I, third successor of Nebhepetra Mentuhotep and first king of the 12th Dynasty, founded a new Residence south of Memphis, and named it Itjtawy-Amenemhat 'Amenemhat seizes the Two Lands' (i.e. Upper and Lower Egypt), abbreviated in most ancient texts as Itjtawy. This continued to be capital of Egypt until the central line of kings retreated to Thebes in the late 13th Dynasty over two centuries later. At the desert edge, Amenemhat I had a pyramid built as his eternal resting-place, on a site near the modern village of Lisht. The Arabic word Lisht may well derive from the old placename Itjtawy, prefixed by the Arabic *el* 'the', frequently set before names in modern Egypt. As long as Itjtawy remained Residence, the kings had their tombs constructed in the area of Memphis and the Fayum, more or less the territory covered by the Old Kingdom pyramids. Around the pyramids of the Twelfth Dynasty stood the tombs of the royal family and the officials of the royal court. The shattered fragments from their walls reveal an exceptional standard of artistic achievement, echoing the outstanding tomb-chapels of the Old Kingdom at Saqqara.

A few texts for the afterlife of the king survive from the later part of the Middle Kingdom, the last years of the Twelfth Dynasty and the first half of the Thirteenth Dynasty. The tips of the pyramids of Amenemhat III and an ephemeral successor named Khendjer preserve texts appealing directly for a passage through the sky in sight of the sun. When the Coffin Texts were revived after a century of absence for officials of the Thirteenth Dynasty, the text of the eastern face of the pyramid tip now surfaces among them. At least in the middle years of the Thirteenth Dynasty, then, at about the time of king Khendjer, both the king and his subjects were using at least in part the same stock of texts. This small overlap occurs at the only point where we have any knowledge at all of the texts to preserve the king in this period. The rest of the royal strategy for afterlife remains lost to us, preventing us from seeing how similar or different the sovereign kept his destiny from that of his human subjects. Yet difference is emphasised by one unique text, from the tomb of not a king but the daughter of a king. This is inscribed upon a superb calcite vessel of unusual form, designated the receptacle for cool water in the course of its texts. It secured refreshment for eternity for the owner of that tomb, the king's daughter Sathathoriunet, and is unique among all surviving burial goods. Perhaps then the survival of king and royal family were kept distinct from the methods pursued for other subjects; the texts on the pyramidia would have started life in the service of the king alone, and have been diverted for

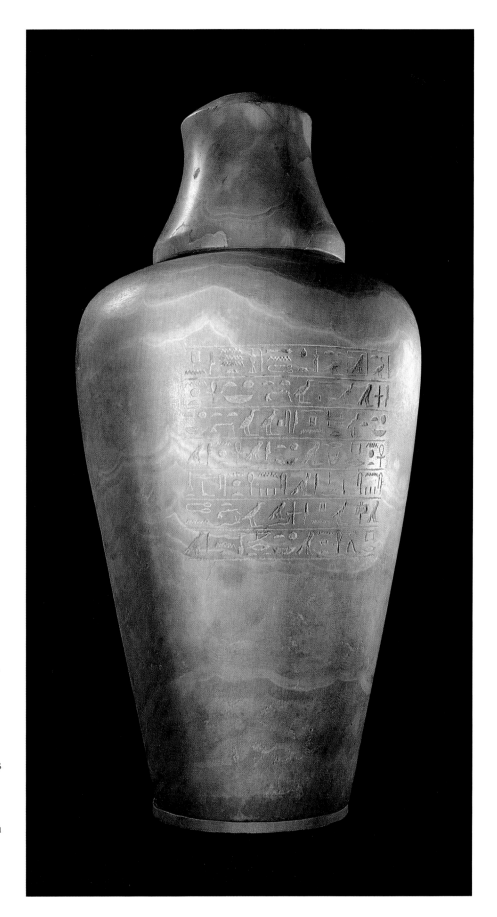

The calcite water vessel of Sathathor-iunet bears a text as unique as the stone vessel itself: 'King's daughter Sathathoriunet, receive this cool water which is from the land that begets everything that lives, all those things that this land gives; indeed it is the land that begets everything that lives, in truth from it everything comes forth. May you live on them, may you revive upon them. May you live and revive upon this breath that is within it. It begets you, and you come forth. You live on all that is desired and perfect that is therein'.

A block from the temple of Karnak illustrates in the Middle as in the Old Kingdom a national network of estates founded to support the royal cult. To the left Amun is seen leading Senusret I toward the sanctuary, and, below the niche for a statuette, kneels an estate in the guise of a goddess bringing 'all offerings, all things'. The estate wears her name on her head, Hut Sekhem-Kheperkara 'the Domain Kheperkara [Senusret I] is Mighty'. One town in Upper Egypt preserves this name today in the abbreviated form Hu.

the benefit of ordinary mortals only after the end of the Twelfth Dynasty. To date there is insufficient evidence to determine the relation between king and subjects in this field. The history of the resurrection of the king and his family lies heavily obscured by the thorough destruction of their burial places.

For better preservation we must turn to the provincial centres of Upper Egypt, where, as never before and rarely since, the courts of the local elite aspired to, and reached, standards of royalty. The tombs of governors rarely survive in good condition, except, until recent years, at Beni Hasan. However, the burials of many officials in the local miniature versions of the royal court were found intact, admittedly most at the turn of the century when archaeologists recorded far less information than can answer our questions today. From these burials of men and women in the upper class of provincial Egypt we gain our first detailed insight into the means by which Egyptians other than the king expected to secure an eternal life, thanks to the new practice of inscribing Coffin Texts on the inner walls of the wooden coffin.

The most striking difference between the mass of new texts and the old body of Pyramid Texts lies in an obsession with the dangers in the earth. Certainly the Pyramid Texts already included means of ensuring that the earth would open, that it would not keep the dead king imprisoned in its depths. Yet they aim constantly at the sky, at the sun and the stars, and their address to the earth to open itself only serves to reinforce their insistent push towards heaven. By contrast the Coffin Texts swarm with chthonic demons, with obstructive forces, often presented concretely as gates blocking the passage of the dead. There within the earth the dead man or woman must spend eternity in at least one aspect, the aspect of the physical body. The dead person is still expected to fly up to heaven, and this detached afterlife could be expressed in the word *ba*, a manifestation of power reserved for divine beings, and so never found among human beings in the Old Kingdom. The Coffin Texts retain with the *ba* the more traditional form of surviving the death, by the *ka*, the spirit sustained by food, and this remains more firmly attached to the body in the burial chamber below the earth. The afterlife now presents two very different faces, the celestial travels of the *ba* and the earthbound destiny of the corpse, sustained in the *ka*-spirit by the offerings of food brought to the tomb. Where the Pyramid Texts addressed eternal life in the sky, the Coffin Texts embrace beside that the darker prospect of eternal life in the earth.

Although the exact dates of individual examples remain problematic, James Allen has recently succeeded in establishing a general history for the whole class of coffins, with and without texts, over the course of the Middle Kingdom. According to this reconstruction the Coffin Texts were in use alongside Pyramid Texts by the time of reunification under Neb-

hepetra Mentuhotep. Renewed political unity encouraged adoption of the same texts across the land, and this trend may have intensified with the creation of a new Residence at Itjtawy at the beginning of the Twelfth Dynasty. At all events the classic phase for coffins inscribed with texts for an afterlife spans the middle years of the Twelfth Dynasty, from the epoch-making reign of Senusret I across the forty-five years of rule by his son Amenemhat II to the brief reign of his son in turn, Senusret II. Under the next king, Senusret III, Egypt underwent a critical transformation in every area of life. We still understand little of this change, but it affected even the texts for the afterlife; for a hundred years they seem to disappear from the burial-place, only to be revived during the Thirteenth Dynasty with a number of new compositions, written on the outer faces of the coffin rather than in its interior. It is not known how long this revival lasted; after the mid-Thirteenth Dynasty Egypt again lost her unity, and the coffins of this Second Intermediate Period preserve few texts.

The earlier part of this history, down to the reign of Senusret I, yields evidence from a range of cemeteries near important towns of Upper and Middle Egypt: from Aswan, Gebelein, Thebes and Dendera in the south, and from a cluster of Middle Egyptian sites – Asyut, Meir, Bersha and

A rare surviving object with a text for the resurrection of a Twelfth Dynasty king is the pyramidion, or pyramid capstone, for Amenemhat III from his first pyramid at Dahshur. A winged sun-disk stretches over two eyes and three hieroglyphs reading *neferu* 'perfection' and a sun-disk faced on either side by the name of the king. The two lines of hieroglyphic text at the lower edge offer the king access to the sun-god, and are found on some non-royal Thirteenth Dynasty coffins.

Beni Hasan. Many of these bear the solid imprint of provincial prosperity from the late Old Kingdom down to the early Middle Kingdom, in the form of great chambers cut into the rock cliffs above the Valley to house the cult of the local governors. The cult chapels over the tombs of governors at Beni Hasan are the only Middle Kingdom monuments to attract many visitors today, but they form only one link in a chain of local wealth strung along the river banks. Lower Egypt is less well represented in this phase, but some of the coffins from Saqqara are doubtless contemporary.

The coffin of the nobleman Ima from Thebes offers a good example for the earlier stage in the history of the Coffin Texts. It contains single horizontal lines of inscription on its exterior, not painted but finely carved in the pure wood, with the requisite pair of eyes toward one end of the eastern or righthand long side. Within the coffin each of the four sides divides into upper registers of detailed painted hieroglyphs and friezes of objects offered during the burial rites, and a lower section of Coffin Texts in cursive hieroglyphs arranged in columns separated by neat dividing lines.

The contents of the texts confirm the thought that went into the layout of the coffin as a whole. As in the pyramids of the late Old Kingdom the coffin compromises the order in which texts were spoken at the ritual in order to place particular formulae close to the appropriate part of the body, such as ointment texts near the head, the main part of the body to be anointed. On the coffin of Ima the head side begins with excerpts from the Pyramid Texts, specifically from the great offering list ritual (PT 77 and 81 from the Unas corpus, and 686 for ointment, first found in the pyramid of Pepy II). These are followed by part of a ritual for transfiguring the deceased, identified on numerous other coffins (CT 30–33). A second funerary ritual to transfigure the dead person dominates the back, that is the inner face of the western or lefthand side of the coffin (CT 1 and 20–25 with associated texts 343, 225–6 and 761–5). This gives a shortened version of a lengthy liturgy which enacted the entry of the dead person into the next world. In its full version, the liturgy opens with four distinct appeals to the deceased to awaken for his justification against enemies in the underworld. These invoke the earth-god Geb, and the creator sun-god, here named neither Atum 'the All' nor Ra 'the sun' but Ruty 'the God of the Two Lions' (the two lions being an expression for the first 'generation' in the unfolding of creation, Shu and Tefnet, or dry and moist air). (In the citations N denotes the name of the deceased.)

O Osiris N, raise yourself on your left side,
place yourself on your right side.
Geb has commanded, the God of the Two Lions has repeated,
that you be given your *ba* in the earth and your shade in the secrets.
O Osiris N, raise yourself to be vindicated against your enemies.

(from the first appeal, CT 1+2)

Of extreme rarity and brilliance, these bronzes demonstrate the power of late Middle Kingdom sculpture. The female torso (*above*) is of a queen or goddess. From its distinctive profile the large head and torso with *nemes* headcloth (*left*) depicts either Amenemhat IV or a king of the early Thirteenth Dynasty and thus perpetuates the cult of a king for whom no funerary texts survive. Probably from a temple in the Fayum.

O Osiris N, take your staff, your loincloth, your sandals,
and go down to the tribunal to be vindicated against your
enemies, against those who would harm you, man or woman,
   who would go to court with you on this good day in the tribunal.
                               (from the second appeal, CT 3)

O Osiris N, the earth opens its mouth for you, Geb throws open
his jaws for you. May you eat your bread, receive your overflow,
pass on to the Great Terrace, and arrive at the great city;
May you light your warmth on earth, may you become Osiris.
O Osiris N, you have seized the sky and inherited the earth.
Who then can take away the sky from you, from this young god,
   the perfect creature ?   (from the third appeal, CT 4+5)

These appeals serve in the full version of the liturgy as introduction to
the rites of vigil proper, called the 'Ploughing of the earth' from the opening words of this main section. The ploughing alludes perhaps to the
digging of a burial chamber in the earth, but this prosaic act here mirrors
explicitly the 'ploughing up' or devastation caused by the combat between
the two Rivals, Horus and Seth, in the battle for succession to the throne.

   The earth is ploughed up, for the two Rivals have battled
   and their feet have dug out the ditch of the god in Iunu.
   Thoth comes adorned in his nobility, for Atum has ennobled him
   with the strength of the Two Great Goddesses who are pleased
      with him . . .

During the heyday of the Coffin Texts, in the early Middle Kingdom, the elite secured a good afterlife by including among their burial equipment models of their estates. One crucial element of a wealthy estate was a fleet of Nile rivercraft, for ferrying, fishing, transport of heavy cargo, and movement of the estate owner both in life and, as here, at his last journey. This example is from the finest surviving set, of the high official Meketra.

Right Over the mummified body of Meketra, women acting as the goddesses Isis and Nephthys mourn the dead, while a man reads out the texts on a papyrus scroll by which the deceased gains eternal life.

Hail officials of the gods ! N is vindicated against his enemies
on this day, as Horus was vindicated against his enemies on
that happy day of the accession.   (from CT 7)

The declaration must go forth that the dead person, like Horus in his battle
against Seth, is true of voice, that he or she speaks the truth, in the tribunal
of the underworld. Vindication is the first requirement for an afterlife, to
remove the opposition of any earthly or demonic adversaries who might
claim that the deceased is not worthy of an afterlife; the dead can only
become transfigured into blessed spirits if they are true of voice in the tribunal, in other words if they have been good in this life on earth.

Once confirmed as true of voice, the deceased is hailed in triumph and
can go forward to enjoy the blessings of heaven; this is the transfigured
condition acclaimed by the second part of the full version of this liturgy.

O Osiris N, the door is opened for you by Seshat,
the good ways are opened for you by Wepwawet (= Opener
    of the Ways)
. . . N has been vindicated against his enemies who went
to court with him on this day.   (from CT 10)

> Go forth from the dispute, go forth from the dispute;
> it is Horus who goes forth from the dispute.
> Be far from N, you who should be far from him.
> Do not approach him, you who would approach him,
> for the Osiris N will judge the Wilful God (Seth)
> in Iunu.   (from CT 14)

The acclamation reaches its climax in the final address:

> O Osiris N, you are a god, you will exist divine,
> you will have no enemies or opponents in the presence
> of Ra who is in the sky, in the presence of Osiris,
> the great god who is in Abydos.   (from CT 19)

Both long and short versions conclude with words to be spoken around the body in its coffin within a chamber called the *henkyt* or chamber of the bier. In part these words are repeated on the sides of New Kingdom coffins as the texts for deities at the burial, and these would have been the same deities with whom men and women at the burial on earth were identified. The reference to sacred cities, to gods and goddesses, casts the entire procedure of mummification and funeral on a different, divine plane; men accompanying the coffin become gods such as Geb, the mourning women become the goddesses Isis and Nephthys, the mourning sisters of Osiris, and the son or chief officiant becomes Horus the avenging son of Osiris. Death is transformed into a drama of the gods, ensuring that the deceased will live again as surely as Osiris lives after death. The intention can be illustrated from a single example among these texts, from the section ascribed to Imsety, one of the four sons of Horus, in the New Kingdom.

> O Osiris N, come then, go forth to the sky.
> The ladder is assembled for you beside Ra among the gods.
> The pestilence of rivers is driven off for you,
> so you may drink water from them.   (from CT 21)

The purpose of the liturgy as a whole finds a typically eloquent, densely figured, expression at the end of the liturgy:

> This is the power of light (*akh*), this is spoken word,
> this is the opening of the West, pleasing to the heart of Ra,
> satisfying to his tribunal, the herdsmen of humankind.
>   (from CT 25)

The front of the coffin contains another funerary ritual, this time known already from the Pyramid Text tradition (PT 213-19) where it accompanies the great offering list. The foot together with that end of the base of the coffin contain a fourth series of texts, found in the same sequence on coffins from Saqqara, and so suggesting another fixed liturgy from the rites of mummification and burial. The remainder of the long series of texts on

This model from Meketra's tomb shows the preparation of bread and beer from barley and emmer wheat.

One of the Coffin Texts records this exchange between the gods and a dead man: "'On what will you live?' so the gods ask this man. 'This N will live on loaves of white emmer, on which the gods live.'" (CT 660).

The grain for the staples, bread and beer, was kept in granaries and, like every instant on an estate, meticulously recorded by scribes under the guard of a doorkeeper. The model of the granary from the burial of Meketra shows (*left*) labourers carrying the sacks of grain past the doorman and two lines of seated accountants, and (*right*) up the stairs to offload the grain into silos.

In one funerary text we read 'I have filled your stores, and brought in your wineracks; your bread cannot grow mouldy, your beer will never sour' (CT 67).

the base and lid appear more miscellaneous, but they too may form at least in part connected strings from specific other moments in the funerary ritual. If the coffin of Ima seems at first sight a mass of disparate and un-connected texts, upon closer inspection it presents more an eternal prolongation of key moments in the funeral ceremonies during which the dead person was helped by the embalmers toward the blessings, and past the dangers, of the afterlife.

Among the most evocative of the funeral rites recorded on the coffins one consists of a series of speeches at the moment of raising the coffin. This moment requires eight men to come forward and lift up the heavy burden for transport to the tomb. By a stroke of imaginative genius the scene, in practice an instant of tension as the vulnerable body is exposed to the risk of violent movement, has been turned by this liturgy into the central act of giving life, giving breath, having power over air. The eight coffin-bearers take on a new guise as the eight gods of Unending, as the deceased lays claim to be the very spirit of air, the god Shu. By delving into the darkness on the eve of creation, the compilers found a perfect metaphor for the lifeless human corpse in which eternal life lay dormant:

> Formula of the *ba* of Shu, for becoming Shu:
>
> I am the *ba* of Shu, the god who came into being of himself.
>
> I am the *ba* of Shu, unseen of form.
>
> I came into being as the limbs of the god who came into being of himself.
>
> I am the one in the side of the god – I came into being as him.
>
> I am the one amid the gods of Unending,
>
> who hears the words of the gods of Unending.
>
> I am the despatcher of my word that comes into being of itself for the multitude.   (from CT 75)

In another passage, the dead addresses the bearers directly, presumably through the words of the lector-priest reciting from his papyrus roll:

> (Formula) for going forth to the sky, for boarding the bark of Ra, for becoming a living god.
>
> O those eight gods of Unending, keepers of the sections of
> the sky, those whom Shu made from the fluid of his flesh,
> who tie together the ladder to Ra-Atum,
> come toward your father in me, tie the ladder for me,
> for I am he who created you and made you,
> just as I was created by your father Atum.
> I am weary of the supports of Shu,
> since I lifted my mother upon myself to give her to Ra-Atum,
> and set Geb beneath my feet so that he might bind the earth
> together for my father Ra-Atum.
>   . . .
>
> It is I, Shu, created by Atum who came into being of himself.
> I was not fashioned in the womb,
> I was not put together in the egg,
> I was not born in birth.
> My father spat me out as spittle (*sheshu*) of his mouth, together with
>   my sister Tefnet.
> She came out after me, and I was cloaked in the breath of life of the
>   throat.
> The *benu*-heron is the form as which Atum came into being of
>   himself,
> in Unending, in Boundlessness, in Wandering, in Darkness.
> It is I, Shu, father of the gods.
>   . . .

One of the model boats from the tomb of Meketra shows the nobleman seated beneath an elegant papyrus-column canopy, while a steward of the estate reads out to him from a papyrus roll. Although the scene is administrative in tenor, it echoes the funerary ritual where a lector-priest must recite incantations from a papyrus-roll to the benefit of his deceased master. The funerary texts themselves include the titles 'for fetching a ferryboat and crossing over in the afterlife' (CT 403), and 'for sailing to Iunu' (CT 616).

O those eight gods of Unending, whom Atum made from the fluids
  of my flesh,
whose names Atum made when the word created Boundlessness,
that day on which Ra spoke with Boundlessness,
as Unending, as Boundlessness, as Wandering, as Darkness.
Come toward me in joy, give me (your) arms,
tie the ladder of Shu for me as you tied it for my father Atum,
  for I am weary.

The liturgy of Shu aims to give life to the dead, and in its course reveals to us some of the most elaborate Egyptian expressions of existence. Here the creative force, the sun, and its offspring, the air, encounter exactly what existence is not, and so that out of which existence must have come. In place of fixed limits, there is eternal Unending. In place of visible internal segments there is Boundlessness. Wandering removes stability, and the light yet to be born is negated by Darkness. These are not so much evil forces as nothingness, four pairs to lift up Shu and relieve him of his task of lifting the sky Nut from the earth Geb. The literal and unpoetic mind might ask how the sky Nut can be mother to her own father Shu. Such questions fail to recognise the many sides of existence; the sky gives birth to the sun, and the son of the sun equates himself directly with his father, and so sky, air and sun are interlocked in motherhood and fatherhood simply as bald human metaphors to embrace mysteries of life and rebirth.

Some of the Coffin Texts are not confined to the early or later part of the period, but occur throughout the three centuries of the Middle Kingdom, and beyond. Among these longer lasting works, one self-declaration stands out, a formula through which the deceased identifies himself with the creator. Already in the early Twelfth Dynasty the formulaic phrasing had attracted the attention of theologians, who inserted as time went by more and more glosses to explain particular references. The ambition of the text may be caught in the opening words of the declaration as they occur on the coffin of Sobekaa from Thebes, now in Berlin:

Formula for Going Forth by Day in the Underworld
by the honoured Sobekaa, who says:

The spoken came into being.
Mine is All (Atum) in my existence, alone.
I am Ra in his first appearances.
I am the great god who came into being of himself,
who created his names, lord of the Nine Gods,
without opponent among the gods.
Mine is yesterday; I know tomorrow.
It means Osiris.
At my word they acted at the battle-place of the gods.
The battle-place of the gods means the West.
I know the name of that great god who is (in) it.
'I am in adoration of Ra' is his name
I am that great *benu*-heron which is in Iunu,
the keeper of controls of what exists.
It means Osiris. What exists means Eternity and Everlastingness.
I am Min in his processions.
I am given the double plume upon my head.
What is the Double Plume?
It means Horus who champions his father.
It means the Double Plume Crown.   (from CT 335)

Rarely are we given such a detailed glimpse of Egyptian scholarship at work. Only recently has a copy from the reign of Senusret I been found without the copious glosses, many of which seem more obscure than the plain declaration of identity by the creator, among the more direct attempts by humankind to paint a verbal image of god.

The later phase of the Coffin Texts, the century of two great kings,

The provision of food offerings and an afterlife of luxury was assured for Meketra by models of food production. In the slaughter-house model a bull is butchered under the direction of an official. The raising of the specially formed *kherep*-sceptre evokes the moment in ritual where king or priest directs that the action of offering begin, a reminder of the repeated hidden but specific references to funerary cult, and even religious texts, in these apparently prosaic 'scenes of life on the estate'.

The portico and pool in the garden of Meketra. The trees recall the shady sycamore trees with their figs, and offer the deceased nourishment as well as respite from the summer sun.

Senusret I and Amenemhat II, is best attested outside the Residence cemetery of Lisht, in Middle Egypt and particularly at Meir, Beni Hasan and Bersha. Model estates were still placed in burials without tomb-chapels, to provide the eternal sustenance of the deceased, although perhaps none are as remarkable as the earlier examples from the tomb of Mesehty at Asyut and the tomb of Meketra at Thebes. The texts on the inner faces of the coffins now reached their peak of development, directly continuing the search for certainty beyond death with exact images and even measurements. If we look outside the world of the tomb for a moment, we find the same increasing emphasis on precision in all areas of life, and nowhere more than in the activity of government. Titles and departments in the state hierarchy become more and more narrowly defined, preparing the way for the minute job descriptions of the late Twelfth and Thirteenth Dynasties.

The most celebrated and most perfect surviving coffins in the classic stage in the history of the Coffin Texts come from Bersha, cemetery of Khemenu, the town of the god of wisdom Thoth. In their every feature these coffins present the peak of artistic achievement, from the joinery of the carpenter and the quality of the wood, imported cedarwood from the northeast, to the magnificent detail of the painted hieroglyphs on the upper registers within the coffins. The images of the coffins begin to take on new life in charting the underworld, most famously in the so-called Book of Two Ways, a set of maps and texts to guide the deceased person along the paths of water and earth through the obstacle of death.

One coffin in particular illustrates the principle that the texts form connected sequences with a direct bearing on the funerary rites, the coffin of a mayor Amenemhat buried at Bersha. Of his luxurious set of three cases to contain the body, the outer presents a carefully arranged series of the groups of formulae to transfigure the body for eternal lfie as a blessed spirit. Between the different groups stands a connecting passage, devised especially for Amenemhat and not found on any other Egyptian monument, in which the idyll of the afterlife is described with explicit reference to three of the very liturgies occurring on coffins. The first is named Ploughing up the Earth, the first words of its principal section, while the second is called the Great Mourned is Come, again opening words, this time of the vigil for the dead, and the third is denoted the Laments of Unison, from the refrain to ritual laments uttered during embalming and burial. The liturgies include moments of high drama in which the human and mortal world become divine:

> The doors of the sky are opened to your beauty:
> may you go forth to see Hathor . . .
> You are risen as lord of the West,
> you ruled the Egypt of those on earth.
> Stand ! Live ! You have not died . . .
> Come to me, rise up to me, be not far from your chapel,
> turn to me.   (from CT 44 and 51).

These laments can contain references to specific procedures or places in Egyptian mummification:

> Be gone, creature of darkness!
> See, the embalming house is guarded.   (from CT 52)

Yet local Egyptian colouring never obscures the guiding force behind the liturgies, which remains the universal human experience of grief and hope:

> Awaken to life! See, day breaks.
> Nephthys has favoured you, anew, anew, every day at night time,
> when you are with the Unwearying Stars.   (from CT 53).

As night gives way to dawn, the light brings relief, but not an end to the vigil, which must pass the seventy days of mummification, the burial and lead on into eternity, as implied in the phrase 'every day at night time'.

The latest court buried at Bersha, that of the governor Djehutyhotep, included one of his chief physicians, Gua, whose coffins are now preserved at the British Museum. As with all Bersha tombs, the quality reflects the high standing of local tradition, not surprising when we consider that the patron god of Khemenu was Thoth, lord of hieroglyphs. We should at the same time remember that these are not the finest products of the area,

The front wall of the garden of Meketra shows a central grand doorway, with a pattern of *djed* pillars and *tiyet* knots, between a narrower trade entrance and a tall, latticed window.

From the same group of Middle Kingdom bronzes as those illustrated on pages 74–5, the kneeling figure of a king may be ascribed by his features to Amenemhat III. The material of the figure appears to be 'black gold', a copper, silver and gold alloy only recently recognised from analyses by Alessandra Giumlia-Mair and Paul Craddock. The blackness of the alloy provides a perfect background for highlighting gold and silver details, here mainly lost but once including perhaps both kilt and headcloth.

The stone statue head on the right is of unknown provenance, but its strong features identify the king again as Amenemhat III. Like other royal statues, they serve the eternal cult of the king, no less than the funerary texts on his pyramidion.

which would undoubtedly have been the burial of the governor himself. His tomb is now being recorded to modern standards by epigraphers from Leiden and the Boston Museum of Fine Arts, but has suffered greatly even in recent times from limestone quarrying at the site. We should also remind ourselves that even the finest monuments at Bersha would have been a step down from the level of the royal cemeteries at Dahshur and Lisht. Recent recording work in the Delta has shown that compositions such as the Book of the Two Ways were copied in tombs north as well as south of the Residence, confirming that the tradition flowed out from that central source. We must be content with the secondary product of a secondary, provincial level, as in the coffin of Gua. The tradition seems all the more extraordinary for retaining such power at so great a distance from its source.

Gua commissioned, or was given, not one but two fine cedarwood coffins. Together these had the task, along with the canopic chest and the now lost funerary mask, of securing eternal life for the wrapped body of the chief physician. Some of the texts do not occur on any other coffin, such as the only surviving Middle Kingdom guide through the portals of the underworld:

The first portal, of which it is said: vigil of fire.
It is its flame which repels from it.
Fifty cubits along its side is its fire,
and the front of its flame traverses the earth from this sky.
The gods said of it – it is charwood.
It came from the arms of Sekhmet.
It stood bound with the dispensers.
It created its body, and made the gods
a light task of plunder afterward.
It stretches its foot to the tomb called
'That of which the horn guides him who is in the secret place'.
Open to me. Make way for me. See, I am come.
O Atum who is in the great sanctuary, O seizer of the gods.
Rescue me from that god who lives on meat-sacrifice,
dog-faced, human-skinned, keeper of the bend of the waterway of
   fire, who swallows shadows, who snatches hearts,
who throws the lasso and yet is not seen.   (from CT 336)

Along the floor of the coffins of Gua stretch more visual guides for passing through the underworld, including the charts which have given these compositions their modern name of the Book of Two Ways. Until the past few years this tradition of maps for the afterlife was known for the Middle Kingdom only from coffins at Bersha, but the more recent work allows us to extend the geographical spread of the text to the Delta. This makes it probable that the text originated between the two areas where it is

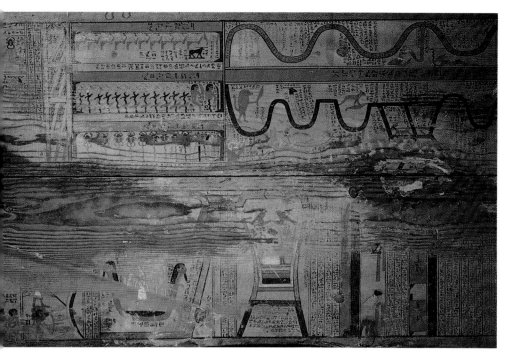
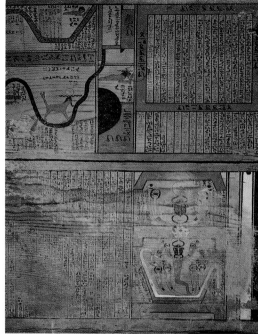

now found, and emanated from the Residence and its cemeteries at Dahshur and Lisht, spreading south to the tombs of the governors of the city of Thoth, at Bersha, and north into the heartland of Lower Egypt. The gap at the centre of this distribution may remind us how much we have lost in the annihilation of the royal court tomb fields. The Book of Two Ways survives in more than one edition, with varying amounts of illustration and of names for demons in the underworld, although the focus of intent remains the same, to ensure the survival of the deceased. The 'Book' opens with a description of the trauma of death evoked even at the moment of birth and rebirth:

> Quaking falls from the eastern horizon of the sky at the voice of
>   Nut as she clears the ways for Ra upon the arms of the
>   Great One whom he circles.
> Raise yourself Ra, raise yourself now, O He who is in his cabin.
> May you lap up the winds, may you swallow the spine,
> may you spit out day, may you breathe Right.
> May the retinue circle when the bark sails to Nut,
> may the great ones be moved at your voice.
> May you count your bones, and assemble your limbs.
> May you turn your face to the beautiful West, and arrive fresh
>   every day,
> for you are that perfect image of gold with shining hair.
> Sky and earth fall before you quaking, as you circle afresh,
>   afresh every day.
> the horizon rejoices, there is jubilation at your tow-rope.   (CT 1029)

Although the layout of Books of the Two Ways varies in detail, notably in the proportion of vignettes to texts and plans, the general impression of a map is common to all. Some demons guarding the features of the underworld take forms reminiscent of later figures on ivory throwstick-'wands'.

See there, the star in Iunu, the sun-people in Kheraha,
their thousand is born, the god whose headband is tied,
   whose oar is taken up;
with them I board the Storm-boat at the quayside of the gods . . .
I go forth in it to the sky and sail with Ra,
I steer in it at the territory of Nut, at the stairway of
Sebeg (Mercury).   (CT 1030)

The proclamation that the journey commences leads to a second section of text, this time within a red rectangle, in each of whose sides the label 'entourage of flame' is written. In these lines the word *shenyt* 'entourage' alludes simultaneously to the circle of flame around the sun-god and to the gods and goddesses in his retinue, who form a protective barrier like the flame itself. The words within are entitled 'formula for passing the entourage of flame', and end with the reassurance:

Pass by, says Horakhty,
   to govern the bark,
   the eye of your father.   (CT 1033).

Before the chart of the two ways, one version presents an extended series of compartments that lead to a building, depicted as in ground plan. The deceased must here confront in turn each door and its keeper, over whom he or she can have power if only they know the names, symbol of essence and identity. The first of these barriers is described in words at once characteristic of the series and unusually revealing of purpose:

The gate approach of flaming front and hidden back,
   with a man within it bound . . .
This the deceased is Nun lord of darkness:
I have come that I may have power over the way . . .
I have come today from Iunu,
   that I may be crowned with the Powerful Goddess,
   that I may see the bull of Iunu in their form,
   that I may see the water that is in the darkness.
I know them by their pictures.   (from CT 1132)

The last phrase identifies the reason for including images with the texts, to complete the knowledge of the deceased in the face of unknown enemies. The general fear of ignorance and its perils is voiced again as the dead person approaches the building at the end of the gates series:

O physicians, protect me every day from those
   whose names are unknown.
Lords of life each day,
   make them benign at my approach.   (from CT 1145)

The final building remains itself an enigma, bearing simply the label 'image of the *hut*-enclosure'. A *hut* can be any edifice bounded by a rectangular enclosure wall, and laid out formally on an initiative of the state. It can be a temple or sanctuary, or an entire town such as Hetep-Senusret, the site near modern Lahun at the mouth of the Fayum, where the original form of the rectangular enclosure is preserved. The word is virtually untranslatable, and we can barely do more than render the phrase 'image of the building'.

The next part of the composition, in all versions, presents its most instantly recognisable feature, the two ways winding through a landscape of named features. The upper way is coloured blue, presumably to indicate water, and the deceased asks for access as the physician of Osiris:

> Make way for me, so that I may pass.
> I treat Osiris – do not mourn his flesh.
> Plough through Shu with the knife . . .

The deceased is then provided with the most important information to enable him to pass, the name of the way through which he must pass, for the name carries with it deeper knowledge and power over that pathway:

> *Its name is the Gateway Approach of Darkness.*
> *This is for perceiving its name.* (CT 1148)

The service rendered to Osiris can include more than the medical:

> My two fields are in the Field of Hotep among the learned,
>   so that I may care there for Osiris . . .
> I am the pure one who cooks for Osiris in the course of the day
>   among the learned in offerings. (CT 1159)

The representation of the Fields of Hotep follow, in a form different to the more common map of Coffin Texts 464 to 468, the text and image taken up in the later Book of the Dead as 'chapter 110'. The upper way concludes with words to carry the deceased past the barrier of flame:

> Formula for passing the way of flame.
>   I am that eye of light in the darkness,
>   the eye of flame in its perfection.

Between the upper and lower ways a band separates the two halves of the map, with the explanatory note:

> This is the channel of flame, called the Great One.
> None exists who might, if fallen into the flame,
> be turned back from it. (CT 1054)

The lower way is marked in black, presumably to denote earth. At the

This exquisite set of Middle Kingdom coffins belongs to the steward Hapy surnamed Ankhtyfy, an official of the late 12th Dynasty buried at Meir in Middle Egypt. His innermost coffin is mummiform, with the head adorned with both a striated false beard reminiscent of the royal beard, and a tripartite headdress in black and gold stripes inlaid with black faience beads. The inlaid eyes intensify the effect of the head, in a relatively early example of the anthropoid coffin. The rectangular outer coffin is inscribed inside and out with incantations on behalf of Hapy.

start the deceased appeals directly to the doors blocking his way:

> Open sky! Open earth!
> Open eastern horizon! Open western horizon!
> Open shrines of Upper Egypt! Open shrines of Lower Egypt!
> Open, O eastern gates of Ra,
> that he may go forth from the horizon.
> Open for him the doors of the Night Bark,
> unleash for him the bolts of the Day Bark,
> that he may breathe Shu, that he may create Tefnet,
> that those who are in his following may follow him,
> that they may follow me like Ra every day.   (CT 1065)

The chart empowers the deceased to overcome specific obstacles on his way to join the sun-god on his Night and Day Barks to sail around the skies, and as such carries the same message as the other funerary texts only with a more visual impact.

The pathways through the underworld continue in the next section, with which one version concludes the entire composition. These are the paths named Rosetau, after the Memphite necropolis and specifically the Giza plateau. Here again the deceased encounters two sectors, one of the 'ways upon land', the other of the 'ways upon water'. Again access is granted to the physician of Osiris:

> I have treated Osiris. Make way for me.   (from CT 1183)

In the versions that continue, another path is associated with Thoth, possibly a local tradition at Bersha, the cemetery of his city Khemenu:

> This is the way of Thoth to the House of Right.   (CT 1093)

More universal in tone is the next, a single formula, the longest in the Book of Two Ways, which contains neither vignette nor plans but a sun hymn, and begins with the declaration 'I am a follower of Ra' (CT 1099). There follow further barriers, seven portals each with a gatekeeper to be named by the deceased in order to gain free passage. Beyond lies the end of the journey, a final chart incorporating the outline of the bark of Ra:

> the entourage of flame (repeated three times) –
> the entourage which is on the prow – Isis, Seth, Horus;
> the entourage which is on the stern – Hu, Sia.   (CT 1128)

Here at the end of the Book, instead of turning again to the deceased, to celebrate his or her successful entry into a blessed afterlife, the text cuts to the words of the creator himself as he confronts the chaotic forces that would overthrow creation. He justifies his passage through the cosmos by recalling the four essential good deeds of creation, devised when he was still unborn within the 'Coiled Serpent', the image of primeval time:

Some of the finest Middle Kingdom coffins survive from Bersha, cemetery of Khemenu. Unlike his contemporaries, but following a custom found elsewhere in these same middle years of the Twelfth Dynasty, general Sep commissioned not two rectangular coffins with texts along traditional lines, but a rectangular outer and a mummiform inner coffin. On this mummy the head is neither wrapped nor a portrait of the deceased as he had lived on earth. Instead it takes directly the attributes of kingship, the headcloth and divine beard, not to usurp kingship in the order of this world, but to follow in the footsteps of the king in procuring eternal life. A funerary text explains the purpose of the headcloth: 'Come, that you may see me adorned with a headband, wearing the headcloth of kings; by this is joy granted me' (CT 398).

Words spoken by the Secret-of-Names, the Lord of All,
saying before the silent ones who rage
    at the sailing of the entourage:

Proceed in peace.
Let me repeat to you the four good deeds which my own heart
did for me within the Coiled Serpent,
of my desire to silence evil.
I did four good deeds within the portal of the horizon.
I made the four winds that every man might breathe in his time;
    that is one of the deeds.
I made the great flooding that the poor might be empowered
    like the rich; that is one of the deeds.
I made every man like his fellow; I did not command that they
    do evil – it is their hearts that destroy what I have said;
    that is one of the deeds.
I made their hearts not forget the West, in my desire that
    divine offerings be made to the gods of the provinces;
    that is one of the deeds.
I created the gods from my sweat, and people (*remet*) from the
    tears (*remyt*) of my eye.   (from CT 1130).

This passage ends with the note 'The End', the first time that such a marker is found in Egyptian texts, demonstrating the self-consciousness of this expression of life and afterlife. By ending with a celebration and defence of the creator, the composition lifts the world of the dead onto a new plane, asserting that only the good is, or should be, eternal.

Perhaps more remarkable still than either the Inferno measured in such detail or the self-defence of the creator, we find on the outer coffin of the general Sep from Bersha a direct portrait of that same creator in word and image combined. A figure in human form is embedded like an embryo within a series of circles in space. He, for the figure is depicted as male, looks out at us, face to face. He grasps the symbol of power and is seated upon a throne bearing the signs 'millions of years', for this is the lord of time. He is crowned with an unfamiliar crown, resembling the *atef*-crown of Osiris, but on which the horns emerge as serpents. The creator sits within circle upon circle of black, white and red, the primordial colours of earthly power, purity, and danger. Around the outermost circle an obscure text invokes the circling of millions upon millions, as if to capture the expanse and mystery of creation.

The creator image stands unparalleled within Egyptian art. If the precise measurements of the Book of Two Ways recall the *Commedia* of Dante Alighieri, we are more likely to think of his Inferno than his Paradise as we confront this core vision wrapped like a foetus in fold after fold. Even the circles around the throned figure seem more reminiscent of the circles of

The rectangular outer coffin of general Sep (*see p.94*) is of exceptional quality. A bold polychrome border defines the area for text and illustration, divided into an upper band of exquisitely detailed hieroglyphs, a central band for the frieze of objects, and a more extensive lower section for the main series of Coffin Texts, the formulae to preserve the deceased for eternity. The frieze on this head end of the coffin depicts items appropriate to the head, notably seven stone vessels for the canonical seven sacred oils. Below is a unique image, within circles of black earth, white, and red flame, of the creator enthroned; his throne is inscribed with the signs 'millions of years'.

hell than the tiers of heaven. Together image and text evoke a force which encompasses death as well as life.

The outer coffin of Gua contains another text of central importance from the Middle Kingdom, known from only two other Twelfth Dynasty coffins, but then taking on a life of its own. This is the address to a figure identified with the deceased and ordered to take his or her place in the case of a summons to do any manual labour in the next world. For a member of the elite, of the scribal class, the prospect of heavy manual work would have seemed a genuine hell. In this life they avoided the demands of the state for help on agricultural and other projects by sending a servant in their stead; this option could of course only be open to the upper strata in society. Records from the temple archive at Lahun from the end of the Twelfth Dynasty include lists of workers fulfilling their national service duties, among whom we find some designated 'man of such-and-such an official', presumably their substitutes at hard labour. In the afterlife the little figure is directed to play the same role, and is named *shabti*, a word of uncertain meaning perhaps derived from *shabet* 'stick of wood'. The text for the figure reads as follows on the coffin of Gua:

Formula for making a *shabti* do work for his master in the underworld.

See him then, gods and blessed spirits and dead,
whether he be in sky or on earth. He has assumed his strength.
He has taken to himself his seats (of office, i.e. his authority).
He has ruled with the sceptres made for this (the deceased)
by order of the gods.
If this (the deceased) is called up for substitute-work of
replacement-land (meaning uncertain), for removal of a sector,
for traversing(?) riverbank lands, for turning over new fields
for the reigning king,
Here I am! you should say to any commissioner who may come for
this (the deceased), as his replacement.
Take up your picks, your hoes, your carrying-poles, your baskets,
see, as does every man for his master.
O *shabti* made for this (the deceased), if this (the deceased) is
counted in for his lot, see the obstacle is struck there
(meaning his name is ticked off on the works roster) for
this (the deceased) as (is done for) a man for his lot.
See us here, you should say.
If this (the deceased) is called up for (work) which is done
there, turning over new fields, strengthening riverbank lands,
ferrying sand to the west that has been swept to the east
and vice versa,
see us here, you should count him for it.

The burial of Neferu, one of the women accorded special status within the cult precinct of Nebhepetra Mentuhotep, contained several miniature wooden coffins, painted with hieroglyphic inscriptions and containing a female figurine in wax, as here, or mud. These were found wrapped in linen and seem to have served as substitute burials in case any harm befell the real body.

The earliest *shabti* text specifies that it is to be pronounced over a figure of the tomb-owner in wood; no such figures survive with the *shabti* text itself, but these contemporary statuettes of a scribe of offerings, Merer, bear Coffin Texts in red or black on the white kilt.

Words spoken over an image of the owner as on earth, made of tamarisk or zizyphus-wood, placed in the tomb-chapel of the blessed deceased.

Actual figures do not appear until later in the Middle Kingdom, but the texts on these three coffins reveal that the practice had already become fully established by the mid-Twelfth Dynasty.

At some point toward the middle of the Twelfth Dynasty, during the reigns of Senusret II and III, in a country moving toward ever more precise means of expression, the Coffin Texts suddenly disappear. Instead of recording even more detailed descriptions of the underworld, the coffins quite suddenly abandon all but the most essential texts. The sides continue to bear on their outer faces a prayer for eternal supplies of offerings, the share in the offerings from the king to the gods. The lid may present a single line with the appeal to Nut to spread herself over the deceased, an appeal first addressed to the sky-goddess by the king in the Pyramid Texts of the Sixth Dynasty. Within, the coffin stands void of the countless lines of text and friezes of objects which had characterised the finest coffins of the early Middle Kingdom.

Senusret III established his southern boundary at the Second Cataract with a series of decrees carved on stone, such as this example from Semna, issued in year 16, third month of spring. The boundary, one of the most precise in the ancient world, stood under the protection of fortresses, and allowed control over traders. The stelae celebrate the achievement of the king in elaborately poetic phrasing, proclaiming in the first person the words of Senusret III himself: 'I am a king who says and carries out what has been planned; what comes to pass by my hand is my intent.'

Part of the reason for the disappearance of the Coffin Texts may lie in the change in appearance of the coffin. From the mid-Twelfth Dynasty, in burials rich enough to afford not one but two coffins, the inner coffin was shaped like a mummified body with its funerary mask. From the time that it first appeared over the head of the body in early Middle Kingdom burials the mummy-mask had been growing in length, and it was natural perhaps that it should eventually envelop the entire body as the form of the inner coffin. The mummiform coffin provides a dramatic visual aid to the task of preserving the body forever, so much so that we think of it as the typical Egyptian coffin. Yet its sides are far less suitable for the recording of regular columns of text along the inside, because the curves of the body are too faithfully observed in the Middle Kingdom. It was more practical to give up the practice of inscribing words of the funerary rituals alongside the body.

The reign of Senusret III brought fundamental change to the organisation of the whole country, breaking local traditions including the funerary traditions to which we owe the bulk of the surviving Coffin Texts. The king launched a concerted campaign to strengthen Egyptian control of Nubia, strengthening the chain of fortresses and the southern boundary itself, and for this momentous military operation he may well have needed to rationalise and centralise the resources of the state. Whatever the reasons, his reign witnessed tighter occupation of Nubia and cutting of a new canal at the First Cataract to facilitate river travel to the border at the Second Cataract. It also saw government titles and departments more clearly defined than at any other period of Egyptian history, strikingly devoid of the ceremonial and religious phrasing which so often obscures the function behind a particular title. Most importantly for our subject, the reign marked an end to the great cemeteries of governors and their courts in Upper and Middle Egypt. Instead the aristocracy were buried near the pyramid of their king; Detlef Franke has shown how the son of the last governor to be buried at Beni Hasan is almost certainly the man buried in a magnificent tomb of Old Kingdom style at Dahshur, the part of the Memphite necropolis where Amenemhat II and Senusret III chose to site their pyramid complexes. When the leading families moved their burial place from hometown to Residence, the local funerary workshops would have lost their link to the world of the literate elite. The world of the Coffin Texts would have come to a natural end.

Beside such worldly considerations there probably lies a less tangible cause for giving up a tradition of text already three centuries old. The increasing precision of the mid to late Twelfth Dynasty may have caused the Egyptians to think again about the logical consequences of placing certain texts, or more specifically certain hieroglyphic signs, so close to the body of the dead person. Although the texts celebrate the triumph of good over evil, they are forced to mention evil if only to state the fact of its defeat. It

One of the earliest surviving *shabti* figures belongs to a prince named Wahneferhotep of the Thirteenth Dynasty, found at Lisht. The gilt figure bears the *shabti* text in mutilated hieroglyphs, bidding the figure to do any heavy labour required of the deceased in the afterlife, and was found in a miniature version of the contemporary vaulted outer coffins.

may have seemed at some historical periods too great a risk to take in the efforts to safeguard survival. If this seems implausible, we have only to consider the last echo of the Coffin Texts, a dramatic but impermanent revival a century after Senusret II, attested only in the area of the Residence cemeteries at Lisht and Saqqara, and, perhaps from the disintegrating years of the Middle Kingdom, at Thebes. In this revival the danger of signs is countered by two simple stratagems, writing the texts on the outer face of the coffin sides, and mutilating the hieroglyphs of living creatures.

The custom of mutilating hieroglyphs in the late Middle Kingdom begins at the close of the Twelfth Dynasty, in the monuments for the cult of princess Neferuptah. The hieroglyphs in the form of birds or snakes have in the one case their legs removed, in the other their necks severed; these are mutilations, rather than the careful selection of harmless signs which marked the Pyramid Texts in the Sixth Dynasty royal tomb. Earlier in the Middle Kingdom the same phenomenon sporadically marks coffins from Asyut, also on coffins with texts confined to the outer faces of the coffin; it was also a feature of the limestone sarcophagi for the women buried in the temple of Nebhepetra Mentuhotep at Thebes. It is not possible to establish a direct link between the two occurrences, separated by over a century. Yet it is interesting to find not one but both special features of the later revival present on the coffins from Asyut, as if that corner of Upper Egypt nurtured ideas that came to their fullest expression over a hundred years later at the Residence itself. The script involved creating on a small scale images on the rules of a perfect harmony, giving each sign at least the potential of life. In most contexts and periods the literal consequences of this act of creation were eclipsed behind the purpose of the whole text to communicate a message, but the potential lingered in each sign. A snake drawn to the specifications of hieroglyphic art could become a snake, and this conjured up a nightmare of the artist's own making, that in his endeavour to ensure the tomb owner's immortality he might be creating also a lethal enemy for the deceased. The simplest remedies were to avoid the sign altogether, or not to include the text. Mutilated hieroglyphs presented a third solution.

The two most striking coffins with mutilated hieroglyphs are the inner and outer coffins of the chief lector-priest Sesenebnef, from the cemeteries of the Residence at Lisht. A chief lector-priest, especially at the Residence, would have been the person best placed to supervise if not the actual renaissance of the texts then at least their use for his own burial. Whether Sesenebnef himself led or took part in the renewal depends on his date; the monuments of Neferuptah date the first mutilated hieroglyphs to the end of the Twelfth Dynasty, about 1800 BC, and Sesenebnef may have been in office only a generation or more later. His coffins are two of a select group produced at Lisht, Saqqara and Thebes, and may well be the earliest at least of those that survive. At present we must admit the frustrating absence of any securely dated burial of the late Twelfth Dynasty which might reveal the point at which burials were again, briefly, armed with texts in profusion.

If the revival of Coffin Texts begins with Sesenebnef, it used the new late Twelfth Dynasty method of mutilating hieroglyphs, affecting all birds and serpents whereas the early Middle Kingdom coffins had dismembered only the horned viper, the *f* of the hieroglyphic script. However, like a

Figures on throwstick-shaped ivory 'wands' or markers vary in quality from hasty sketches to meticulous carvings of the highest quality. This fine fragment presents on one side the crocodile, on the other the frog and the jackal-headed staff reading *user* in the hieroglyphic script. Although the forces invoked may be more generic, the crocodile perhaps indicates the god Sobek, while the frog denotes the birth-goddess Heqet and the staff suggests Usret 'the Powerful Goddess', as in the common Middle Kingdom name Senusret 'man of Usret'.

This scarab is dated to the late Middle Kingdom by the names on two similar hardstone heart scarabs with human face in the British Museum. In this example, in the Louvre, the text on the base has been erased, leaving only a few ghost traces of the appeal to the heart not to testify against the dead man in the judgment; over the erased text a column of hieroglyphs gives the name of the person for whom the scarab was recut, Useramun, an official of the early New Kingdom.

This the only complete example of a rod with square section shows how the several other extant segments or animal figures fitted together to form a particular staff of power in the apparatus of the healer. Symbols of regeneration, such as the frog, unite with emblems of destructive power, such as lion and crocodile, to fight off attacks on health and life. The forces enlisted to aid the healer appear in three-dimensional form on top of the segments, and in relief along the sides and at the end. This rod is said to have been found at Iunu, one of the rare survivals from a key centre of Pharaonic tradition.

Late Middle Kingdom burials included faience figures of animals outside the settled life of agriculture, from desert mice to lions and, most famously, the hippopotamus, sometimes with the head raised, and usually with depictions of marsh plants and even butterflies and grasshoppers.

number of examples from Asyut, the Thirteenth Dynasty coffin designers took the precaution of placing the texts on the outer faces of the coffin sides, to avoid the slightest danger that the hieroglyphs might rebel against their master. When we read the contents of his coffin, we find that these do not coincide exactly with those of the early Middle Kingdom. Instead they include a number of unique formulae and, most intriguingly, a high proportion of previously unknown texts which later surface again in the New Kingdom as part of the Book of the Dead. These two coffins bridge the gap between the funerary literature of the Middle Kingdom, extinct in the written record by 1850 BC, and that of the New Kingdom, not otherwise found before 1600 BC.

At the same time, marked by the same dismembering of serpent and bird hieroglyphs, a small number of unprecedented objects with their texts enter the burial place. Most celebrated of these are the early *shabti*, funer-

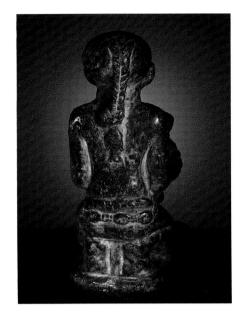

The small steatite vessel to hold the black eyepaint *kohl* is presented as a miniature sculpture, a jar held by a young girl, whose single lock is clasped by a fish-shaped pendant. Fish pendants survive in burials of young girls, and are generally of gold, but an example in Baltimore includes red and blue inlay. The blue colour recalls the turquoise fish pendant in the following episode from a set of late Middle Kingdom tales: king Sneferu is enjoying watching the most beautiful girls of the palace rowing in the garden pool, clad only in net dresses, when the lead rower on one side of the boat, fiddling with the pendant in her hair, drops it into the pool; she refuses to continue, even when the king offers her a replacement; suspicious of receiving a mere paste imitation, she declares 'I want my pendant, not a copy of it'; the day is saved only by the chief lector-priest Djadjamankh, who recites words of power to fold back the waters of the lake, and discovers the fish-pendant on the lake-bed.

ary statuettes, which bear the text cited above from the Coffin Texts in which a wooden figure is told to do any hard labour for the deceased in the next life. Curiously the earliest surviving examples are of hard stone rather than wood.

Another bulwark of the grave, even rarer than the early *shabti*, is the heart scarab. The first examples, of which perhaps as few as three survive, take the form of an exquisitely carved scarab with a human face in place of the head of the beetle. The underside is carved in mutilated hieroglyphs with a text appealing to the heart not to bear witness against the deceased at the judgment of the dead.

> The high steward Nebankh. He says:
> Heart of my mother, heart of my mother!
> Do not stand up against me, do not witness against me,
> do not oppose me in the tribunal,
> do not incline against me in the presence of the
>   keeper of the scales.
> You are my *ka*, the one within my body,
> the Khnum who makes my body whole.
> You come to happiness with me.

Although the text is short, its significance is immense, for this is the earliest dated reference to the judgment of the dead. Other monuments place the high steward Nebankh in the reign of the brother kings Neferhotep I and Sobekhotep IV of the Thirteenth Dynasty, as Detlef Franke has documented. In the New Kingdom the image of judgment produces a dramatic illustration, one of the most frequently repeated from ancient Egypt; the heart of the deceased is weighed in the presence of Osiris against an emblem of the goddess of Right, to determine whether the

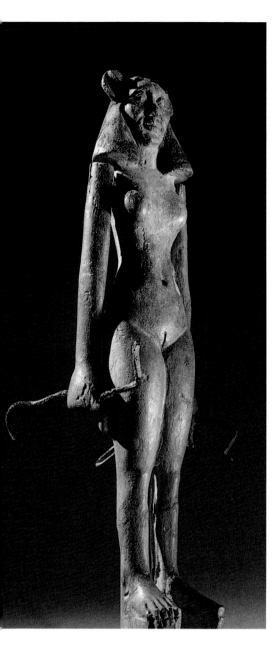

There are parallels for, but no rivals to the fragile wooden figurine of a naked woman or goddess, with the mask or face of a lion. It was found at Thebes with a bronze serpent staff and a chest full of papyri, mainly bearing incantations and prescriptions to secure good health.

owner may pass on to enjoy everlasting life. The magnificent heart scarabs of the Thirteenth Dynasty do no more than imply this procedure, but their existence carries evidence for this belief firmly back from the fifteenth to the eighteenth century BC.

Beside the coffins of the Thirteenth Dynasty, in place of the models of workshops, boats and gardens of the great estates of the early Middle Kingdom, appear small faience figures of animals and plants, symbols of rebirth and the triumph of order over chaos. Occasionally these creatures are carved from steatite and set along a wooden rod, rectangular in section, made of segments each of which bears on the sides further depictions of the evocative animals in relief. A single example survives intact, from an extraordinary group of objects buried with an unknown person at Iunu, the ancient centre of the cult of the sun. Although the item is never depicted in ancient Egyptian scenes or sculpture, its purpose for the defence of the vulnerable can scarcely be questioned. A more frequent find among burial goods of the new age is the ivory stick, curved like a boomerang, and inscribed with the figures of the demons which defended mother and child at birth. These 'wands' were wielded like knives, and perhaps also used as markers to draw protective lines on the ground around the bed of the child. In the tomb-chapel of a governor at Elkab, in southern Upper Egypt, one wall relief depicts each child of the governor with his or her own nurse, and each nurse grasps in one hand a curved stick and in the other a short staff in the shape of a coiling serpent.

Although birth became the model for surviving death, some items seem to have been kept for children, such as the fish pendants worn at the end of the single lock of hair by young girls. A tomb at Haraga produced three fish pendants for a single child, and their value to the child even becomes the central motif of an episode in the literary Tales of the Court of King Khufu, preserved on a single papyrus of c.1600 BC but apparently composed in the late Middle Kingdom c.1750 BC. In the relevant episode king Khufu is told how his dead father, Sneferu, had been enjoying the spectacle of the most beautiful girls in the palace rowing across the lake clad only in bead nets. His pleasure was interrupted when a rower fiddled with her hairlock and dropped her fish-pendant into the water. When the king offered to replace the lost pendant, the girl indignantly refused, preferring, she stated, her genuine article to some copy – probably a bald accusation that the king would palm her off with a faience copy of the real turquoise pendant. At this point the chief lector-priest Djadjamankh came to the rescue by parting the waters, finding the fish-pendant lying on the pool bed, and returning it to its owner.

One remarkable statuette from a Middle Kingdom tomb at Thebes develops the theme of birth and the defence of life to the extreme. It presents a naked female figure with the face of a lion, with a serpent in each hand. The lion face recalls a canvas mask of the same period, found with other items for healing or defence of the body in a house at Lahun, a town site at the mouth of the Fayum. In the same find an actual serpent staff was found, along with the usual faience figurines of animals and plants, and this second unparalleled object confirms the existence of serpent staffs in defence of birth, of new life and of birth into new life after death. From the early New Kingdom another Theban burial preserved a staff in the shape of a serpent not coiled but stiffly outstretched, and a gilt wooden example was found among numerous other amulets on the mummy of Tutankhamun, of the end of the Eighteenth Dynasty. Two further outstretched serpent staffs are now in the Louvre, but of unknown date or origin. The evidence is sparse, but it evokes at once the Biblical story of Moses at the court of Pharaoh, when the staff of Aaron was turned into a snake, swiftly followed by the staffs of the court, which were promptly devoured by the serpent staff of Aaron. Although the episode is probably separated from the serpent staffs of the late Middle to early New Kingdoms by several centuries, it is tempting to take both sets of snakes as two outlets for one and the same motif.

This coiled serpent staff of bronze was discovered at Thebes in the same find as the statuette opposite, tangled in a mass of hair.

The Theban burial defended by the serpent staff and serpent-wielding figurine also yielded the most precious single find of papyri from the late Middle Kingdom. These were deposited in a wooden chest with a lid adorned by the figure of a jackal, perhaps Anubis, god of mummification. They contain notes concerning business affairs on an estate, literary manuscripts, and, in largest number, a series of liturgies for rituals and texts to defend good health. One papyrus bears the words and, without surviving precedent, illustrations of a ritual of kingship for the cult of Senusret I at Thebes. That king had transformed the temple of Amun at Karnak, the site of Middle Kingdom Thebes, into a sanctuary of fine limestone walls housing, beside the image of the god, statues of the king and his outstanding high officials such as the first minister Mentuhotep. Among the few surviving monuments of his reign at Thebes the finest must be the White Chapel, a small shrine with open pillared walls and steps leading up to the central stand on both sides. The monument in Egypt can never stand alone as an empty commemoration; it implies an active life of ritual all in the service of maintaining order. The papyrus preserves, albeit in appallingly fragile fragments, that forgotten dimension of the monuments. It dates not to the reign of the king, but some two to three centuries later, a reminder of the success with which kings could imprint their names on posterity with their monuments.

Other ritual papyri in the group contain hymns to Sobek, the god in the form of a crocodile, who attained national importance in the late Middle Kingdom, when his cult centre in the Fayum attracted the same attention as Thebes would assume in the New Kingdom. The hymns to Sobek at Thebes celebrate the strength of the cult across every part of the country, citing every major centre of worship. The extent of its importance is con-

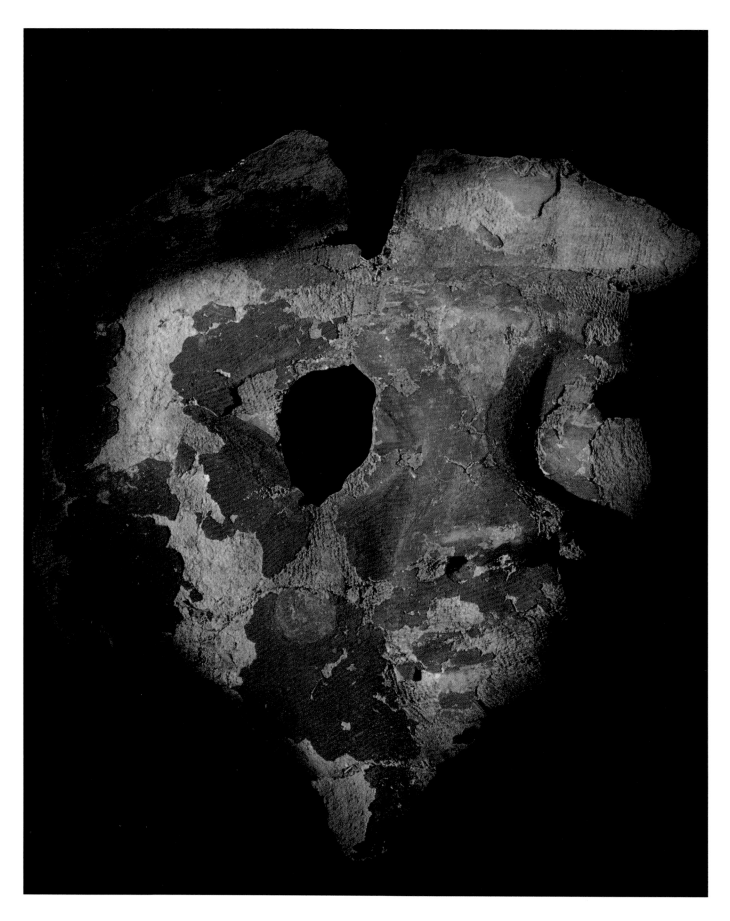

firmed by numerous late Middle Kingdom amulets in the form of cylinder seals, with the name of the reigning king and the epithet 'beloved of Sobek' followed by a specific place of worship. The insistence on national unity through the cult of the crocodile-god may strike us with the hindsight of history as ironic; the late Middle Kingdom gradually retreated into itself in southern Upper Egypt when the northeast became part of the Western Asiatic world.

The third ritual papyrus in the group concerns the rites of burial, and is written like the other two in cursive hieroglyphs, a script legible only to the innermost circle of specialists within the literate elite. The texts for healing in this ancient library are written in some cases in cursive hieroglyphs but mainly in the more accessible everyday hieratic script. All three types of healing text occur here, the treatments, prescriptions for medicaments, and formulae to be recited in defence of good health, but the latter outnumber the other two. Together the collection of ritual and healing texts would be exactly the professional toolbag of a lector-priest involved in reciting ceremonies and formulae for healing.

All we lack in our rediscovery of this one ancient Egyptian is his name; the tomb had been reused, and the coffin destroyed, in antiquity, so we do not know whether any texts were inscribed on the sides of the coffin, or even what shape it took. Nevertheless the find sums up an epoch, in which men and women alike used the imagery of birth and its defence in their quest for eternal life. The period becomes increasingly more obscure as we move toward and past the traumatic but unrecorded moment at which Egypt lost her unity. In the middle of the seventeenth century BC the country became divided into two parts, a northeastern area under the control of *heqau khasut* 'rulers of foreign lands', and the old line of kings now based at Thebes with power over no more than southern Upper Egypt. In local burials at Thebes we find almost no hint of this fatal turning-point. Yet there are one or two hints that the world of the dead too was affected by the death of the Middle Kingdom. Within a century the kings of the south were able to restore the unity of Egypt and drive out the northerners. By the time they succeeded there already existed a new body of text to survive death, that known today as the Book of the Dead.

Left This plastered linen mask bears signs of ancient repair; it shows a leonine face, painted black with green forehead triangle and red cheek spot, white teeth and a hole at the eye pupil. No other such mask survives from ancient Egypt; it was found at the late Middle Kingdom town at Lahun.

Above During the late Middle Kingdom the lion and sphinx are among the more common forms of stamp-seals of shapes other than the scarab; this example of glazed steatite bears a general hieroglyphic motif combining the *ankh* sign of life and the *was* sceptre, denoting dominion. The upper side takes the form of a maned sphinx. In the Second Intermediate Period scarabs and other stamp-seals are virtually the only bearers of hieroglyphs, and many kings and lesser rulers are attested only on scarabs.

CHAPTER 4

Surviving Death in an Age of Empire

THE reconquest of the Delta by Kames and Ahmes I brought Egypt her third classic age of unity and prosperity, the New Kingdom. In this new era the successors of Ahmes I, above all Thutmes I and III, took their armies deep into Syria-Palestine, as if to ensure that never again would Western Asiatic princes like the Hyksos control a part of Egypt. In the course of this massive military intervention, following a period in which the more advanced technologies of the Levant had already been introduced into Egypt by the Hyksos, Egypt felt foreign influence as never previously in art, religion and literature. The one area which resisted the flavour of the new cosmopolitan East was the funerary domain. This may seem surprising, given Egyptian control of Nubia to the south and the wealthy Asiatic trade routes to the northeast, beside the large numbers of Asiatics in Egypt who played such a large part in New Kingdom life, ranging from the taste for colour in costume to the vocabulary of daily life and even the way in which words were spelled. Inscriptions in the burial chamber, among the most traditional recesses of the land, delayed any apparent influence from abroad a further six centuries. Rather than experiment with strategies for an afterlife, the elite put their faith in a revised and condensed version of the Coffin Texts and their last formulation in the coffins of Sesenebnef. We call this New Kingdom edition the Book of the Dead.

Book of the Dead is not a name that would have meant anything to an ancient Egyptian. In the early decades of the last century, local villagers of Gurna, on the West Bank at what had been Thebes, scoured the forgotten cemeteries around their houses to find antiquities for foreign travellers, and they noticed the 'scrolls of the dead' in many of the burials. The phrase was not a title for a particular group of manuscripts, merely a means of referring to any papyrus roll buried with a dead person. However, the overwhelming bulk of those papyri were New Kingdom, Third Intermediate period and Ptolemaic selections from a single pool of formulae derived for the greater part from the Coffin Texts. In 1842 Richard

In the New Kingdom the walls of subterranean corridors and chambers within the royal tomb were covered in an explosion of text and image to describe in detail, and so to ensure, the safe passage of the journey of the sun through the night.

Lepsius, the founder of German Egyptology, brought some order to the confusing mass of formulae by publishing the most extensive example known to him, the papyrus of a Ptolemaic Theban named Iufankh, preserved in the Egyptian Museum of the kings of Savoy and Piedmont at Turin. He used the phrase of the Gurna villagers to entitle the manuscript Book of the Dead, and this name has ever since denoted not any papyrus found in a burial but only those with formulae from a particular stock less than two hundred in number. The papyrus of Iufankh presents a sequence of formulae which is more or less the same as that found in most other Books of the Dead after 650 BC; Lepsius numbered the formulae as chapters 1 to 165, and these numbers are still used. Before 650 BC there was less regularity, and sequences rarely follow such a set format; we also find in the earlier manuscripts some texts which do not occur later, and vice versa. In order to extend the orderliness of Late Period Books of the Dead to their New Kingdom and Third Intermediate Period precursors, the Egyptologists Edouard Naville and Wallis Budge continued the numbering by Lepsius to the other formulae of the New Kingdom, reaching 'chapter 190'. Although the numbering is modern, it is kept for convenience, but the reader should remember that 'chapter 1' of the Book of the Dead is not an ancient Egyptian title, but simply a convenient way to denote a particular text.

The Egyptians themselves adopted a title used for some of the Coffin Texts of the Middle Kingdom, Formulae for Going Forth By Day. The dead were to go forth from the burial to secure their perfect afterlife. Like the elite of the Middle Kingdom they were equipped with formulae to receive offerings, to have power over the body itself and the elements of air, fire and water, to take the forms appropriate to immortals, to know the beings and landscape of the underworld in order to pass by them unscathed. They reinforced this tried and tested core with emphatic declarations of purity at the moment of judgment, with hymns to Ra the sun-god and Osiris king of the dead, their two main promises of resur-

Numbering of texts by nineteenth-century scholars can cause confusion. The text numbered by Naville as 'chapter 168' of the Book of the Dead does not belong to the central stock of 'Formulae for Going Forth by Day', but is a separate composition in which the deceased appeals to different deities of the underworld for survival, noting that they receive offerings on earth from him.

This text is therefore better titled 'Chapter of Offerings'; one copy is found on a papyrus from the tomb of Amenhotep II, perhaps placed there not in the Eighteenth but the Twenty-first Dynasty when the royal tomb was used to house other burials. The detail shown here comes from a more colourful manuscript belonging to a Twentieth Dynasty assessor of revenues Setnakht.

rection, and with a greatly extended use of vignettes, the illustrations that expand and expound the precision of each formula of words. Various Coffin Texts had been given illustrations, but the Book of the Dead transforms the vignette from a marginal, even optional feature to a central feature of the manuscript. In part this may have seemed less necessary on the rectangular coffins of the Middle Kingdom, already richly laden with depictions of offerings and objects in the elaborate friezes around the upper bands of the interior. The New Kingdom tradition retained the core of text, but its presentation was quite different; instead of having the coffin inscribed, the tomb-owner commissioned or bought a special book, which in ancient Egypt means a papyrus roll.

The shift from coffin to papyrus took several stages, which reveal at least a part of the obscure early history of the Book of the Dead. The new stock of texts first appears on the interior walls of the coffin of a queen Mentuhotep, written not in the cursive hieroglyphs, mutilated or otherwise, of the Middle Kingdom, but in the everyday hieratic script. Her coffin was found in 1822, according to one account, and then disappeared, fortunately not before John Gardner Wilkinson, the English traveller and indefatigable recorder, had prepared a careful copy of the texts. He presented his copy to the British Museum in 1834, and it confirms that the revision of words to be spoken in burial had continued after Sesenebnef. The coffins of that lector-priest straddle the two traditions, Coffin Texts and Book of the Dead, but the lost coffin of Mentuhotep stands firmly in the new world. We do not know the exact date of the queen, but she did not belong to the royal family of Seqenenra Taa and Ahmes I, and so can be set with her coffin at least a generation earlier, perhaps c.1600 BC.

Since the Thirteenth Dynasty coffins with formulae for new life had reached only halfway to this stage, we have to look elsewhere for the moment of revision into what we call the Book of the Dead. Possibly the stock of formulae was revised already for the kings and royal family of the late Thirteenth Dynasty, a blank in the surviving record. However it seems more likely that the Book of the Dead was born at a specific time for a reason; if there was a single moment of change, we might expect it when the kings of Egypt forsook the north and the Middle Kingdom Residence at Itjtawy, and moved south to Thebes. We call the kings of Egypt at Itjtawy the Thirteenth Dynasty, and their successors at Thebes the Seventeenth Dynasty. The Seventeenth Dynasty probably had no access to the ancient centres of learning at Memphis and Heliopolis. Deprived of those sacred libraries, they would have required a new edition of the texts for surviving death. The creation of the new stock of sacred texts would then reflect the division of Egypt into a reduced Middle Kingdom government at Thebes and a northern realm dominated by foreign rulers from Western Asia.

The coffin of queen Mentuhotep lies almost alone in the century before the wars of Seqenenra Taa, Kames and Ahmes I against the foreign rulers of Lower Egypt. The coffin of a king Intef contained a shroud with hieratic signs scrawled large in horizontal lines, but the surviving scraps are too small and too few to identify the text. The only other text of any length in a burial of the period is a version of a Coffin Text used in the Book of the Dead, in hieratic on the inner face of part of a coffin naming a king's son and general Herunefer. These tantalising fragments demonstrate that the queen Mentuhotep was not alone in having formulae inscribed in her tomb for her afterlife, but they do not take us any further.

The period of war between south and north, marking the beginning of the New Kingdom, has left more substantial, though still fragile, evidence of the preservation of the dead by written word. Sons and daughters of the royal family were buried in the desert wadi now named the Valley of the Queens, and their mummified bodies were wrapped in linen shrouds covered in cursive hieroglyphic texts from the Book of the Dead. The custom of placing a shroud with texts, but no vignettes, over the body survived into the reign of Thutmes III, over a century later. When that king died, his son and successor Amenhotep II had made for the burial a shroud covered in formulae from the Book of the Dead and a part of the Litany of Ra, a hymn to the sun-god in his seventy-five forms, covering all divine creation. In the same period shrouds were made with the additional feature of coloured vignettes, one for almost every formula. In the most striking case a man named Senhotep was buried within a linen covering much wider than it is tall, with an introductory vignette depicting the family in adoration. This extraordinary elongated shape, suitable neither for the narrower bands of mummy wrappings nor for the body-sized outer shroud, can only reflect the primacy of place allotted to a new surface for the formulae of eternal life, the papyrus roll.

The revised stock of texts was then well established in the grave by the time that the major changes in burial custom, as in the other materials of life, took hold of Egypt after the reign of Thutmes I. The immediate suc-

During the New Kingdom the Amun temple at Karnak underwent massive expansion, and earlier monuments often had to be dismantled to make room for new projects. The growing temple complex became one of the most important centres for copying and composing funerary texts, and remained vital into the Roman Period fifteen centuries later.

cessor of that king was his son Thutmes II, but he reigned no more than a handful of years, leaving his infant son as Thutmes III in the care of the court. The mother of Thutmes III was queen Iset (the Egyptian form of the name of the goddess Isis), but his father left behind another queen, his halfsister Hatshepsut. We still do not understand why kings of the early Eighteenth Dynasty married sisters and halfsisters, but it may be useful to consider the role of the king's sister in the rituals of kingship. Marriage is perhaps the wrong word for these relations. Their prototype is not the earthly contract of man and woman to produce children, itself never a religious ceremony in ancient Egypt, but the myth of creation.

The connections between the original features of existence are expressed as family relationships 'father' to 'son' and 'daughter'. If the creator sun-god Ra or Atum 'All' produced of himself Shu 'Dry' and Tefnet 'Moist', and they then produced Geb the earth and Nut the sky, the family relationships must on the literal level be incestuous; as in every Genesis, two to three generations into creation there are only brothers and sisters to marry. This mythic prototype offers Egyptian kingship a model for the earthly kinswomen of the king at court, but the role applies to the title of the woman and her active part in cult. It need not imply sexual relations between king and consort to produce children, and indeed the children of the king are rarely, perhaps never, born of union between king and sister. This then is the mythic plane on which Thutmes II married Hatshepsut.

115

With her husband the king dead, and her nephew a child on the throne, Hatshepsut proceeded to acquire exceptional status within the court, until she stepped beyond all bounds to be declared, perhaps in the seventh year of his reign, king of Egypt. The revolutionary breach of a cardinal rule, that the king be male as the sun-god, called for the heights of artistry to legitimate the female 'king'. In the campaign for kingly status, her sages revived texts of the Twelfth Dynasty king Amenemhat III, whose accession in the reign of his father Senusret III had been recorded as an act of divine inspiration on the walls of the then national sanctuary of Sobek at Medinet el-Fayum. From the same period Hatshepsut found the precedent of queen Sobekneferu, the first woman known to have claimed kingship as a female Horus. Coupled with the first aftershock of the conquests in Western Asia, the joint reign of Thutmes III and Hatshepsut brought changes in every branch of Egyptian life. Even the form of scarabs, the smallest artistic products, is affected by the wave of innovation, making it easy to date a scarab to before or after the reign. This is precisely the moment at which the Book of the Dead on papyrus becomes widespread in elite burials at Thebes. It is also the moment at which two other texts, the Litany of Ra, and the Amduat, first appear in the surviving record.

The funerary texts for the first kings of the Eighteenth Dynasty are unfortunately lost, and even the tomb of Hatshepsut has not been published in full. However, her highest officials included in their tomb-chambers texts which were for the next three hundred years reserved for the burial of the sovereign. The most influential minister Senenmut had a second, more hidden tomb-chamber prepared in the immediate approach to the cult temple for queen Hatshepsut, her famous terraces on the West Bank at Thebes. The chamber before the final descent into the burial chamber bears a ceiling inscribed with astronomical charts and texts, not found again until the reign of Sety I, and then only in the monuments of the

From at least the reign of Hatshepsut with Thutmes III, the network of estates funding the cult of king and gods continued to be expressed on the lower register of temple walls, reinforcing the physical support to the building. In this example from the Karnak pavilion of Hatshepsut a female figure personifies the estate, wearing its name within the *hut*-hieroglyph on her head, and alternates with the androgynous image of Hapy 'Inundation'.

king. The only precursors for these extraordinary devices for eternal life are the inner faces of coffin lids in the early Middle Kingdom. The group aspires to immortality through the same emphasis on stars that never sink below the horizon, the circumpolar stars, as we find in the Pyramid Texts.

The texts and images in the tomb of the first minister Useramun occur more frequently in later reigns, although they, like the star charts, were for the rest of the New Kingdom confined to the tomb of the king. One text comprises a Litany of Ra in which the sun-god is identified and worshipped as seventy-five forms, some with obscure names but others as familiar as Horus and even goddesses such as Isis. At the heart of the series stands the otherwise unmentionable, unpresentable image of the pig. That animal represents the unclean incarnate because it not only scavenges but, worse, devours anything it finds, thereby breaking all the borders of carnivore and herbivore, as does humankind. Here we encounter the single thread underlying all religious thought in Egypt, a belief in a single creation unravelled through a myriad single features but present in all of them. The sun-god unfurls himself into every feature of creation, but remains its visible source of energy, of heat and light, distinct and aloof from the level of the rest of existence.

The second text of Useramun, later exclusive to the sovereign in the later Eighteenth and Nineteenth Dynasties, is the Text of the Hidden Chamber Which is in the Underworld, a title abbreviated after the New Kingdom to Book of What is in the Underworld, in the Egyptian language Amduat. In this series of images predominating over text, the sun-god undergoes a journey through the twelve hours of the night, in each overcoming opposition through his power, expressed as knowing names. The title lays out the purpose of the text with remarkable clarity:

The text of the hidden chamber:
the positions of the *ba*s and deities,
shadows and transfigured dead, and (their) duties.
The start is the Opener of the West, door of the western horizon;
the end is deepest darkness, door of the western horizon.
To know the *ba*s of the underworld, to know their duties,
to know their transfigurations for Ra, to know the secret *ba*s,
to know what is in their hours, and their deities,
to know his summons of them.
To know the doors and the road travelled by this great god,
to know the course of the hours and their deities,
to know those who sing praises and those who are destroyed.

The dead person, preeminently the dead king, was to merge with the sun-god at death, and therefore this description of the night journey and morning resurrection of Ra applied with equal force to the deceased. The

analogy is underscored by the continual reference to the sun-god as Flesh, and his depiction as a human figure with the head of a ram, symbol of eminence. In this vision of the night secrets of rebirth the sun-god is accompanied by a full crew of deities on his bark, and the underworld around him teems with the names of guardians, gates, enemies and other vivid features. The texts in the tomb of king Thutmes III make explicit exactly where this resurrection of the dead takes place, by identifying the section on the eastern wall of his burial chamber as texts to be written on the east wall of the Hidden Chamber. Similar directions are inscribed for the sections of the night on the other walls of the same chamber, marking it out as the Hidden Chamber itself, the secret domain where Osiris and Ra share their immortality with one and another and with the deceased.

Each of the twelve hours of the night is presented in a section of tomb wall divided into three registers, except for the first hour which is given four. At the first hour the entry of the sun-god into the underworld of night is greeted by the jubilation of baboons, a species noted for its noise levels at the appearance of the sun in the morning. Farther into the night, the deeper darkness of nothingness before creation is evoked in the fourth and fifth hours, the terrain of the earthbound god Sokar mirroring the Memphite cemeteries already of great antiquity, and named like the plateau of the Giza pyramids Rosetjau. There in the recesses of existence the hope lay of regenerating life within its opposite, Nun, the emptiness of non-existence. Indeed immediately in the next hour, at midpoint in the night journey, the sun-god meets his corpse, a union of cosmic force which renders possible in the seventh hour of the night the decisive triumph over the enemies of order, personified as the serpent Aapep.

During the journey the sun-god passes through the waterway of Ra in

Blocks of red quartzite from a pavilion of Hatshepsut have survived through reuse, and illustrate the claim of the queen to be king. In one scene (*above left*) she joins the goddess Seshat 'Writing' in the foundation ceremony 'stretching the cord' to demarcate a construction site. In another scene (*above*) the queen appears wearing the Blue Crown between Amun, enthroned, and his consort Amunet, standing to the left.

the second hour, a region named Wernes and including the Fields of Reeds where the blessed dead spend their afterlife. The journey through the realm of the blessed dead continues into the third hour, with the waterway of Osiris. By contrast those who died by drowning receive their own immortal space in the tenth hour. The punishment of evildoers is shown in the eleventh hour. At the end of the voyage, the twelfth hour witnesses the resurrection of the sun-god by being towed with his bark through the very body of a giant serpent named Life of the Gods. Again a force from the dark world below the earth, a serpent, brings about the regeneration of life.

Although other compositions grew out of the Amduat, and were copied in the tomb of the king from the reign of Tutankhamun onwards, they abandoned the insistent naming of each feature of the underworld. Even the style of drawing in the first copies of the early Underworld Books differs, with the careful proportional full figures of Egyptian formal art replaced in the tombs of the Eighteenth Dynasty kings by a rapid sketch of figures and text in black and red outline only, echoing the smaller scale illustrations on ritual books. The message of a full-blooded battle for rebirth seems all the better communicated by these simple strokes of the brush in the dark of the burial chamber. From the reign of Tutankhamun the dramatic outline figures disappear, and the less underworldly forms of canonical Egyptian art are used to depict the journey through the night. When they came to choose their strategy for resurrection, the Thebans of the Third Intermediate Period returned to the texts and images of the Litany of Ra and the evocative sketched forms of the early copies of the Amduat.

In the burials of those other than the king after the death of Hatshepsut, the Book of the Dead stands alone as the guarantor of new life, and it offers no such confrontation with the stark outline of death and birth. Within the Book of the Dead, a number of new texts compensate for the considerable reduction in the total stock of formulae. The formulae for

Below From the reign of Hatshepsut, among many other innovations, shrouds bearing funerary texts begin to receive illustrations. These details of the judgment and the hieroglyphic texts are from the Book of the Dead on the linen shroud of Meh, an official under Thutmes III or Amenhotep II.

taking divine forms are among the most severely curtailed, but even here we find innovation, as in the formula for becoming a lotus, a perennial symbol of solar rebirth because the flower opens for the sun:

> Formula for taking the form of a lotus.
> I am that pure lotus that comes forth from light,
>> who is at the nostril of Ra.
> I made my descent. I sought him out for Horus.
> I am the pure one who comes forth from the marshes.
>> (BD 81A, from the papyrus of Nu,
>> early Eighteenth Dynasty)

Another new formula on a well-established theme is the appeal to become a divine scribe:

> O Elder who sees his father, keeper of the book of Thoth.
> Bring me the mud of Aker (an earth-god), in which is Seth (=red
>> ochre?).
> Bring me the waterpot and palette in that writing-kit of Thoth,
> and the secrets of their contents. See, I am the scribe!
> Bring me the rotting of Osiris with which I may write,
> to copy down what the great and good god says every day,
> the goodness which you decreed for me, O Horakhty.
> I have done Right. I run errands for Ra every day.
>> (BD 94, from the papyrus of Nu)

The most notable addition to the funerary texts from the Coffin Text tradition must be reckoned the judgment of the dead, above all as painted in chapter 125. The formulae that cover this stage of the entry into the underworld present the deceased in the broad hall of the two goddesses of Right, before Osiris, king of the underworld, among forty-two gods and goddesses who sat in judgment over the men and women who had died and wished to become eternally blessed spirits. Before Osiris, as chairman of the tribunal, the deceased declaimed a series of misdeeds of which he or she protested innocence; a similar procedure was repeated before the forty-two assessor deities, before each of whom the deceased had to swear his or her innocence of a particular sin. The whole declaration of purity appears in Late Period temples as the oaths taken by the priest entering his period of service, and it is possible that priestly oaths of purity provided the model for this 'Negative Confession' of the dead. Three examples from the papyrus of Nebseny, of about the reign of Thutmes IV, illustrate the type:

> O enveloper of flame who comes forth from Kheraha –
>> I have not stolen.
> O breaker of bones who comes forth from Henensu –
>> I have not spoken lies.

Tomb of Sennefer, mayor of Thebes under Amenhotep II, is a rare exception to the rule that burial chamber walls were unadorned. The scenes present Sennefer with his family in rituals such as the purification of the deceased with water.

The Book of the Dead for the high official Nebqed contains the clearest illustration of Egyptian beliefs in the afterlife: the funeral procession ends with the Opening of the Mouth of the coffin in front of the chapel above ground, and inside the vertical tomb-shaft the *ba* is seen as a human-headed bird flying headlong down toward the subterranean chamber, holding in its human arms a loaf of bread and jar of water. Within the underground chambers the coffin is represented again within, while an outer room offers a chair and lotus flower for an afterlife as leisurely as a rich home.

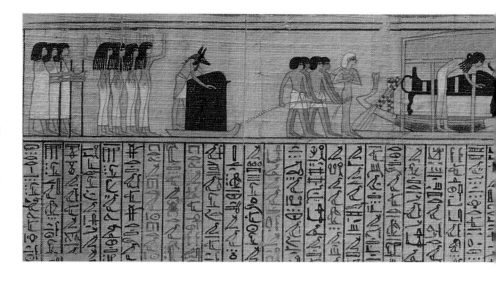

The Book of the Dead for Nebqed includes one of the earliest images of the monster 'Swallower of the Dead', part crocodile, part lion, and part hippopotamus, ready to devour any soul found unworthy in the judgment after death.

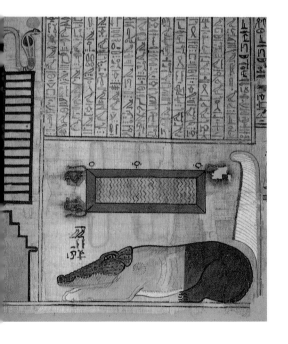

O floodwater who comes forth from Nun –
My voice has not been raised.

In conjunction with these most expressive of Egyptian moralistic texts the Book of the Dead conjures up the scene of judgment, the fulcrum of existence, in a remarkable image taken from not myth but accountancy and the marketplace. The heart of the deceased is set in the balance quite literally against an image of Right, either the form of the goddess or her feather alone. The gods attend to the probity of the operation; Anubis and Horus set the scales in motion, and Thoth records the outcome exactly as would a scribe measuring an amount of precious or other metal.

The earliest manuscripts tend to omit the most colourful character in this picture, Amemet 'the Swallower' or 'Swallower of the Damned', a hybrid form ready to gulp down the heart if it proves impure against the figure of Right. The monster takes the three animals of voraciousness who could be depicted in Egyptian formal art, the crocodile for the head, lion for the forepart, and hippopotamus for the rear. Exactly the same animals in a somewhat different configuration provide the icon of the defending goddess of childbirth, Taweret. A fourth voracious creature lurks in the background of the consciousness of the artist – Reret, the female pig who can devour not only animal or vegetable matter but even, if provoked, her own children. The monstrous swallower of the dead is included in virtually every scene of judgment after a particular turning-point in Egyptian history, the reign of Akhenaten.

Jan Assmann has christened the radical departure of Akhenaten as the crisis in Egyptian polytheism, a conflict between two visions of god. In the name Ra the Egyptians perceive a physical and natural life-giving power in their experience, the sun. In the name Amun the creator turns into a hidden, invisible, but everpresent and all-knowing, all-seeing deity. At a point early in his reign Amenhotep IV decided that the name Amun

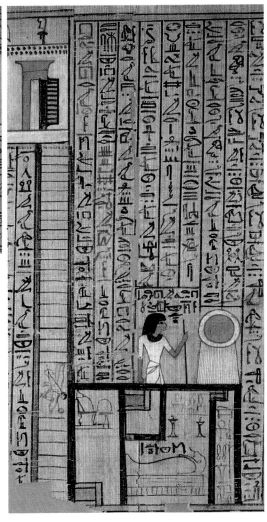

could not present god, and must be removed from worship of the creator; that even the name Ra failed to hone in on the specific physical form of god in the sky; and that therefore a new cult must be installed to the Aten, the solar sphere itself. At a stroke the ancient metaphors of animal and bird become forbidden idols, and the supernatural plane is converted from a populous home of innumerable gods and goddesses into the empty prospect of a single celestial being moving visibly across the sky, devoid of any company or echo save the presence of the king on earth. Where every Egyptian had been able to approach his or her deity directly, including the deities of state, the Aten smiled only on the king and his wife Nefertiti, the double channel of all divine blessings to humankind. The name of the king could no longer include the proscribed form of expressing god as Amun, 'Invisible', and was changed to Akhenaten, servant of the Aten; the word *akh* cannot be rendered in a single word in our language, conjuring up the ideas of service, of piety in the Latin sense of filial duty to father, and much more of the light and transfiguration that only the sun-god can provide.

In this world there can be no Osiris or Isis, no Amun or Mut, and no Book of the Dead. At the special new Residence city dedicated to the Aten, Akhetaten 'Horizon of the Aten' (modern Amarna), the household shrines and tomb-chapels replace the personal contact to deities with images of the royal family worshipping and blessed by the Aten, and every person other than the king must bow low not to usurp the light granted by god to king. In the tomb of the king the scenes of night journeys disappear, yielding to some of the most intimate depictions of Egyptian art, in which a royal birth and royal death cover the walls of the chambers. Even around the canopic chest of the king the goddesses of protection have no place, and instead the queen herself stands with arms outstretched to defend the mortal remains of her husband.

So personal and exclusive a royal cult of one god, the sun-disk, could not withstand the change of reign. When Akhenaten died, the boy-king

Right In this statue of Amenhotep III, the royal cult finds its logical extreme, the statue of the king as a statue. As manifestation of the sun-god on earth, the king received worship already during his own lifetime. In the reign of Amenhotep III it was thought appropriate to show the king offering to himself as divine being. His image might be transported on a sledge during ceremonies, and this statue presents Amenhotep III divine on such a sledge. The veined quartzite evokes the hues of the sun, and survived ungrazed in the Luxor cachette of temple sculpture.

Below Ivory palette with six blocks of pigment. At the top, a cartouche encloses the throne-name of king Amenhotep III; the palette demonstrates the luxury and sense of form that characterise the reign.

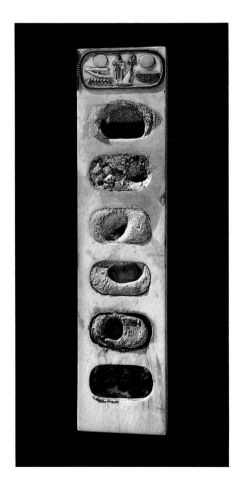

who followed him shortly on the throne of Egypt presided over a restoration of the Amun temples, including the replacement of the statues smashed by the agents of Akhenaten, both general images of Amun and more specific figures of the fertility of man and river. The name of Amun was restored on the thousands of monuments where Akhenaten had had it erased, and the reverse programme began to remove from hieroglyphic and eternal existence the king who had disobeyed creation. In the Book of the Dead and the texts for the afterlife of the king the restoration generated a new energy. The judgment is consistently given its monster, and the papyri now begin and end with dramatic visions of worship, covering the full height of the roll, whether of the sun-god or the goddesses of birth and re-birth, Taweret and Hathor. In the tomb-chapels at Thebes and Saqqara, the funerary texts begin to intrude into the pattern of scenes, which had concentrated in the Eighteenth Dynasty on the motifs of official life and estates conducive to rebirth, such as the scenes of fishing and hunting wild birds in the marshes. In the Twentieth Dynasty cult temple for Ramses III at Medinet Habu, one of only four Theban West Bank royal temples to escape destruction, the king is depicted ploughing his fields as in Book of the Dead chapter 110, and other texts and images from the formulae for going out by day occur for the survival of the king, in addition to less unexpected scenes of festival, ritual and triumph over the foreign enemies of Egypt.

If the reforms of Akhenaten and their rejection caused certain changes in the Book of the Dead, the effect was far greater in the tomb of the king. At the end of a decade of rule Tutankhamun was buried in a small tomb, in size more appropriate to one of his courtiers than to a king, even a boy-king. The burial-chamber was not large enough to contain a composition as long and complex as the Litany of Ra or the Amduat, and instead the royal craftsmen chose evocative excerpts from the Amduat, such as the baboons of the night, and placed them alongside a unique depiction of a royal burial, in which the highest officials of the land accompany the dead monarch on his last journey, and his successor the courtier Ay is shown in the role of pious son, performing the rite of opening the mouth on a Tutankhamun mummiform and crowned like Osiris. The remainder of the texts and images for his survival cover the walls of the gilt shrines set tightly fitting one inside the other within the burial chamber around the sarcophagus. It is not known whether all other royal burials contained such shrines, but it seems likely that those of Tutankhamun were exceptional devices to compensate for the lack of necessary wall space. However, the shrines bear not the usual Litany and Amduat, but instead a series of texts, some from the Book of the Dead, others as yet unidentified and written in cryptographic hieroglyphs, that is to say in hieroglyphs outside the normal repertoire of signs and meanings, and therefore still difficult for us to decipher.

One text and image found later, and intelligible to us, presents the sky

Akhenaten and Nefertiti alone were permitted to offer directly to the sun-god, in his form as the physical celestial sphere. In this relief queen Nefertiti is depicted in the extreme style of the earlier part of the reign of Akhenaten, with the names of the sun-god imprinted upon her torso, waist and upper and lower arms. She offers a vessel upon which stand the two names of the sun-god, spelling out the identity of the divine being in which Akhenaten and his court professed belief: 'Ra-Horakhty jubilant in the horizon, in his name as the light (Shu) which is in the sun-disk'.

as a star-studded cow, lifted aloft by the eternal chaos-gods, and supporting the journey of the sun-god on his bark, swallowed by the sky in the West at evening, and born from her in the East at dawn. The text demonstrates the departure of the sun-god from his direct rule on earth, leaving the king to act as his champion of order. This can be read as a reply to the claim of Akhenaten to see the sun as king over earth in a more pressing sense. When the text of the heavenly cow occurs for the second time, in the reign of Sety I, it contains a first part in which a rebellion of humankind is given as the cause for an attempt by the sun-god to destroy all people. The sun sends his eye, metaphor for all-seeing power, to devour every human being that she meets. As the slaughter continues, the sun relents, but the goddess has become addicted to human blood, and the gods are forced to resort to a simple ruse, colouring a lake of beer with red ochre to make it look like blood; the goddess duly drinks the liquid, turning from the fury, Sekhmet, into the mistress of drunkenness, Hathor, and the remnants of the human race are saved. However, the sun-god feels weary of rule, and leaves the earth to sail in the sky at a distance from his creation. It falls to the king, son of the sun-god, to keep his order.

In the tomb of Horemheb, second successor of Tutankhamun, the new texts and the old alike disappear, to be replaced by a new composition, named by Egyptologists the Book of Gates because each of the twelve hours of the night presents a fortified and inhabited gateway. At first sight the new 'Book' appears similar to the Amduat, with the same number of divisions and registers, but it contains new elements, notably the great judgment scene. There a monkey beating a pig from a boat encapsulates the theme of order over chaos, while Osiris enthroned upon a stepped platform presides over the judgment of the dead. At the end of the 'Book' a scene summarises the circuit of the sun-god around the world, and his rebirth through the forces of the earth. Extracts from this new version of the night journey also takes the place of the Amduat in the tomb of Ramses I, founder of the Nineteenth Dynasty, but thereafter both compositions were used in portions of varying length in the tomb of the king. Sety I, the successor of Ramses I, had the longest and most richly sculpted tomb in the valley cut for himself, culminating in an imposing burial chamber with a vast star chart laid out over the ceiling, taking up the innovative astronomical design in the ceiling of the Deir el-Bahri tomb of Senenmut.

Among the most unusual of royal monuments must be reckoned the second tomb or cenotaph of Sety I at Abydos, sunk in the desert behind the royal cult temple of that king. The ceiling of the eastern chamber includes another celestial image on a grand scale, the first depiction of Nut arched over the earth-god Geb, separated by their father Shu, with detailed cosmographic explanations written around to record the characteristics of different regions of the world at the horizon. The complex centres on a pillared hall with the second tomb of the king, a primeval

The rear wall of the innermost gilt shrine of Tutankhamun bears the earliest known vignette of the sky as a cow supported by eight gods of Unending. The scene illustrates a text explaining the decision of the sun-god to withdraw into the heavens, marking the separation of gods and men.

mound surrounded by corridors that flooded during the inundation of the Nile. The layout echoes the plan of chambers within the pyramid of Senusret II, and at least one other Twelfth Dynasty king, his successor Senusret III, constructed a vast, now ruined cult complex farther south at Abydos, including a rock-cut burial chamber.

The gently sloping western access corridor to the pillared hall of Sety I was decorated in the reign of his grandson Merenptah with a new Underworld Book, named today the Book of Caverns. Here the twelvefold division of the underworld gives way to two sets of three major sections, still in three registers. In place of the bark of the sun-god, or in addition to it, the scenes present the sun as a disk alone. The 'Book' formed a regular part of the repertoire on the walls of the royal tomb in the Twentieth Dynasty, though only the tomb of Ramses VI gives a full version. Its final scene became a separate unit dominating one wall of the burial chamber in the tombs of kings Merenptah and Ramses III, and of the Nineteenth Dynasty queen Tausret who, like Sobekneferu and Hatshepsut before her, became king.

The later Ramesside tombs of kings produce a number of arrangements of new scenes and, less prominently, texts, which have been christened by Egyptologists with names such as 'Book of Night' and 'Book of Day'. The two last named compositions may have belonged to a litany from the rites of the royal court, in which the king, or officiants acting on his behalf, spoke the appropriate words at the onset of each hour of day and night. This ritual is preserved in fragments from the open court, for sun worship, in the terraced temple of Hatshepsut, and then twelve centuries later in the Ptolemaic temples at Edfu, Philae and Dendera. The images and part of the accompanying text in the so-called Books of Night and Day echo and reinforce that essential royal duty, to maintain the course of the sun through the sky, upholding order against chaos.

In some cases the decoration of the wall itself may have dictated an expansion or contraction of the familiar stock of motifs at the disposal of the artists and scholars on the project. However in one case a fuller sequence of scenes for the twelve hours of the night does survive, in the tomb of Ramses VI, from which single images in the tombs of kings from Merenptah to Ramses IX are taken. The composition aims toward the rebirth of the sun at dawn, as do the other Underworld Books of the New Kingdom, but concentrates to an exceptional degree on the dark regenerative forces of the earth, and has therefore been given the modern name 'Book of the Earth'. Three earth gods play a part in the journey of the sun through the night sky below the earth, Geb the predominant earth-god familiar from other texts, Tatenen 'the weary earth', a god associated primarily with Memphis and its god of creative craft, Ptah, and, the third and most mysterious, Aker, a primeval deity depicted as a double headed lion. As in the Book of Caverns, the sun appears as a simple disk, but the proportion of texts to images is sharply reduced, some scenes entirely lacking texts. In the first part of the fourth section, the 'Book of the Earth' provides us with the only ancient Egyptian view of the Hidden Chamber to which the Amduat alludes in its original title 'Text of the Hidden Chamber'. The space encloses a 'secret chest' in which the corpse of Osiris lies. On a second level, the Hidden Chamber is the burial chamber itself; in the Amduat the text specifies that particular hours belong to a particular wall of the hidden chamber, and those hours do indeed occur on the appropriate wall, southern, western, northern or eastern, in the burial chamber of the earliest full example, the tomb of Thutmes III.

The various compositions were not confined to the walls of the tomb of the king. We have already seen their use in the cenotaph of Sety I at Abydos, and on the gilt shrines of Tutankhamun as support or replacement for the burial chamber walls. The material closer to the body of the king might also bear texts to ensure his afterlife, much as the coffins of the early Middle Kingdom enveloped the dead with their guides to surviving death. The shroud lain over the mummy of the dead sovereign survives in a single instance, that of Thutmes III, and it bears in early Eighteenth Dynasty style an array of funerary texts. One part of these texts belongs to the Book of the Dead, that is the Formulae for Going Forth by Day; the other completes in an extraordinary example of planning the Litany of Ra from the pillars of the antechamber of the royal tomb. This reminds us how incomplete the burial of each king reaches us, with the exception of Tutankhamun; even in the latter there are gaps in our knowledge. If we know now, thanks to the most recent scientific analysis, that the statues guarding the entrance to the burial chamber did not conceal papyri, we will never know what texts or images covered the small papyrus folded and tied like an amulet to the neck of the king, for it disintegrated at the first touch in the twentieth century.

After the death of Akhenaten the task of restoring almost limitless defaced monuments began in earnest under Tutankhamun, but continued in the reigns of his successors Horemheb, Sety I and Ramses II. In many respects they returned to models and unfulfilled plans of Amenhotep III, such as the hypostyle hall at Karnak, and doubtless benefited from the great quantities of half-quarried stone blocks intended for that king's projects. The cache of temple statues at Luxor included among its outstanding pieces the sculpture of the king with the goddess Mut, along with her consort Amun one of the principal targets of the agents of Akhenaten. Her face echoes the polish of the reign of Amenhotep III, but displays already features of the later Eighteenth Dynasty and Ramesside period. This is one of few works of art which can be ascribed to Horemheb, in contrast to the large number of Tutankhamun statues upon which he had his own name inscribed.

From the reign of Hatshepsut with Thutmes III the sarcophagus of the king took the shape of a cartouche, the name-ring expressing rule over the world created by the sun-god, and was cut from a single block of red or golden hued quartzite, one of the hardest stones of Egypt and redolent with the symbolism of rising and setting sun. Amenhotep III abandoned the material in favour of red granite, and this was used by most other rulers of the New Kingdom, though Tutankhamun was laid to rest in a fiery orange quartzite sarcophagus with red granite lid. The sarcophagus could contain up to three mummiform coffins, and this is the number found in the intact burial chamber of Tutankhamun, the innermost of solid gold, sign not merely of wealth but of the untarnishable eternity of the sun-god. The outward appearance of the sarcophagus changes under Akhenaten, who used a rectangular form with an image of his queen Nefertiti with arms stretched out in protection at each corner. Tutank- 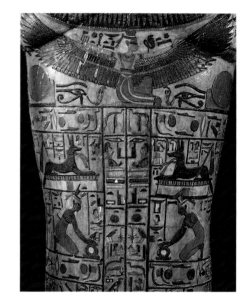 hamun, Ay and Horemheb returned to the traditional deities, but retained the new model, replacing Nefertiti with the goddesses Isis, Nephthys, Serqet and Neit, who were entrusted with the deceased, and in particular with the soft inner organs that had to be removed for separate embalming, and were thus in need of extra attention. After Horemheb the Ramesside kings went back to the cartouche form of the earlier Eighteenth Dynasty, but a dramatic new feature was introduced under Sety I, the sculpted image of the dead king as Osiris upon the lid.

From the beginning of this tradition in the reign of Hatshepsut and Thutmes III, the sarcophagus of the king reinforced the protective outward appearance with images and texts. The texts before Akhenaten draw from all three phases of the general tradition in texts for life after death, the Pyramid Texts, Coffin Texts and Book of the Dead. In the Ramesside period the inscriptions take a new and elaborate turn, for which the magnificent calcite sarcophagus of Sety I may be taken as representative and epitome. Its fine veined white to golden surface was inscribed inside and out with texts and images inlaid in a rich lapis-coloured blue, now sadly disintegrated in all but a few fragments. The lid was almost completely destroyed in antiquity, but enough survives to confirm that its upper side bore a sculpted image of the king, and its underside included the closing section of the Litany of Ra, in which the deceased presents himself as the heir of Osiris and guardian of Ra. Also on the underside of the lid appear two formulae from the Book of the Dead, 'chapter 72', the Formula for Going out by Day and opening the Tomb, and 'chapter 89', the crucial Formula for causing the *ba* to unite with the corpse in the Underworld; both occur frequently on coffins, particularly the upper side of the lid, in later periods.

The floor of the sarcophagus bears a full-length image of the goddess Nut, with a second rendering of 'chapters 72' and '89'. The side walls present perhaps the most important composition for the king, a complete

Funerary texts were not confined to papyrus. In their community at the Theban site now known as Deir el-Medina, the craftsmen of the royal tomb used their art to provide themselves with the finest coffins, such as these examples from a Nineteenth Dynasty family burial discovered in the 1880s. On the breast of the coffin of one man in this family, Khons (*left*), the goddess Nut spreads her wings over the deceased, echoing the appeals of the Pyramid Texts, while Anubis sits as a guardian jackal above the kneeling goddesses Isis and Nephthys.

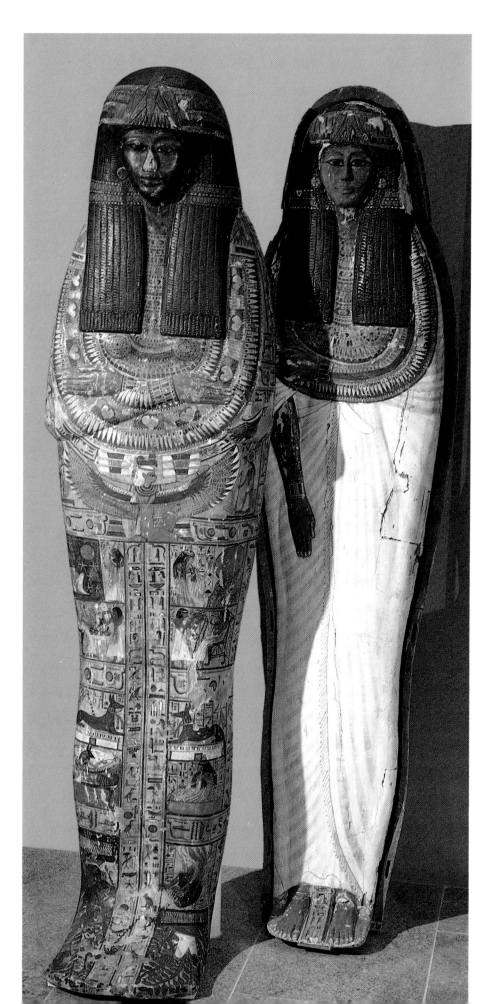

version of the Book of the Gates in its twelve hours over three registers, beginning at the outer face of the foot end, and running clockwise around the outside to the fifth hour; the sixth and seventh hours are inscribed along the edge of the lid, and the remaining five hours cover the inner walls from the eighth hour at the left shoulder of the deceased around to the twelfth hour to the right of the head. The remaining space, exactly behind the head of the dead king, bears the concluding scene of the rebirth of the sun, where the sun-god is raised out of the primeval waters of Nun. Armed with these repeated affirmations of daily birth on the walls and ceilings of both tomb and sarcophagus, together with a panoply of now lost protective devices among the grave goods, the king could rely on his burial for as firm a guarantee of eternal life as could be devised.

During the Twentieth Dynasty the restriction of the Underworld Books to the tomb of the king appears to have been relaxed. The tomb-chapel of a man named Tjanefer, third priest of Amun in the hierarchy at Karnak, bears a number of scenes excerpted from the Book of Gates, and is apparently dated to the reign of Ramses III. In addition, the sole surviving funerary papyrus from the period, the Book of the Dead of Anhay, closes at its left end with a pair of scenes of regeneration. One is the final scene of solar rebirth from the Book of Gates, while the other presents the following unique image; a mummified body rests on a stepped platform between two ram-headed gods, hands raised in adoration, beneath eight

The calcite sarcophagus of Sety I has lost most of its lid, but remains one of the most perfect expressions of Egyptian art for the afterlife. Its base bears a full-length figure of the sky-goddess Nut (*far right*), while the sides record the journey of the sun through the twelve hours of the night sky. In each hour the sun-god appears on his bark accompanied by Sia 'perception' and Heka 'creative power', and generally takes the form of a ram-headed man in a shrine; on the outside foot end (*far left*), the entry into the underworld is depicted with the same bark and the sun-god as disk containing scarab beetle, symbol of regeneration, beneath a pole in the form of the hieroglyph *user* 'powerful' attended by personifications of the desert into which the sun sets. This composition is named by Egyptologists Book of Gates, because each hour is entered through

a portal guarded by fire-spitting cobras (*centre left*). Half-way through the sequence of hours, a separate scene is inserted (*above left*) in which Osiris appears in judgment on a steep-stepped dais before the animate judgment scales; to the side, a monkey beats a pig away from a boat, denoting the victory of good by reducing evil to the absurd. In the ninth hour the drowned are shown in the Nile (*above*); not suffering eternal damnation but rather forever blessed; those who drowned in the Nile were considered to share the fate of Osiris, and therefore to be particularly close to the gods. The twelfth hour closes the journey with a resurrection scene (*centre*) in which the scarab and disk emerge from the primeval waters, Nun, to be received by a minute figure of the sky Nut, standing upon a figure labelled 'Osiris circling the Underworld'.

white circles. The whiteness of the disks suggests the moon, and specifically Thoth, the god most anciently associated with the lunar crescent, while the number eight may allude to the eight primeval deities in the nothingness before creation, who account for the name of the cult-centre of Thoth, the city of Khemenu 'Eight' in Middle Egypt. Anhay and her papyrus cannot be dated with certainty, and the manuscript is exceptional in every way. It is a papyrus roll of unusually large format, at 42 centimetres in height, and presents one of the only instances of gold leaf in papyrus illustration, on the sun-disk at the opening scene of adoration. Moreover, this would be the first funerary papyrus known to belong to a woman since the reign of Hatshepsut; all others in the intervening three centuries present the man with or without his wife and mother, and always as owner of the manuscript.

The extraordinary character of the papyrus, and above all the inclusion of excerpts from Underworld Books, might provide grounds for dating Anhay to the period immediately following the New Kingdom, but there are strong reasons to resist this. The style of the figures of Anhay and the gods seems closest to those from the Twentieth Dynasty. In particular they recall the figures of king and gods in three illustrations on a papyrus compiled under Ramses IV to list the good deeds of his murdered father Ramses III and appeal for legitimacy. Another Twentieth Dynasty feature is the title of the husband of Anhay, a man named Nebsumenu who is confined to helping at agricultural tasks in the scene for 'chapter 110' of the Book of the Dead. Despite his humble role in the manuscript, he bears the important position of Master of the Stable of the Residence, evoking the period of the Residence city of Ramses II and his Nineteenth and Twentieth Dynasty successors at Per-Ramses in the northeastern Delta.

It would seem that both Tjanefer and Anhay represent a trend toward wider use of the Underworld Books in the Twentieth Dynasty. This need not be taken as an automatic token of loss of royal authority. Without intact examples of contemporary kingly and non-royal burials it is extremely difficult to assess just how distinct the burial of the king might be. For the period of Tjanefer and Anhay, we should note at least that the Valley of the Kings became home precisely in the mid-Twentieth Dynasty to a variety of new scenes, typified by the grandiose scheme of the tomb of Ramses VI. New compositions such as the scenes which we entitle Books of Day, Night and Earth would mark the destiny of the king, immediate son of the sun-god, apart from the afterlives of his subjects. At all times in Egypt the king sets the model in the quest for eternal life. If his subjects emulate the royal example, this seems never to detract from the distinctness of the king. It simply demonstrates how firmly kingship lay embedded in the core of Egyptian expression of the world in religion, art and script. If the king chose a path of renewal, it acted at once as a beacon for all beneath him. As soon as a text or image ceased to be the point of distinction between king and subject in the tomb, as soon as another composition arose to mark the difference, the elite subject might be allowed, strictly within the limits of the tomb walls, to arm himself with the same defences as had been tried and tested by his king. The themes of the non-royal tomb must then lag behind those of the tomb of the king.

Down to the end of the New Kingdom we have the royal tombs at Thebes to compare with burials of the subjects of the king. After the death of Ramses XI, with the abandonment of the Valley of the Kings, the kings were buried in the Delta, where far fewer ancient monuments have survived. With a handful of exceptions we have no information on the design and contents of a king's tomb for the entire millennium before Christ, and this deprives us of the chance to compare strategies for the afterlife of the king with those of his subjects. Yet the images and texts for persons other than the king demonstrate that, as long as the hieroglyphic tradition survived, the dead person sought eternal life by taking the status of Ra and Osiris, the gods of resurrection, and that this involved of itself taking the status of the dead king. Even when the kings themselves have disappeared from our sight, kingship remains crucial to all aspirations for life after death.

The craftsman of the royal tomb, Amennakht, and his wife Nubemsha are aligned in this idealized version at a simultaneous burial, in front of the steep pyramid of their tomb-chapel against the grained ground of the desert hills. They are shown mummified, with mummy masks topped by cones to indicate scented oils. In a Nineteenth Dynasty tomb at Deir el-Medina.

CHAPTER 5

Revivals of the Past in the First Millennium BC

THE New Kingdom ended in strife and disunity. The line of kings in the north showed less and less interest in Upper Egypt, until the royal tomb in the Valley of the Kings was left as the last link between the two halves of the country. During the middle to later years of the Twentieth Dynasty the Theban area sank into near anarchy, with marauding desert nomads threatening security from the west, and outright conflict between the leading officials of the local administration, notably the mayors and the high priest of Amun. Security could no longer be provided for tombs outside the Valley of the Kings, and reports of theft led to a royal commission in which every king's tomb outside the Valley was inspected. The commission found every tomb intact except for that of the Seventeenth Dynasty monarch Sobekemsaf. Although no documents survive to continue the story to the recommendations of the commission, most of the other kings whose tombs were checked were probably gathered together into one group burial, where they survived until they were found by local villagers in the 1820s.

Over the following decades, the Theban authorities pursued the same course to protect the burials within the Valley of the Kings, removing every last gram of gold and every object of value, partly to discourage potential tomb-robbers from taking any interest in the royal corpses, partly to bolster the faltering balance of account. One main reason for the neglect of Upper Egypt by the kings in their northern Residence, and a principal cause of the end of the New Kingdom, was the exhaustion of the goldmines in Egyptian-controlled Nubia. The last tomb prepared for a king in the Valley of the Kings was for Ramses XI, last king of the Twentieth Dynasty. It was never finished, and it is not clear whether the king was buried there.

In the name of Ramses XI a general named Payankh, of unknown origin and connections, went to war against the viceroy of Nubia, Panehesy. Despite the upheavals of the age, it still comes as a shock to read the

There is no exact parallel for this schematic depiction of the world, from the exterior decoration of a Late Period sarcophagus. The sky-goddess Nut arches over a circle representing the world. It is uncertain to what extent Western Asiatic or Greek influence may have contributed to the depiction of the world as a circle, but the motif has evidently been deemed appropriate to the imagery of the burial place.

original letters of Payankh to his civil servants at Thebes, a miraculous survival on the West Bank at Thebes that preserves for us in graphic terms the end of the New Kingdom. In one letter Payankh orders the murder and disposal of the bodies of some policemen, and in another he orders the seal of the necropolis to be held in readiness for himself, an ominous hint of semi-official tomb-emptying to pay for the campaign against Panehesy. Most startling of all, Payankh does not seek to conceal his contempt for the divine king, as his words in one letter flagrantly reveal: 'Pharaoh! Of whom is he master these days ?'

Within a few years Ramses XI had died, and the rulers of Egypt became at Thebes another general, named Heryhor, and in the north another man of unknown origins, Nesbanebdjed. The division of Egypt did not cause conflict, but had on the contrary been celebrated as the Repeating of Births, Renaissance, as if an opportunity to revive the land after the chaos of late Ramesside rule. The northern kingdom centred on a new Residence city, Tanis, perhaps because Per-Ramses silted up and could no longer function as a harbour, and perhaps also because the new rulers wished to distance themselves from the last Ramses. The southern domain of Amun was governed by the general, who took the title of high priest of Amun and, on certain monuments, the status of king. Although the two parts of the country seem to have maintained good relations with one another, and documents in Thebes seem to have been dated by the king in the north, this partition of the land marks the decisive end to the New Kingdom. During the next four hundred years, the city of Tanis acted as centre of a kingdom to which it is geographically marginal, and not surprisingly it never provided any effective unity for Egypt.

The particular role of Thebes as centre to the cult of Amun brought about a separate and flourishing religious tradition at that city, in contrast not only to the northern kingdom but also to the rest of Upper Egypt. Admittedly the ground of the Delta does not favour survival of organic material such as wooden coffins and funerary papyri. Nonetheless it seems from the lack of evidence across the entire rest of the country that at this period Thebes alone produced the dazzling explosion of creativity in the workshops for the afterlife. Suddenly, as at no other moment in Egyptian history, the output of richly decorated coffins and illustrated papyri veered toward a crescendo of innovation, in which no one papyrus or coffin exactly copies another, and instead the craftsmen and designers explore every path suggested by the five centuries of New Kingdom experience in preserving life beyond death.

The new age begins without a great quantity of evidence even at Thebes. On the bridge of old to new stands a pair of papyri for survival in the innovatory style of the Third Intermediate Period. They belong to a woman named Nedjmet, who bore the title king's mother, and appears on the longer papyrus together with the general Heryhor of the late

Twentieth Dynasty. It is not known exactly how Nedjmet was related to Heryhor, or who had her papyri prepared. It seems most likely that she was the wife of Heryhor, but we have no idea which king might have been her son. Heryhor himself claimed royal status during his decade and more of high office in Thebes, but Nedjmet never calls herself king's wife. One of her two papyri presents formulae from the Book of the Dead in cursive hieroglyphs. As in nearly all New Kingdom Books of the Dead, the hieroglyphs face to the right, which normally indicates that the text is to be read from right to left, but these sacred texts for the afterlife read from left to right, as if to highlight their more secret nature by reversing a cardinal rule of the script.

The Book of the Dead for priest and treasury scribe Userhatmes, of the tenth century BC, ends with the vignette that closes papyri three hundred years earlier in the 19th Dynasty, a scene of the deceased adoring Ipy, goddess of rebirth, at the edge of the desert. Behind her, Hathor appears in the guise of a cow emerging from a papyrus thicket, and on the lower slopes of the desert hills can be seen the round-topped stelae of tomb-chapels.

The Book of the Dead of Nedjmet is richly illustrated with coloured vignettes, and Heryhor in the guise of king takes a prominent role, although the scene of judgment and a vignette of the coffin make it clear that the papyrus belonged to Nedjmet. Certain scenes could only be played out by a man, as has already been seen in the vignette to chapter 110 of the Book of the Dead of Anhay, where her husband had to be introduced to hold any agricultural tools with blades, a threat to male potency and domination. In the papyrus of Nedjmet, Heryhor replaces his kinswoman at the scene of playing the boardgame *senet*, a test of skill and fate symbolic of the battle with life and death, much as chess could be in the Middle Ages in Europe.

The second papyrus of Nedjmet does not begin to rival her Book of the Dead in either length or the sumptuous coloured illustrations, but is nonetheless more innovative in two important respects. First, it can be seen with hindsight as the beginning of a new tradition of funerary manuscript, of the scheme for preserving life with text, a tradition of placing not one but two papyri in the burial, and not of the same type but complementary. This practice is confined to Thebes and to the two centuries from 1050 to 850 BC. The second papyrus of Nedjmet complements her Formulae for Going Forth by Day, her Book of the Dead, with scenes from various Underworld Books, in particular the Book of Caverns. The images on the papyrus include presentations of Nedjmet in adoration, at the beginning of the papyrus at the right end with the titles 'king's mother, she who bore the strong bull (i.e. the king), Mistress of the Two Lands' before the gods Amun-Ra-Horakhty, Theban version of the falcon-headed sun-god, and Osiris the lord of the underworld.

The second outstanding feature of the smaller papyrus of Nedjmet is the script. The texts between the various scenes derive mainly from the Formulae for Going Forth by Day, with one extra formula 'for bringing a garland of justification on the day of the Wag-festival' (an important funerary festival for the necropolis) related to some of those formulae ('chapters' 18 to 20). Their contents seem, then, less surprising than their juxtaposition to scenes from the Underworld Books. Yet their script opens an entirely new phase in the practices of preparing for the afterlife. Previously the hieroglyphic and cursive hieroglyphic scripts alone sufficed to record for eternity the sacred formulae to enable the deceased to survive death. The few exceptional uses of the more cursive hieratic script evidently occur only where an inferior or rushed scribe went to work on a restricted passage within a predominantly hieroglyphic manuscript. Since the reign of Hatshepsut with Thutmes III, when the papyri of Hatnefer, mother of Senenmut, included a finely written hieratic papyrus, hieroglyphic had been used for all funerary texts. In reviving the careful calligraphy of the earlier New Kingdom, the early Twenty-first Dynasty craftsmen who produced the papyrus of Nedjmet set a model for the last

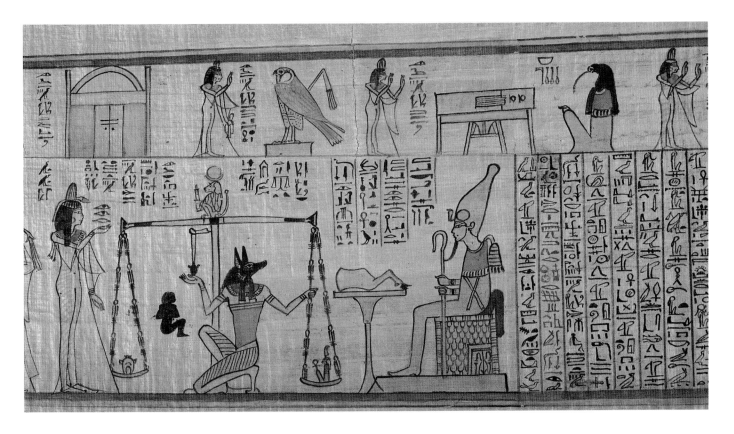

The judgment of Nany takes place before Osiris, with the jackal-headed Anubis checking the scales, and a figure of the goddess Right in the balance against the hieroglyph for a heart. Nany herself addresses Osiris from the far side of the scales. Between her and Anubis a small black figure crouches with hands crossed, evoking her shadow, essential part of her eternal life. Directly in front of Osiris an offering table is laden, unusually, with a single item, a haunch of meat. Vignettes along the upper register of the papyrus include that for 'chapter 94', the formula in which the deceased asks for a scribal palette in order to serve as secretary to the gods; Thoth, ibis-headed, is given the label in hieroglyphs 'lord of the words of god' (i.e. hieroglyphs).

thousand years of the tradition. It should also be noted that the quality of the hieratic texts so beautifully written out for the afterlife extends beyond the forms of the signs to the standards of text; whereas many hieroglyphic manuscripts contain formulae garbled almost beyond recognition, with numerous errors in understanding and in copying, the hieratic papyri of the Third Intermediate Period present among the most reliable versions of funerary texts known to us.

Curiously the two papyri of Nedjmet seem to stand alone in their generation, and the next group of manuscripts to survive, from the middle years of the Twenty-first Dynasty, do not select exactly the same scenes or texts or even the hieratic script so perfectly refined for her rebirth. The new stock of texts for the afterlife follow only the general principle that the burial should contain two papyri, of which one selects formulae from the Book of the Dead, while the other derives inspiration from the Underworld Books of the New Kingdom. Both manuscripts were written in hieroglyphs, and one placed in the coffin, the other in an extra piece of burial equipment rarely attested in the New Kingdom, a wooden figure of Osiris. In the Nineteenth Dynasty the Book of the Dead of Hunefer was placed in such a figure, as was that of Anhay from the Twentieth Dynasty, but otherwise the custom of concealing the papyrus within a wooden statue seems characteristic only of the Theban renaissance in the Third Intermediate Period. A further example, in the tomb of Amenhotep II, would be the oldest, as well as being the sole surviving royal papyrus of

the New Kingdom, but it may date instead to the Third Intermediate Period, when the tomb of the king came to house several other bodies in the course of dismantling royal burials in the Valley of the Kings.

The earlier group of Third Intermediate Period manuscripts presents a standard pattern of pairing, with a Book of the Dead in the cursive hieroglyphic script and brightly coloured vignettes, and a papyrus given the title Amduat, dominated by illustrations taken not from the 'Book of the Hidden Chamber Which is in the Underworld' but from the Litany of Ra. The Books of the Dead in this phase often take their inspiration from early Eighteenth Dynasty examples, sometimes so faithfully that only such details as the title of the owner can distinguish them from the earlier originals. Even personal names at this period hark back to the first part of the New Kingdom, testifying to the real power felt in a bygone age, when the first recorded oracles of the god Amun were delivered to confirm the legitimacy of the sovereign.

The Litany of Ra, named in Egyptian 'Book of the Adoration of Ra in the West', was often inscribed near the entrance to the royal tomb in the Ramesside period. The papyri deriving their design from this more accessible of the royal texts contain up to sixty, but not the full seventy-five, forms of the sun-god, mostly as mummiform bodies with the heads of various creatures, though some are smaller figures of other symbols and animals such as the cat or goat. In addition to the known series of forms of the sun-god the preparers of the new papyri composed new shapes, first indication of an endless inventiveness in Theban texts and, above all,

The second papyrus of Nany belongs to the new eleventh century BC complement to the Book of the Dead. Entitled Amduat 'What is in the Underworld', the eleventh and early tenth century BC manuscripts present a series of mainly mummiform deities, as found in the Litany of Ra in New Kingdom tombs of kings. On this papyrus each is directly identified in hieroglyphs by the name Nany, assuring her eternal existence by merging with the god.

images over the next two hundred years. The two papyri of a lady named Nany illustrate the new custom of pairing Book of the Dead with an 'Amduat' papyrus of Litany of Ra vignettes.

The burial of Nany was discovered by the Metropolitan Museum of Art, New York, excavations under Herbert Winlock, as he reported in 1930, and are now preserved in that museum. The titles of Nany include beside the usual designations of Theban noblewoman of the time, lady of the house and chantress of Amun-Ra, the unexpected title 'king's daughter'. We do not know to which king this could refer, although it may have been a Theban general and high priest of Amun who had taken royal titles, such as Heryhor. Both papyri are dominated by their paintings, with an especial emphasis on the colours yellow, for daily solar resurrection, and green, for the annual renewal of plant life.

The Book of the Dead of Nany presents ten formulae through vignette and text together, and a further twelve in vignette alone. Among these we find the fundamental depiction of the judgment and of the cultivation of fields, but also two vignettes not known from the New Kingdom papyri. The same spirit of experiment brings new forms to the series of figures in the Litany of Ra, where the creator takes shape in a variety of forms principally with mummiform body. Both manuscripts clearly serve one aim in obtaining for Nany her eternal life, yet they are kept physically apart on two separate scrolls. Evidently the Book of the Dead, for 'Going Forth By Day', could be complemented by texts from the Valley of the Kings such as the Litany of Ra, but it could neither be replaced by, nor merged with them. These two strategies for life are intended to remain distinct from one another.

After perhaps half a century, toward the end of the Twenty-first Dynasty, a new pairing of funerary papyri began to replace the standard combination of hieroglyphic Book of the Dead with Amduat papyrus of images based on the Litany of Ra. Formulae from the Book of the Dead were introduced by an offering scene in which the deceased worships or offers to one of the principal gods of rebirth, generally Ra or Osiris, as before, but now they were written in hieratic as the second papyrus of Nedjmet had been. Coloured vignettes were still added for the various formulae in the more sumptuous examples but these are outnumbered by the abbreviated manuscripts, in which the opening scene of adoration is the only illustration for the whole book. In a single example, the papyrus of the priestess Nestanebetisheru, an extremely extended series of formulae in hieratic runs beneath an even longer sequence of illustrations of outstanding draughtsmanship but left in black outline without any colour. The second papyrus in the pair for the afterlife also changed dramatically in appearance, although the name Amduat was retained. In the new pairing the Amduat abandoned the Litany of Ra and turned instead to the eastern wall of the burial chamber of Amenhotep II, bearing the last four

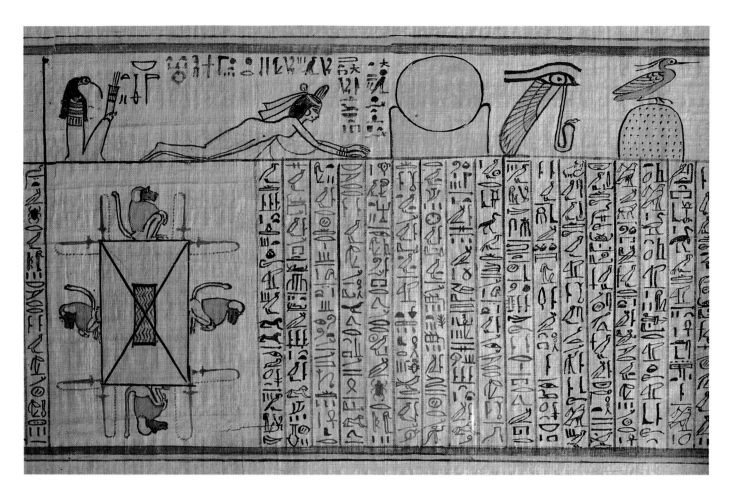

hours of the 'Book of the Hidden Chamber Which is in the Underworld'. The texts accompanying these final and crucial hours of resurrection seem to have been checked against the versions in the tomb of Amenhotep III, to judge from detailed variants.

The opportunity for examining the tombs of Eighteenth Dynasty kings in such a painstaking manner arose in the continual moves of the royal corpses around the West Bank at Thebes into ever larger and more secret group burials. These manoeuvres are recorded in ink notes on the bodies and coffins themselves, dated to years ranging from the end of the Twentieth Dynasty more than two and a half centuries into the early years of the Twenty-second Dynasty. Although the exact motivation for each move remains to be researched, the entire operation must have given the kings at Tanis and, more immediately, the high priests of Amun at Thebes considerable opportunity to bolster their own claims to rule as divine agents of the order of the sun-god on earth. During the moves, scribes evidently had time to record minutely the most favourable series of images for their own afterlife, and they seem to have found in the tomb of Amenhotep II, specifically in its burial chamber on the eastern wall, side of each sunrise, the most attractive models to follow.

Careful copies of the Amduat on papyrus use the same division into

This section of the Book of the Dead for princess Nany displays the characteristic combination of neat columns of hieroglyphs with clear coloured vignettes. To the left appears the lake of fire, which sustains the blessed dead but consumes the wicked in flames; each side is guarded by an image of the baboon, emblem of Thoth, and each corner is marked by two hieroglyphs denoting fire. Above Thoth is shown with ibis head, clasping a scribal palette and labelled 'lord of the words of god [hieroglyphs]', an illustration to 'chapter 96+97' of the Book of the Dead in which the deceased is enabled to be beside Thoth. In front of Thoth Nany is shown prostrating herself before the hieroglyph for the sun at the mountains of the horizon. Egyptian artists rarely presented the human body in pure profile, and this aspect here reinforces the dramatic effect of her posture.

three registers, but numerous less exact versions either garble the texts or the sequence of hours, or reduce the number of registers to two or even one. It is not certain exactly when the decision was taken to convert the scenes of the Eighteenth Dynasty tombs into designs for the funerary papyri of the Theban elite, but the evidence points to the tenure of office of a high priest of Amun named Menkheperra, the throne-name of Thutmes III. Menkheperra held his supreme position at Thebes for over forty years, and had gathered to himself enough authority by the later years of his life to claim royal status. At this time the king at Tanis was a young nephew of Menkheperra named Amunemipet. The circumstances could not be better for the deepest possible intrusion into the royal secrets of eternal life from the most glorious years of the New Kingdom.

At exactly this time the variety of the papyri, and of decoration on the ornate wooden coffins, reaches its peak. Instead of restricting the theme of each manuscript to a single source, the Theban craftsmen began to experiment with a wide range of ingredients from every type of image. This is an age in which the visual effectively triumphs over the written word, without abandoning it entirely. Many papyri swarm with motifs from the Book of the Dead and the different Underworld Books, sometimes adding new variations on the existing forms, in a whirlwind of active invention. The boundary between the two papyri, Book of the Dead and Amduat, becomes so blurred that, with two manuscripts full of mingled motifs, it becomes difficult to be sure which is the Book of the Dead and which is the Amduat. The titles Going Forth by Day and Amduat were still regularly written on the manuscripts, but sometimes papyri of all but identical appearance bear different titles. In this plethora of images, texts sometimes disappear completely from one manuscript, but it seems unlikely that any burial would have contained two manuscripts with no text, if only for identifying the owner, unless that function were to be left to the coffin or Osiris figure. It is to this age of colour that we owe most of even such supposedly typical Egyptian images as the scene of Nut arched over Geb. Far from being routine or typical, these are rare motifs infused with vitality at the most productive era of the quest for life after death.

In the midst of the storm of creativity, the Twenty-second Dynasty descends, all of a sudden curbing the frenetic pace of the afterlife designers. It is not at present possible to gauge whether the rapid disappearance of most types of illustrated manuscript in the grave reflects the disapproval of the new dynasty, or whether it stems simply from a stylistic exhaustion, prompting a return to simpler models. Although of western nomadic origin, the Twenty-second Dynasty kings lent particular prominence to their home in Egypt, Per-Bast 'the Domain of Bast' in the central Delta. For this reason they are sometimes called the Bubastite kings (Bubastis is the Greek form of Per-Bast), although they maintained the Residence city of Tanis and were buried there. Bast was a feline goddess of protection, originally the protective power of ointment in the *bas* or stone vessel for cosmetic oils. From the Third Intermediate Period she enjoys national popularity as protectress in the guise of not lion but cat, much as the crocodile Sobek had acted as national patron during the late Middle Kingdom.

Instead of ignoring Thebes, the kings of the new dynasty imposed sons of the royal line as high priests of Amun, and revived the New Kingdom practice of adding to the already fabulous monumental complex of the Amun temple at Karnak. Under the first kings of the dynasty, Sheshonq I and Osorkon I, the strong rule of the north led to effective unity, for the first time since the early Twentieth Dynasty.

During this period the Theban funerary workshops continued to produce papyri, limited now to the straightforward pairing of hieratic Book of the Dead with Amduat. Often the Book of the Dead consists of no more than five or six formulae, written still in the clear and beautiful forms of the hieratic style first encountered in the Amduat papyrus of Nedjmet. These abbreviated versions of the Book of the Dead allow us to discover which formulae the ancient Egyptians themselves considered most important to survival. Some present the ancient text in which the creator declares his identity, 'chapter 17', while a greater number select the formulae to prevent loss of the heart, *heka*-power, or name of the dead, 'chapters 23' to '28'. The emphasis on the heart can be detected at all periods, perhaps because it had to be removed for separate embalming and then reinserted into the body. At this period the techniques of mummification reached their height of refinement, and this may have reinforced the attention to the heart, always considered the seat of the intelligence as well as of the emotions. Some burials of the late Twenty-first and early Twenty-second Dynasty add to these illustrated manuscripts a novel brand without any vignette, either a series of funerary ritual texts, or more commonly a decree for good health from an oracle. The decree consists of a long strip of papyrus rolled up and tied around the neck, sometimes placed in a special container such as the gold cylinders of Shaq. Its texts could have been used by the living as much as by the dead, and insure the bearer by name against every imaginable danger in life, from the sprites at pools and glades, to the risk of falling walls or the strike of lightning.

The latest dated funerary papyri in the now traditional pairing come from the burial of a grandson of Osorkon I, of the same name. These were the first papyri recorded by the expedition of the French army under Napoleon Bonaparte, opening the modern history of Egyptian papyri, and they were preserved by the expeditionary scholar Vivant Denon. At the sale of his collection the agent of the Tsar purchased them for the imperial collection, and they are today housed in the National Library at Saint Petersburg. Back in early ninth century BC they close the colourful history of the Theban papyri in the Third Intermediate Period.

The scene of Nut arched over Geb is sometimes now considered the classic Egyptian conception of the world, but it is rare before the late tenth century BC. In one of the examples on Third Intermediate Period coffins (*see page 11*), the message of rebirth allows the artist to present Geb with erect phallus below Nut, below the soul of the sun-god, shown as a ram-headed winged scarab holding the hieroglyphic group 'perfection'. In this one Shu intervenes to hold aloft Nut, and is supported by two ram-headed deities, with the word 'perfection' written above head and womb of the goddess. 'Perfection' is also written beside the heavenly cow on the great vignette in the gilt shrine of Tutankhamun and later royal tombs.

It is not clear why the output should have suddenly ceased altogether. A similar fate befell the crowded ornamentation inside and outside coffins of the same century. The abrupt simplification of coffin design, and the utter disappearance of funerary texts, including even the Formulae for Going Forth by Day, coincides with a turbulent phase in the history of northern rule over Thebes. An account of the deeds of prince Osorkon at Karnak refers to open warfare and to attempts at suppressing Theban opposition. The funerary workshops may have been unable to function in the old style if their clientele, the Theban elite, faced impoverishment in war or disgrace. It is also possible that the northern kings acted directly to close down the workshops producing texts and images on the earlier scale, perhaps in the energetic reign of Osorkon II. A third possibility would be a change in style on more elusive aesthetic grounds, in which profusion of word and image was finally discarded in favour of a purified simplicity.

For the remainder of the ninth century the only funerary texts are found not at Thebes, but in the north, and especially at Tanis, in the latest royal tombs to survive into modern times. The French excavations under Pierre Montet during the Second World War uncovered the burial chambers of

During the late ninth to eighth centuries BC, when funerary texts and monumental projects seem lacking, the expression of kingship finds new forms. In an openwork spacer bead of faience, the king brings a defeated foreigner to Sekhmet under the protection of Mut.

four kings of the Third Intermediate Period, Pasebakhaemniut I and Amu-nemipet of the Twenty-first Dynasty, and Osorkon II and Sheshonq III of the Twenty-second Dynasty. The same group of tombs, in the corner of the Amun temple of Tanis, included some chambers of unknown persons and the burial of a general of Pasebakhaemniut I named Wendjebaundjed. Like the tomb of that official, but in contrast to the earlier royal tombs of Tanis, the burial chambers of Osorkon II and Sheshonq III both contain reduced excerpts from the Formulae for Going Forth by Day and the Underworld Books of the New Kingdom. During the same period the sons of kings who held the office of high priest of Ptah at Memphis also received burial in chambers adorned with scenes from the New Kingdom compositions.

Against the imperfect survival of royal and noble tombs in the north, and the slim chances of survival of papyrus in the damp soil of Lower Egyptian cemeteries, it is impossible to reach definitive conclusions, but on present evidence it seems that the Book of the Dead and the Underworld Books were no longer included on the surface of grave goods or tomb chamber walls after 800 BC even in the north. Every last formula, even the appeal to the *shabti*, vanished, and instead the Egyptian elite secured its life after death with the help of virtually no text and only a small number of symbols drawn large and clear over the coffin: the figure of Nut or the goddess of the West, and the falcon-headed Sokar or Osiris painted full length over the lid and floor of the coffin, and a simple formulaic prayer for a share in the offerings from the king to the gods. During this period, after the reign of Osorkon II, Egypt gradually unravelled into a system of more or less competitive principalities, with minimal recognition of the originally central kingship of Per-Bast and Tanis. In the face of the political fragmentation of the country, more than the funerary text tradition might appear already dead. The Pharaonic kingship itself no

On the other side of the spacer bead the king is suckled by Isis, as if he were her child Horus, between winged goddesses. New focus on the divine child fostered names such as Ankhosorkon 'May king Osorkon live' and Ankhhorpakhered 'May Horus the child live'.

longer existed in practice, a development that imperilled the religious and artistic expression which depended on a king to maintain order for the sun-god.

This peril can be exaggerated. At local level local princes used the Pharaonic titles, and supported the Pharaonic arts at least on the smaller scale. The country did not sink into poverty, and the eighth century saw the Iron Age firmly implanted in Egypt, confirming the spectacular advances in metalwork and, above all, faience production. The bronze sculpture and faience chalices of the late Third Intermediate Period face no rivals for the brilliance of their conception and execution. In many respects the disunity of this age prepares for a new rebirth, and without the disruptive century the rebirth could not have taken place. Nevertheless, in the funerary domain, there is no hint of any chance of a coming revival in the ancient texts used to secure an afterlife.

When the fortunes of the texts for an afterlife revived, rescue came from a most unexpected corner, invasion by kings of Kush, the area that is today the northern Sudan. In the late eighth century, Piy, king of Kush, took up the mantle of Pharaonic kingship, embracing beside the cult of Amun the formal canon of proportions for Egyptian art, hieroglyphic script and even the language of Egypt, in his bid for the throne of the ancient enemy to the north. Already his predecessor king Kashta had moved in the same direction, toward domination of Thebes and Upper Egypt, but by the reign of Piy the cause had become more urgent. In the northwest Delta one Tefnakht, a ruler of the city Sais, had assembled sufficient force to reach out beyond his terrain and threaten both the kings at Tanis and the princes of Middle Egypt. Only direct action could prevent Sais from emerging as a new and more powerful Egypt, and the kingdom of Kush must have felt impelled to take energetic and drastic action. A triumphal stela, now in the Egyptian Museum in Cairo, celebrated the

Late Period workshops in the Delta produced hollow cast bronze figures of the goddess Wadjyt as a lion-goddess (*left*) and of Horus as her son (*right*), and these contained mummified bodies of the Egyptian mongoose, the ichneumon. Wadjyt is usually represented as a cobra, defending the king and the northern borders of Egypt; as the

passage of Piy and acknowledgment of his rule by kings in Upper and Middle Egypt as well as, to a lesser extent, those in Lower Egypt. Yet it took further action under the next rulers of Kush to ensure that Egypt obeyed the south.

In this same generation, toward the end of the eighth century BC, the Formulae for Going Forth by Day begin to reappear on the surfaces of coffins. Already before the Kushite intrusion, Egyptian workshops began to goddess of Buto in the northern Delta she could provide maternal protection for the child Horus in the marshes there, and the figure of the god as a falcon or a child appears incised on the back of the thrones of Wadjyt bronzes. The ichneumon is an efficient snake killer, and denoted to the Egyptians the ability of Good to defend itself.

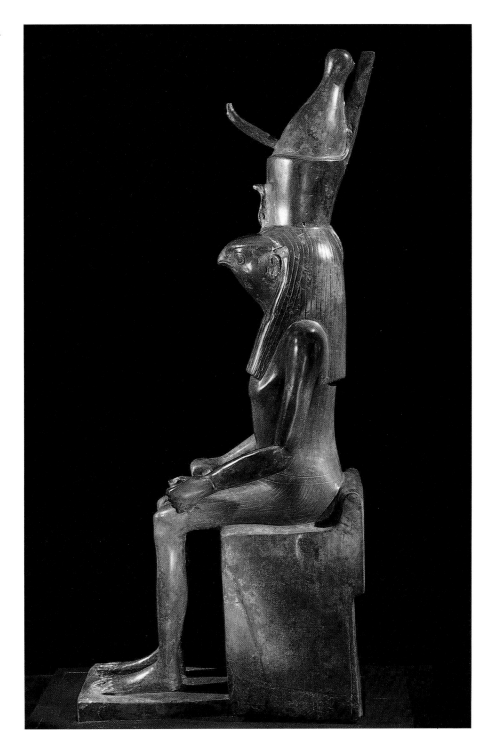

devise new forms inspired by remotest antiquity, with an outer coffin of wood but evoking the massive stone sarcophagi of earlier ages, adding a vaulted roof and cornerposts in a design reminiscent of the sign for a shrine of Upper Egypt, found already in the First Dynasty. The new shape did not yet bear texts beyond the simple offering formulae, but the inner mummiform coffin now began to expand its simple repertoire of image and words. One example of the late eighth century BC presents, after a gap of over a hundred years, texts from the Book of the Dead ranging from excerpts of the judgment scene to a formula for breathing air and having power over water in the afterlife ('chapter 59'), and a formula for free entry and exit ('chapter 12'). It is not possible yet to date this coffin, now in Grenoble, to the time before rather than after the conquest by Piy, and so we cannot be sure that its revival of the past precedes Kushite rule in Egypt. Yet it can be taken at least as a sign that the seventh century renaissance rested on a reawakening already in the eighth century.

Once installed as kings of Egypt as well as Kush, two rulers in particular impressed their presence on Egypt with an exemplary revivification of ancient custom. The earlier, Shabako, is famous for having a slab of basalt inscribed with an account of the creation from the point of view of Ptah, a text said in the introduction to have been found wormeaten in the archives of the temple. Possibly the phrase forms a part of the hyperbole of restoration, on a theme of carving order out of chaos, but the preceding century of Memphite neglect might encourage us to believe the Kushite king. This spirit of revival can be felt more tangibly still in the reign of the later active ruler of Kush in Egypt, Taharqo. Under his patronage, in the first two decades of the seventh century BC, Egypt underwent a rebirth of Pharaonic order. In the temple of Amun at Karnak, the then facade of the main complex, now within the later First Court, was embellished with the tallest kiosk or pillared open hall in the land. Less visible but perhaps more revealing of the restoring zeal, a stone edifice beside the sacred lake of the temple contained ancient texts such as the description of the king as champion of the sun-god, revived from the Theban temples of the New Kingdom.

At Thebes the principal authority at this period was the daughter of first the Tanite, then the Kushite king, with the title god's wife of Amun. This woman lived as an unmarried high priestess for the cult at Karnak. The holders of the title were buried in the open space between the royal cult temple of Ramses III and the temple to the primeval Amun at Medinet Habu, within the enclosure built to demarcate the terrain of the Ramses III temple. The tomb-chapel of Amenirdis I, daughter of Kashta and in office under his successors down to Shabatko, includes the first Pyramid Texts inscribed in stone since the New Kingdom. However the decoration of the relevant part of the chapel may not date as early as Shabatko, for it was undertaken under her successor Shepenwepet II, the daughter of Piy. Shepenwepet II remained in office throughout the reign of Taharqo and into the reign of the last Kushite king of Egypt, Tanutamani. The earlier tomb-chapels of god's wives of the eighth century were of brick. These have not survived, and seem unlikely to have contained funerary texts inscribed or painted on architectural elements. This leaves the chapel of Amenirdis as the earliest evidence for a revival of exceptional vitality, a dawn for which the modern label 'Late Period' seems almost deliberately inadequate.

152

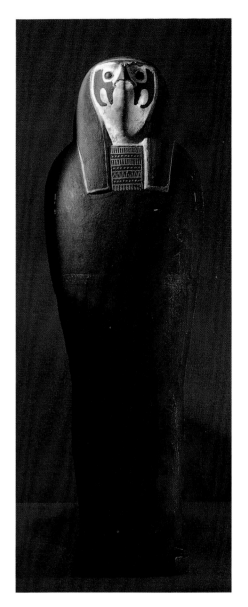

The falcon-head of this mummiform case refers to Sokar, god of the Memphite necropolis, and thus an appropriate form for a container of the figure of the god of the dead, Osiris. The figure of Osiris itself (*right*) is made of earth with germinated grains, symbolising resurrection.

In the Late Period such figures were fashioned every December, and buried after germination of the seed in a ritual designed to ensure the fertility of the earth after sowing in anticipation of the harvest.

The Book of the Dead returns now with greater insistence to resume its task of securing eternal life for the elite, as on the *shabtis* of Harwa, manager of the estates of the god's wife Amenirdis. These are the first *shabtis* since the ninth century to bear the text for avoiding hard labour in the underworld, and they find a royal echo in the tomb-complex of king Taharqo deep in the Sudan, at Nuri. Instead of the fine sculptures in wood and faience, the craftsmen of this brief period in the early years of the seventh century BC returned to the Middle and New Kingdom custom of carving funerary figurines from stone. The *shabtis* of king Taharqo, and of the Theban high officials who were his contemporaries or near-contemporaries, are masterpieces in the hardest and most beautiful stones of Egypt. The *shabti* text written upon them heralds the return of the Book of the Dead to its central role in the Egyptian life after death.

Harwa left his own imposing tomb-complex in the approach to the temple of Hathor at Deir el-Bahri. That temple seems to have been still the focus of the main Theban cemetery festival, the Festival of the Valley, at which Amun of Karnak crossed the river to visit the great sanctuaries of the West Bank. Under Kushite rule the approach from the fields to Deir el-Bahri began to offer the most important dignitaries of Thebes a home for their eternal cults. Harwa and his successor as manager to the god's wife, Akhamenru, each had tombs constructed with cult chambers above; the largest, that of the overseer of Upper Egypt Montemhat, ranks as the greatest non-royal structure set up at any period in ancient Egypt. These exceed mere chapels in size and defy modern attempts to label them; the phrase tomb-temple has been applied to these monuments, and a nineteenth century scholar, Duemichen, tried the term tomb-palace, evoking majesty if not purpose of the chambers above the tomb. The vast scale of these projects for the eternal life of select individuals prompted an exhaustive search for the most effective means of surviving death, wherever they might be found on monuments of the past or in the living rituals of the principal temples of Egypt. If we can name one man responsible for this massive task of research and re-edition, it would be Padiamenipet, the man to whose cult complex Duemichen was referring when he devised the term tomb-palace.

Padiamenipet held the title chief lector-priest, the same unassuming token of office which Sesenebnef had held just over a thousand years before him. The title evidently conceals the very kernel of Pharaonic tradition; these were the men who brought back into use the texts of their past. Just as the coffins of Sesenebnef mark a revival and extension of the Coffin Texts, on the path to becoming the Book of the Dead, the great tomb-complex of Padiamenipet reaches back beyond the textless century of the late Tanite kings, beyond the religious ferment of art in the earlier Third Intermediate Period, and into the classic ages of kingship. The walls of his tomb contain extracts and revised versions of Pyramid Texts from the late

Old Kingdom, friezes of objects and Coffin Texts from the early Middle Kingdom, and both Book of the Dead and the full range of royal Underworld Books from the New Kingdom. His resting-place would be a virtual library and history combined for the funerary tradition, had it escaped its appalling ruin in antiquity and over the past one hundred years. Even the surviving fragments have not been recorded or published, despite the intentions of Duemichen, but the existing accounts demonstrate clearly enough the extent to which the programme of image and text matched the ambition in sheer size of the complex. Here we touch a nerve-centre in the history of a nation.

In 671 BC war broke into this calm idyll of renewal. The Kushite realm was invaded as far as Memphis by Esarhaddon, king of Assyria, then at the peak of her imperial power. Taharqo was able to restore his authority over Egypt, but the Assyrians returned under a new king, Ashurbanipal, in 667 BC, and installed as their governor a certain Nekau, prince of Sais, the traditional enemy of Kush. When the Assyrian armies withdrew, the next Kushite king Tanutamani reconquered Egypt and slew Nekau, but the Assyrians returned in 664 BC to exact terrible vengeance, laying waste to Thebes so cruelly that the episode was recalled by the later compilers of Biblical texts. The Kushite forces retired to the south, leaving Egypt to the northern rivals. Psamtek, son of Nekau, became governor and slowly, as Assyria faced more and more serious problems on her eastern flank, made himself independent ruler, taking the titles and powers of Pharaoh. The violent Assyrian incursions effectively brought southern rule over Egypt to an end, and enabled the Saite dynasty to introduce a new period of independent Egyptian power.

The last trace of Kushite rule lay at Thebes, where the principal civil authority Montemhat had held office under the southern empire, and where Amenirdis II, daughter of Taharqo, was high priestess. By one of the strokes of fate with which Egypt is particularly blessed, the details of the contract of union survive on a stela celebrating the arrival of a daughter of Psamtek, Nitiqret, for adoption by the 'god's wife' as her successor. The notables of Thebes, including Montemhat, participated in the ceremony, at which the ancient unity of Egypt was asserted with more force and hope than had been possible since the death of the New Kingdom. With Kush banished to the south, and Assyria in death throes, the new dynasty of Sais could build on the restoration of the past to entrench a solid and self-conscious renaissance. The beneficial impact of the reinvigorated order is apparent in the funerary texts.

Within one or two decades from the departure of the Kushite king from Thebes, a man named Nespasef from a well-established priestly family was buried on the West Bank at that city, with the first papyrus of formulae for Going Forth by Day in two centuries. This new manuscript does not seem remarkable at first glance, a cursive hieratic text beneath blank

The New York section of the papyrus of Nespasef contains spaces for the insertion of vignettes after completion of the hieratic text in a separate studio. The space at the right includes the hieratic note 'add the prescribed images'. This is the first known funerary papyrus after a gap of two centuries.

spaces for vignettes which had never been filled in by the artist. We need to recall their place in time to recognise the importance of these unadorned sheets of papyrus. This is the first roll on which an entire stock of over one hundred and fifty formulae have been arranged in a sequence that was applied to the books for eternity across the next six hundred years. The spaces which stand blank, waiting for the images which were never added, seem to capture the very moment at which that new edition was being prepared. At one point a vignette space even contains the instruction in the same calligraphic writing as the main text 'add the prescribed images'. The draughtsman is on the point of walking in to make the addition, the design is being drawn up while we wait; time suddenly means nothing. One or two shadowy outline figures in red pigment have been drawn on other spaces, but this Book of the Dead keeps its atmosphere of experiment, of being the first in a radically new way of formulating the path to eternity.

That path has best been explained by Paul Barguet in his analysis of the Late Period sequence of the Book of the Dead. In the more complete versions of the period, the first fifteen formulae are placed beneath a single long vignette depicting the burial ceremony. A full height scene of the sun-disk follows, so strong a break that the nineteenth century Egyptologists gave it a number of its own as 'chapter 16' of the series, although it bears no text. This introductory group can be taken as the procession to the tomb, texts to ensure the safe burial of the deceased. The next group begins with the Middle Kingdom self-declaration of the creator, 'chapter 17', beneath a second long series of illustrations, and is followed by texts for justification and for power over the parts of the body and the elements of air and water. The next grouping of the formulae begins with another key statement of creation, 'chapter 64', still more obscure than 'chapter 17', and introduces a series of texts in which the deceased displays his divine power, either through a number of supernatural forms into which he can transform himself, or through the knowledge of holy places and their inhabitant forces. This section includes the scene of the harvest for the sustenance of the deceased in the Field of Hotep, taken from the Coffin Texts of the Middle Kingdom, 'chapter 110', and culminates in the great judgment hall of the Two Goddesses Right before Osiris, 'chapter 125'.

After the judgment the deceased knows his way past the caverns of the underworld, aboard the bark of Ra for his daily resurrection, and on the paths leading by the portals, gateways and mounds of the journey through the night sky. The texts for sailing with Ra stress the phrase *siqer akh* 'to invigorate a transfigured spirit', echoing the term *sakhu* 'transfiguration' or being transformed into a blessed spirit of light. This is the underlying theme and goal of every funerary text, and these particular formulae derive in part from that original recorded guide to the underworld, the Book of Two Ways. Equipped with knowledge of every corner of the darkness, the deceased can escape the fishermen of souls, here not benign but a threat to the survival of the dead. There follow the texts for amulets protecting the deceased, taken from the New Kingdom, with headrest, *tiyet* and *djed* amulets and the protective bricks at each of the four cardinal points of the burial chamber. To the earlier types the Late Period added necklace collars and *wadj* 'freshness', expressed by columns of papyrus.

The Book ends with a set of four previously unknown formulae echoing the healing recitations of the Ramesside period. Many of the words are written as if foreign, a tactic for increasing mystery and so power in the New Kingdom world. Here, nine hundred years after Egypt entered into close contact with Western Asia, after the wideranging effects of that contact, the foreign influence finally catches up with the funerary tradition, to become an inalienable part of the central texts for life after death, the Book of the Dead itself. The vignettes for these final 'chapters' recall the schematic, tenergetic sketches of composite demonic forms from Ramesside healing books, and present a stark contrast to the sobriety of the preceding formulae. The goddess Mut grows a phallus, and the heads of Amun multiply over a dwarflike body, in grotesque units designed to frighten away enemies at birth, in this life or, in their new service, the next. According to the heading on this manuscript, these texts were added from a separate papyrus roll in the Residence city of the Third Intermediate Period, Tanis, a rare indication of the place where manuscripts, if not

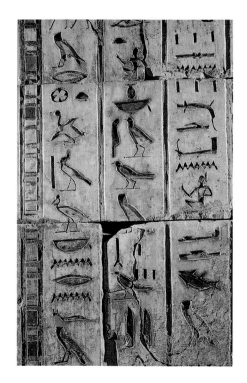

The tomb-chapel of Bakenrenef at Saqqara contained hieroglyphic inscriptions from both Pyramid Texts and Book of the Dead. In this section the titles and name of the vizier occupy the first column, while the rest contain the assertion of innocence, beginning 'I am free from sin'.

Quality of carving varies considerably in the burial chambers of three Twenty-sixth Dynasty officials discovered at the turn of the century at the bottom of a deep shaft immediately to the south of the pyramid of Unas at Saqqara. The Pyramid Texts for the admiral Tjanhebu contain formulae kept alive in temple ritual on hieratic papyri, and here given the hieroglyphic forms found in the tomb of Unas, expertly sculpted in the limestone (*right*).

The burial chamber of Padiaset, reached by the same shaft as that of the tomb of Tjanhebu, includes uneven lines and irregular forms even at the most visible, central points of the walls (*far right*).

texts, were compiled.

After the unfinished, unillustrated papyrus of Nespasef, a handful of seventh to sixth century manuscripts survive to demonstrate that the promise did not go unfulfilled, that the images were devised, and the entire scheme for eternal life launched afresh. These rarest of funerary papyri range from the provincial but magnificent coloured Book of the Dead of Iahtesnakht from Middle Egypt, now in Cologne, to the more formal and superbly executed manuscript of Psamtek, an official of the end of the Twenty-sixth Dynasty known also for his sky-blue glazed *shabti* figures as well as a coffin with exceptionally fine hieroglyphs, containing a revised version of a passage first encountered in the Pyramid Texts. Seventh to sixth century coffins build on those of the eighth, as if ignoring the devastation of war between Kush and Assyria. The first dated vignettes for the Book of the Dead in the Late Period are on not a papyrus, but a pair of coffins in which the floor bears the words and the new images of formulae for repelling serpents, insects and any other physical enemies of the deceased. Even within the constraints of space and anthropoid shape, the coffin selections of formulae tend to take the same sequence as the papyri, evidence of the conviction that the new order held in the Late Period.

The revival of ancient texts did not remain confined to Thebes. The few papyri with Book of the Dead texts derive from both halves of the country, and both sarcophagi of high officials and coffins of less wealthy members of the elite at Saqqara, Giza and Iunu (Heliopolis) bear appropriate selections such as 'chapter 72' and 'chapter 89', texts to allow the body to receive nourishment and the *ba* to join the body. A number of the most impressive monuments in the revival belong to leading members of court buried near the pyramid of Unas or along the escarpment east of the Step Pyramid at Saqqara. Among the latter the most prominent belongs to a vizier Bakenrenef, while the Unas group includes the chief physician Psamtek and the overseer of ships Tjanhebu. All are characterised by an inventive combination of ancient texts and new ideas for their arrangement in defence of the deceased. Edda Bresciani has drawn attention to the disposition, remarkable for its clarity as much as its scholarship. Indeed it may be noted that the texts themselves do not owe their use to probing in ancient tombs so much as continual life in the temple and funeral rites of the age. By contrast the very forms of the hieroglyphs seem to have been inspired if not quite specifically modelled on the crisp blue outlines of the Pyramid texts against a white background in the Old Kingdom royal burial chambers. In other words, the renaissance revives not the texts themselves, but the practice of inscribing them for eternity.

Into the renaissance of art, script and text, invasion from Asia burst for a second time. In 525 BC Cambyses launched his successful attack against Psamtek III, only a few months king of Egypt. Like the armies of Esarhaddon in 671 BC the Persian forces crushed any opposition swiftly, but unlike the Assyrians the Persians came to stay. At first they maintained at least some Egyptian cults, and had themselves depicted within Egypt as Pharaohs. The statue of an Egyptian official, Wedjahorresnet, bears an hieroglyphic text in which he narrates at length his services to the Persian king, from devising the Egyptian throne name for his accession, as 'creature of Ra', to restoring the temple of the goddess Neit at Sais in a display of piety at a leading national sanctuary of the period. At the death of Cambyses, rebellions elsewhere in the Persian Empire did not seem to produce the same level of military activity within Egypt, and the Pharaonic facade of kingship continued, with the construction or at least decoration of the temple at Hibis in the Kharga oasis and hieroglyphic inscriptions at the greywacke quarries in the Wadi Hammamat under both Persian officials such as Atiyawahy and Egyptians like Khnumibra.

Despite such tokens of traditional kingship, in general Egypt became a province like any other, the Sixth Satrapy of the Persian Empire. If we look for the Egyptians themselves in the monumental record, they have all but disappeared. Statues are often ascribed by modern scholars to the Persian Period, but there is a remarkable vacuum of inscription to support this. The statue of Wedjahorresnet stands in striking isolation proclaiming that Darius I had him restore the department for healing in the House of Life, institution at the heart of Pharaonic tradition, at Sais, the recent home of Pharaonic kingship. No other monument survives to demonstrate the effect of this restoration. Still more striking is the utter dearth of any burials dated to the fifth century BC. Of course Egyptians were still being buried, but the tomb-chapels, sarcophagi and coffins, the *shabtis* and

Most texts and scenes on Thirtieth Dynasty sarcophagi derive from the Amduat. At one end of a sarcophagus two hours are included, the tenth, with those who died by drowning and thereby became divine, and, above it, the eleventh, with the enemies of the sun-god burnt in desert pits.

papyri, in a word the entire Egyptian afterlife disappears under Persian rule for a hundred years.

Greek victory against the odds at the Battle of Marathon in 490 BC undermined the confidence of the Persian Empire, producing a brief interlude of independence in Egypt about 486 BC around the death of Darius. Although his successor Xerxes succeeded in reconquest, he did not resume temple inscriptions, and the occupation lost its Pharaonic veneer for the rest of the fifth century, despite occasional quarrying inscriptions in hieroglyphs, and occasional legal documents in the new cursive Egyptian script, demotic. Periodically an Egyptian nobleman at one or other of the rival Delta cities secured independence from Persian rule. The most determined of these is known only by the Greek version of his name, Inaros, son of a certain Psamtek, perhaps scion of the line of Sais, and controller of much of Egypt from about 463 to 454 BC The following generation saw peace, but more persistent revolts returned in the reign of Darius II from 424 BC, and Greek support helped a certain nobleman, again recorded only in Greek as Amyrtaios, to expel Artaxerxes II and his forces in a campaign from 404 to 402 BC.

Over the next sixty years Egypt was ruled by a succession of Pharaohs from the Delta, under constant threat of internal rivalries and continual attempts at reconquest by Persia. Such conditions seem scarcely ideal for monumental activity on the traditional Pharaonic scale, yet the land underwent its most thorough programme of temple building, surpassing even the plans of Ramses II. In the world of the tomb, the new Pharaohs revived the renewal of the seventh century, producing a second renaissance. Workshops for relief, temple sculpture, burial goods, took up where the Saite period had been interrupted. Certainly there appeared nothing on the scale of the tomb-chapels of high officials from the seventh century BC. Indeed, the ransacked burial places of the vizier Bakenrenef at Saqqara and the Theban magnate Ankhhor became second home to the bodies of new families of leading figures at Memphis and Thebes. Nevertheless, the fourth century sharpened its focus within the burial chamber, where we find the most intricate inscriptions of image and text on sarcophagi in the hardest stones from any period. These were selected from the lengthy Underworld Books of the New Kingdom, in particular the Amduat, but also the larger scenes from the Book of Gates, such as the judgment and the opening vignette. The practice of writing out the Formulae for Going Forth by Day resumed, with a new twist at Memphis, where the texts and vignettes were drawn directly onto the linen mummy bandages before a final layer of sweet-smelling resin, or less fragrant bitumen, was poured over the body in the culminating step of deification. Beneath the head of the deceased a disk of metal or plastered linen guaranteed the future life of the deceased by appeal to the force of the primeval floodwaters, in the words of 'chapter 162' of the Book of the Dead. Again the Egyptian dead went armed into their next life.

Egypt herself was no less meticulously defended on a spiritual plane with a girdle of temples founded or extended under kings Nakhtnebef and Nakhthorhebyt, stretching the full length of the country to the island of Philae, where a new temple rose to house the cult of Isis. Under the same kings a growing number of healing figures appear with the image of her vulnerable child Horus given power over the forces of nature. The finest of these contains an extended selection of the formulae against noxious creatures, a type of text first encountered in the pyramid of Unas. At the same time high officials such as Djedher had statues made with texts of the same nature completely covering every available space, even the hair of the man. Here piety already claims its reward, as the owner of the statue promises the healing power of the texts on the stone to any who would partake of it. Against the shadow of Persia the entire country, its king and court became more explicitly than before a machine defending good against evil.

In this Late Period sarcophagus detail, the judgment hall of Osiris is seen at the moment when Horus extends the sign of life to revive his father. Osiris sits enthroned in the presence of eighteen standing deities and a further twenty-nine gods with their hands raised in the act of adoration.

In 343 BC the Persian king Artaxerxes III reconquered Egypt, and for an unstable decade Persian armies again controlled Egypt. It is not known what befell Nakhthorhebyt, the last Pharaoh; his magnificent hard stone sarcophagus survives, with the last funerary texts known for a king of Egypt, selected from the Amduat of the New Kingdom, but the date of his death and even the location of his tomb is unknown. Alexander the Great arrived in triumph to claim the throne of Egypt as son of the sun-god, in 332 BC, and put an end to Persian rule in Egypt and over the rest of Western Asia. Yet he retained the system of satraps, and, even if he had temples restored and hieroglyphic texts carved, the land was in practice occupied by another foreign army, the Macedonian. When Alexander died, his empire disintegrated into the hands of his generals, leaving general Ptolemy in charge of Egypt and her western oases. This Macedonian satrap declared himself Pharaoh Ptolemy I in 305 BC, and ruled, as did his successors for the next three centuries, from the new Mediterranean port Alexandria.

During the second half of this fatal fourth century, Egypt and her texts struggled to survive the uncertainty over who ruled. The fate of the country left a direct impact on the temples and the texts preserved within

At the corner of the sarcophagus the jagged path of the sandy domain of Sokar stretches across the fourth and fifth hours of the Amduat.

them, as we see in two separate sets of manuscripts from burials at Thebes of about 300 BC. In each case the manuscripts bear texts from temple liturgy, in many cases formulae reaching back over two thousand years to the tradition of Pyramid Texts, in the same order found on the coffins, and thus in the funeral rites, of the Middle Kingdom, one and a half thousand years before the manuscripts were written. These texts belonged in the Late Period to the temple rituals performed in defence of the god of the dead, Osiris, or the creator sun-god, Ra. They do not form a part of the Book of the Dead, and would not normally be expected outside the walls of the temple at this date. The reason that they were copied can be detected in the dates recorded by the copyist, for in each set of manuscripts these coincide with national catastrophe or change, first the Persian invasion of 343 BC, then the crisis out of which the satrap Ptolemy declared himself king of Egypt in 305 BC. We owe these manuscripts, and thus the survival of the rituals upon them, to the very disasters that threatened their existence and prompted an ancient Egyptian first to copy them and then to take them to the grave.

The new government spoke and wrote neither Egyptian nor Macedonian. Instead it used Greek, one of a series of new kingdoms building on the heritage of classical Greece and the military success of Alexander in destroying the Persian empire. Its capital was perhaps the first city on the seashore in Egypt, and faced out to the Mediterranean traderoutes as much

On this detail of a Late Period sarcophagus appear the angular pathways through the sandbanks of the early night, on which the sun-god had to be dragged according to the description of his nocturnal journey in the royal Underworld Books of the New Kingdom. Goddesses hold the towrope of the divine bark, while gods clear the way in advance, and the serpents imply an area deep in the earth, both rocky and dark.

as in to the substantial traffic on the Nile. In every respect the Ptolemaic kingdom stood removed from its Egyptian subjects, even in the magnificent institutions that it founded in Alexandria, the Museum and the Library, centrepoints of the Hellenistic world. There seems to have been neither an Egyptian book in that library, nor an Egyptian-speaking Greek in the country, at least as far as our sources reveal. A thousand years of Greek as the language of government in Egypt had begun in exclusion of the native tongue.

Yet the arrival of Alexander and Ptolemy did not extinguish Egyptian tradition in the dramatic way that Persian rule had seemed to affect the land. The families of prominence at Thebes continued to commission new statues for the temple courts and halls of Karnak, and to bury their dead in the shell of the tomb-complex of Ankhhor and other ancient sites on the West Bank. Near Khentmin in Upper Egypt the flourishing new city of Ptolemais came into being, and the cemeteries of the old town on the opposite bank of the river continued to nurture the millennial funerary traditions with magnificent coffins and full-length papyri for the dead. At Khemenu in Middle Egypt the dignitaries of the town expanded the city of the dead, at a site now called Tuna el-Gebel, with offering-chapels in which Greek style meets the ancient art and texts of Egypt. Many of the finest works of the funerary craftshops in the third century follow their

models so faithfully that it can still be difficult to distinguish them from the output of the fourth century BC.

At the end of the third century every corner of the Ptolemaic realm, inside and outside the Nile valley, burst into revolt against Ptolemy IV, who left little more than Alexandria itself to his child as Ptolemy V. On behalf of the young ruler the Alexandrian court and army proceeded step by step in the reconquest of Egypt, and thwarted attacks from abroad. Upper Egypt underwent a generation of separate rule with a king Ankhwennefer and then Horwennefer, before succumbing to the return of the Ptolemaic forces. In the reconquest the Alexandrian cause used more than military force, enlisting the aid of the royal cult by having the young king proclaimed a god in every temple. The text of this decision was drawn up and promulgated by the priests of all the temples, necessarily so, since the Greek government could not speak, compose or write Egyptian. The young king was crowned in Egyptian style at the Old Kingdom capital, Memphis, and stelae were set up throughout Alexandrian territory to immortalise the establishment of the royal cult. The stela known as the Rosetta Stone, famous for its assistance to scholars in the decipherment of the hieroglyphs, belongs to this series of temple texts.

Nothing illustrates more clearly the efforts of the Ptolemies to be Pharaohs, and the gulf between them and the Pharaonic world. Under the Egyptian Pharaohs, no priest would have been allowed to take a decision concerning the royal cult, much less issue the text as a decree. Still more important, every Pharaoh was automatically son of the sun-god, and therefore became the object of a cult from the moment of his accession, his first appearance as champion of the divine order. There would be no need for a decree to promulgate the cult. From this point the weakness of royal support for hieroglyphic tradition begins to have its impact. The Books of the Dead start to use hieroglyphic as well as the cursive hieratic script again, but the quality of the text and images loses the standards of fourth and third century scholarship. *Shabtis* disappear from burials and the coffins move away from the classic forms of Pharaonic Egypt. In the temples reliefs were still sculpted, and the cults of the gods did not fade, especially the attention to animal 'heralds' of the major gods such as the Apis bull of Ptah. Yet the royal court did not revolve around Egyptian cults in their original form, and the Egyptian nobility had begun to adopt more Mediterranean customs, with less firm support for the traditional forms in funerary and other workshops.

In 30 BC the last Ptolemaic dynast, Cleopatra VII, took her own life after defeat with Mark Antony at the Battle of Actium. A new ruler of the world had risen, Octavian, named in 27 BC Augustus. Egypt returned to the status of province in a wider empire, and her traditions became still more marginal. Under the new regime her ancient texts take their last flourish of revival, just as a new creed is voiced in a neighbouring land.

Left The tomb-chapel of Padiwesir, high priest of Thoth, yielded a magnificent coffin inlaid with coloured glass. Below the line of stars in the central column the name and titles of the deceased appear within an appeal to Ibuwer, a guardian of the slaughter-house found already in the Coffin Texts. Here the text is taken from chapter 42 of the Book of the Dead, and guarantees the deceased against being butchered by identifying each part of the body with that of a deity. In his tomb-chapel Padiwesir claims that the several cases protecting his body, including the wooden one, are inlaid with precious stones; this is presumably evoked by the colourful glass inlays.

Above In Upper Egypt the Ptolemaic dynasty continued to invest heavily in the massive building programme begun by the Pharaohs of the fourth century BC, as exemplified by this inscription at the temple of Sobek and Horus at Kom Ombo with the cartouche of 'Ptolemy, living forever, beloved of Ptah and Isis'.

CHAPTER 6

The Last Flowering: Preserving Afterlife in Roman Egypt

THE reign of Augustus did not destroy Egyptian tradition along with the Ptolemaic dynasty. Already the first century BC had brought a marked drop in the length of papyri with formulae for preserving life after death. The length of a papyrus roll may seem a mundane feature in literature, but we learn much of the economic climate among those commissioning a traditional burial when we consider the general disappearance of the fuller selections of over a hundred texts. At about this time the funerary tradition underwent its last major revision, as if adapting the armoury of phrases in the Formulae for Going Forth by Day to a less abundant supply of papyrus in the funerary workshops.

In the new edition the deceased went into the next world not with a book of formulae, but with a passport, a travel document for free access. Such travel documents are known in the original from the far ends of Egyptian history. The Old Kingdom archive discovered in the 1980s by the Czechoslovak expedition to Abusir included the earliest surviving sheet of papyrus on which the carrier is declared entitled to enter a restricted zone. From the opposite end of time, after the Islamic conquest of AD 641 Coptic monks were given passes to allow them to travel from one monastery to another in the sensitive desert margins. In this same frame of mind the Thebans of the first century BC named their new shorter means of access to life after death the Documents for Breathing.

The earliest manuscripts may not compare in length with the older and most extensive selections of Formulae for Going Forth by Day, yet they witness a continued vitality. Other than a single papyrus said to come from Esna, a short distance to the south, only Thebes has produced examples of funerary compositions in hieratic on papyrus from the Roman period. The few papyri found in Roman period burials at Saqqara bear instead of funerary texts other compositions, notably the ritual for the Opening of the Mouth, copied out on behalf of the deceased man or woman. That ritual served to bring life to inanimate objects in human

Funerary traditions remained alive well into the Roman period, above all in the practice of mummification and accompanying arts such as the production of mummy masks. The most expensive of these were gilt, as in this example.

form, originally the statue and only by extension the coffin and the mummy itself. The central role of the Opening of the Mouth in Pharaonic civilisation is seen again in its latest use at Saqqara as the preferred text to attain eternal life. For Documents for Breathing Thebes appears to stand alone, much as it had in the Third Intermediate Period. As then, we cannot be sure that this geographical restrictment reflects better conditions of preservation at Thebes, and yet papyri from other periods have survived at other cemeteries, and the record may accurately reflect a preeminent role for Thebes in equipping the dead for a new life.

One of the earliest and finest Documents for Breathing is the manuscript made, perhaps in the first century BC, for a priest of Amun named Osirwer (the papyrus is now in the Louvre). The roll presents the Egyptian in a Mediterranean costume, with a garland around his head in the Greek manner. Yet he bears the Egyptian name Osirwer 'Osiris is the great (god)', and participates in scenes familiar from the earlier books of

At the feet of the coffin shown on page 166 there is a vivid scene of Isis and Nephthys lamenting, and thereby revivifying, the murdered Osiris. Over Osiris hovers a falcon holding a fan and the *shen*-ring of eternity, and beneath the funerary bier can be seen the forms of the Red Crown, Double Crown and White Crown. Even the unusual posture, as if reclining on a couch, can be paralleled from Pharaonic depictions of the resurrection of Osiris.

Formulae for Going Forth by Day: an opening vignette of adoration of Osiris, the hall of judgment, and the offering of incense to a goddess represented as a cow, here identified as Hathor. In the judgment scene, as had been the rule since the New Kingdom, Osiris presides over the weighing of the heart of the deceased, with Isis at his back, Thoth recording the outcome, and the monster Amemet poised ready to devour any evil soul.

The texts set over and between the traditional scenes belong to the new series adapted as document for eternal life. The signs are written in a carefully spaced hieratic with rounded flourishes, and their angular precision betrays the influence of the Greek and Roman world. These distinctive forms evolved as the Egyptian scribes gave up their traditional reed pen, a single stem with bruised end like a brush, and adopted the Greek writing tool, a pen made from a shorter, thicker reed with a cut nib. The change accompanied even a change in pigment, from the carbon black and red ochre of Egyptian manuscripts to the lead inks of the Greek world. These alterations in material may appear superficial, but they form part of a sea-change in the very substance of living in Egypt. Under the Romans iron tools and weapons enter the ordinary Egyptian home on a new scale, including, for the first time in the Nile valley, devices which we take for granted, most notably the lock and key. Each slight innovation joins together to create a new lifestyle, heralding the end of ways of experiencing, seeing and expressing the world. The funerary texts, among the most steadfast corners of tradition, may not switch to the new ink and pen so readily, but even they are affected by the flow of time in the very forms of the hieratic signs.

Three bands of larger signs run along the full two metres of the papyrus of Osirwer over the rest of the texts and illustrations, and give the words of a hymn to the king of the dead. Typically for this last stage of funerary literature, the hymn opens with a phrase that had opened scores of earlier manuscripts, as the first words of 'chapter 1' from the Formulae for Going Forth by Day, deriving in turn from a Coffin Text of the early Middle Kingdom. The familiar phrase, 'Hail O bull of the West', does not lead on to the rest of that formula, but instead develops its own series of variations in the creative spirit that remains the hallmark of this history. According to a demotic tale of the first century BC, the Document for Breathing was found under one of the last Pharaohs in the tomb of a king Psamtek, presumably one of the kings of the Twenty-sixth Dynasty. However such pedigrees were often inserted into formulae for the tomb, in an expression of their known antiquity and uncertain origin. The text of the heart scarabs, from the Formulae for Going Forth by Day, was ascribed to a discovery by prince Hordedef of the Fourth Dynasty, c.2550 BC, although it is written in the Middle Egyptian idiom not current before c.2100 BC, and does not occur on any surviving object older than the Thirteenth Dynasty, c.1750 BC. In the case of the Document for Breathing there is no evidence

Glass image of a serpent with the head of a bearded man, fusing Egyptian and Greek iconography. The serpent represents Agathodaimon, the guardian spirit and patron deity of Alexandria. In this form the grain god Serapis defends the home with his female counterpart Isis.

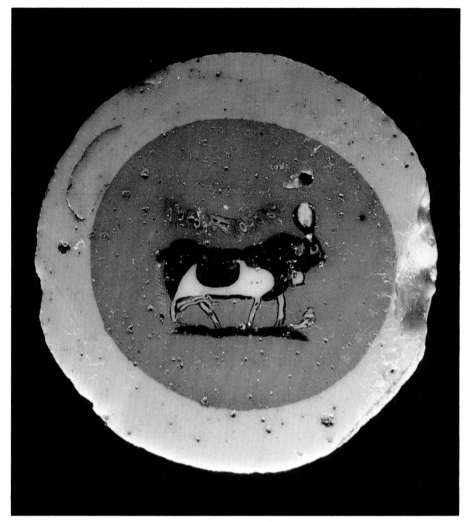

The technological advances of Mediterranean civilization enabled Egyptian craftsmen of the Ptolemaic and Roman periods to produce glass inlays of traditional motifs, on a breathtakingly miniaturist scale, such as the falcon (13mm diam.), the *wedjat* eye of wholeness (18×22mm), and a figure which cannot be recognised but for whom the miniscule hieroglyphic text seems to provide the name Hapy 'Inundation'. The glass inlay showing the Apis bull is an example of the late occurrence of purely Pharaonic motifs in Ptolemaic and Roman Egypt. Despite its miniature size, the craftsman has miraculously included the blue *wedjat*-hieroglyph above the sacred bull.

that it came into being before the late Ptolemaic period. The motive for compiling the new text would seem to be the need for funerary papyri shorter but no less comprehensive than the Formulae for Going Forth by Day. That need arises after the second century BC.

The composition found on the papyrus of Osirwer is not alone in the new and last outburst of invention at the Theban workshops for eternity. In a second and final echo of the turbulent outpourings at the same place in the tenth century BC, a series of manuscripts plays out a kaleidoscope of assemblages from the phrasing with which Egyptians had for centuries sought to secure their existence through time. One composition cites a title emblematic of that group, the Document for Outlasting Eternity:

May your soul live in the sky before Ra,
may your *ka* be divine at the fore of the gods,
may your body rest in the underworld before Osiris,
may your mummy be a transfigured spirit (*akh*)
  at the fore of the living,
your name secure on the mouth of those who are on earth,

in this book of outlasting eternity;
may you go forth by day,
may you join the sun-disk, may his rays illumine your face.

The same text occurs on stelae from the early years of Roman rule in Egypt, one from Hawara in the Fayum, the other perhaps from Tjebennetjer in the Delta. This suggests that the texts were used across the whole country, but that they were taken to the grave on papyrus apparently only at Thebes.

The Document for Breathing provides the heading to the two most common sets of text, full of variations but clustering in families of manuscript. The earlier Documents are presented as recommendations from the goddess Isis to the tribunal of the underworld on behalf of the dead man. Later examples range from elaborate compositions to simple pairs of sheets of papyrus, and specify that the Documents for Breathing are written by the god Thoth to enable the deceased to pass, like the sun-god, through the stomach of Nut, sky-goddess and coffin in one, circuiting the underworld, of which the burial chamber provides a microcosm. The deceased is recalled to earth by the memory of his name, in the most characteristic passage of the text, in which his name is declared to be made as enduring as that of any major deity. The goddess Nut returns him to the world as a living *ba* endowed with the breath of life from Amun himself.

Where the text has been reduced to two sheets, one bears the instruction to be placed at the head, while the other is marked for placing at the feet of the dead man or woman. For the first time the sexes are made distinct in the afterlife, the man identified with Osiris and the woman with Hathor, where previously, since the Coffin Texts in the Middle Kingdom, all the dead had asserted their identity with Osiris regardless of their gender. The abbreviated manuscript of a Theban noblewoman named Tentdjemet opens in typical vein with extracts from the full Document for Breathing:

I am Ra in his rising,
I am Atum in his setting,
I am Osiris Foremost of the West at night.
I am the ibis, black-headed, white-bodied, blue-backed.I am he before whom the decree is issued at Iunu,
for his voice to be heard in the place Secret of Plans.Turn to me, O doorkeepers of the West,
O guardians of the Underworld, let me come and go.

The latest dated burials with funerary texts come from a family tomb, deep in the labyrinthine underground passages of an Eighteenth Dynasty tomb. The head of the family was a man named Soter, with the title governor of Thebes, and some of the burials of his family, including teenage and younger children, contain year-dates referring to Roman

emperors of the late first and early second centuries AD. The coffins and shrouds over the mummified bodies mingle classical Greek and Roman style in the features and costume with the Western Asiatic motif of the zodiac, in the frame of a traditional Egyptian coffin over which the ancient Egyptian gods preside. In this group the texts for eternal life on papyrus occupy no more than two small sheets per burial, and present typically individual variants of the Document for Breathing. After these finds from the early second century AD, we meet no later funerary manuscript. Even the concept of a text with which to survive death seems to evaporate. A number of coffins and one or two wooden boards, apparently to be set beneath the mummified body, bear inscriptions in demotic with formulae in similar vein, but none of even these final gestures can be dated later than the second century AD.

The choice of script is also significant. The Theban scribes had maintained an accurate, if increasingly amorphous, hieratic, but some later funerary papyri lapse into demotic, as if the more sacred scripts were already being gradually lost. This central part of the Pharaonic tradition had always been confined to a handful of centres. Even in the first century of Roman rule, the few funerary papyri produced at Khentmin (Akhmim) were in the demotic script alone; they combine motifs from the Opening of the Mouth with the Documents for Breathing and even the self-justifications of texts on funerary stelae in hieroglyphic. One of the Khentmin texts found on more than one papyrus bears the revealing name 'Book of Opening the Mouth for Breathing'; here the funerary tradition is alive, but it has been transferred to the demotic world, and seems to disappear before the end of the first century AD. During the second century AD at least one or two temples witnessed a revival in the knowledge of ancient texts. At Esna schemes of decoration were being devised that were still being executed under the Roman emperors of the third century, and which included two cryptographic texts, one with ram signs and the other with crocodile signs, that continue to defy attempts at decipherment. At the other end of the country the Egyptian elite at Tebtynis in the southern Fayum, within the sphere of the ancient city Henensu (in Greek Heracleopolis) produced an outburst of writing no less vibrant and intense, and covering all three Egyptian scripts, hieroglyphic, hieratic and demotic. In neither location did the sages write for the afterlife, but their writings prove the vitality of their heritage in its final century. The Tebtynis papyri include even copies of autobiographical and religious texts from Middle Kingdom tombs at Asyut, hundreds of miles to the south, and some coincide by an irony of history with the very texts selected by the early twentieth century scholar Kurt Sethe for teaching hieroglyphs.

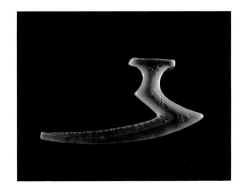

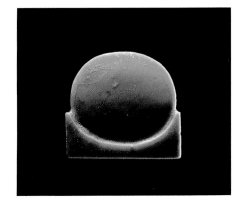

In the second century the death of Pharaonic tradition cannot have seemed particularly imminent. Temple libraries and their Houses of Life, places of copying and composing, of handing down knowledge, were producing Documents for Breathing for the Egyptian nobility at Thebes, copies and commentaries on Middle and New Kingdom monuments at Tebtynis, and some of the most complicated plays on signs and words ever devised at Esna. Yet the next century apparently produced not one innovation to maintain that momentum. Without new input the tradition dies. The loss of creativity may betray a political change. At the end of the second century AD, Lower Egypt rebelled against Roman rule, and the revolt was suppressed with customary brutality. At Tanis, the flourishing port that had been Residence for the Pharaohs of the eleventh to eighth centuries, Petrie noted destruction by burning at the late second century levels, and suggested that this was the material evidence for the end of that enigmatic Revolt of the Herdsmen. Among the ruins, one structure in particular stood out for the quantity and diversity of its finds, ranging from a stone statue inscribed for a certain Ashaikhet, to manufacture of glass and faience, to a hoard of papyri in hieroglyphic, hieratic, demotic and Greek.

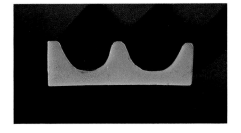

Only two of those papyrus rolls were loose enough to be unrolled, and the rest await advances in treatment, but the unrolled pair give at least a glimpse of the manuscripts in the building. One is an hieroglyphic signlist, the other a series of observations on the religious geography of Egypt, and it is possible that these belong to the sacred books of the hieroglyphic scribe, heir of the lector-priest, from the inner circle of those who could

The Meroitic pyramids take the steep angle of New Kingdom non-royal tomb-chapels, rather than the form of Old Kingdom royal pyramids, and so present a somewhat foreign appearance to us, although they derive entirely from Egyptian models.

read and write not just the daily shorthand but also the sacred signs. Although the building was too badly destroyed, the damp Lower Egyptian soil too corrosive, and the standard of recording in excavation insufficient to allow any definitive view, we might recognise in the so-called House of Ashaikhet a late repository of ancient Egyptian tradition, a House of Life if not in name then in practice. Whether the structure was destroyed in the Roman onslaught against local rebels or from more everyday causes, its death would kill with it the traditions that it upheld. The end of hieroglyphic texts may not have been so dramatic in every case, but the fate of Tanis reminds us of the pressures against the in-dependent voice of provinces in the Roman empire.

During the third century AD military tensions throughout the empire mutated into a continual bloodthirsty struggle for power. Diocletian left a firmer mark than others, with a monumental impact in Egypt as in other of his provinces. For his visit the entire temple of Luxor was transformed into a vast military complex centred on a chapel to house the cult of the emperor. That hall, where a different cult of the ruler had been celebrated by Amenhotep III in the fourteenth century BC, contains traces of fresco, well preserved up to a hundred years ago, which are often presented to visitors today as early Christian. Instead they enshrine the exact opposite to Christianity. In this hall the early Christians of Thebes would have been forced to worship the emperor or face death. The scenes over the walls represent not Christian saints, but the retinue of the persecuting emperor,

Theban temple walls bear testimony to the latest phase before conversion to Christianity, when the state no longer supported hieroglyphic workshops, but the monuments continued to provide a focus for faith. Even crudely incised Greek letters with the last pagan prayers, juxtaposed to the finest art of Pharaonic Egypt, required hours of laborious work.

from whose bloodied reign the Coptic church still reckons its years as the Age of Martyrs. In the new battle over eternal life, Pharaoh lies behind a wall of plaster, forgotten.

Distinctively Egyptian practices and products suffered active destruction and passive indifference on the part of Rome. The latest dated hieroglyphic text is inscribed on the north wall of a river gateway to the temple of Isis on the island of Philae, from 24th August AD 394, and the last known demotic texts are two graffiti carved at Philae in AD 452. This evidence is located at the southernmost boundary of Egypt, indeed slightly outside the country by the classic definition of Middle Kingdom texts, which place the border at the island of Senmut. The mainstay of the ancient script, art and religion was no longer Egyptian but foreign. By this period the Nile valley had lost its security as nomads began to use the camel instead of the donkey to cross the desert. Raids became easier, and the authorities were forced to treaty with the new land pirates of the southeastern ranges. Long after the temples had ceased to attract Egyptians, a tribe called the Blemmyes continued to venerate the goddess at Philae, keeping tradition alive after its death farther north.

Deeper in the south, the rulers of Kush had maintained the Egyptian model of kingship even after the Assyrians had expelled Taharqo and Tanutamani from Memphis and Thebes. They built pyramids for their kings and temples in Egyptian style for their gods. At the pyramids of Meroe the offering chapel walls bear some of the latest depictions of the judgment of the dead before Osiris. Yet there too the strength of tradition grew steadily weaker, partly under classical Alexandrian influence, from which evolved temples in a remarkable mixed Egyptian to Greek style. Kush itself began to fade, and its days of monumental building had already passed by the third century AD. Along the length of the Nile, the world of the Pharaohs was coming to an end.

The final blow must be reckoned the arrival of Christianity. At the same time that the Theban temple scribes were elaborating the later Documents for Breathing, and the first members of the Soter family burial were being laid to rest, a new faith landed in Alexandria, by tradition in the person of Saint Mark. At first, during the late first and second centuries AD, the Christian community in Egypt seems confined to a Greek-speaking elite in the major cities, as variant on the Jewish faith which had been present in Egypt for centuries. During the third century this aristocratic circle widens to embrace the opposite of the Hellenes, the Egyptians who spoke only Egyptian, humble townfolk and farmers excluded from power. The symbol of this spread of faith is Saint Antony, an Egyptian who withdrew to the desert on a pattern set in the Middle Kingdom, if not before, by workers escaping from national service, from being *shabti*s. Although Saint Antony is known as a first monk, the monastic tradition begins in earnest with Saint Pachom, another Egyptian, this time with an Egyptian name. Saint Pachom gathered together many of the Christians who had moved into the desert to escape Roman city life, and founded a community with strict rules inspired perhaps by the regulations for temple guilds in Ptolemaic Egypt, but probably more by the stern order of the Roman army.

The fourth century brought Christianity to Egypt as the official religion, under the emperor Constantine, but it stood on a firm popular ground. The scriptures were spread in the Egyptian language, but the early Church fathers faced a dilemma. Greek was a language for the elite, which could never reach the masses, but Egyptian had been written hitherto only with hieroglyphic signs identical with the abhorred graven images of Pharaonic art, or the offshoots of the same script, hieratic and demotic. They solved this problem by using a strategy already open to their enemies, the practitioners who spoke formulae invoking ancient deities for healing and health. Those healers had needed accurate renderings of sounds, but at the same time used numerous foreign or rare words which were always in danger of being mispronounced by the speaker, and so losing their efficacy. Therefore manuscripts with such texts were provided with occasional glosses in Greek script. The Greek alphabet lacks several of the most important consonants in the Egyptian language, but it provides vowels, and could thus supply the information missing from hieroglyphic, hieratic and demotic texts. When the Christian fathers came to adopt the Greek alphabet to translate scripture into Egyptian, they

could overlook some of the missing consonants, but needed to supply six, for which they took variants of signs from demotic, as the least pictorial, and therefore least contaminated of the pagan scripts. The resulting script is nearly identical to Greek in capital letters, like Cyrillic, another adaptation of the Greek alphabet for Christian missionaries. Church, script and this the latest phase in the history of the Egyptian language are all named Coptic, a term current in European languages since the seventeenth century and thought to derive via Arabic from the Greek word Aiguptios 'Egyptian'.

Inscriptions from the final centuries of paganism in Egypt already bear little resemblance to the sophisticated control of Pharaonic art, but Christianity added to this distance the resolute intent to avoid and destroy the past. Coptic sermons and tales of saints rail violently against pagan temples and their adherents. In their hyperbole, so often shocking to the modern reader, we witness the scars of a struggle for the soul of Egypt. Nevertheless even the diametrically opposed faith of the early fathers allows inevitably for Egyptian traits, some of which we might label Pharaonic. The hordes of demons in the Coptic hell recall the myriad shapes of the Underworld Books, but a line of direct descent is difficult to establish, because the Amduat and similar compositions had not been used in Egyptian burials since their inscription on sarcophagi of the fourth and third centuries BC, five hundred years before the conversion of the land to Christianity. Possibly any link is less direct; the hermits who withdrew to Pharaonic tombs and converted them into churches may have been influenced by the figures around them.

A Pharaonic connection seems equally slight for the origins of the monastery rules fixed by Saint Pachom. The regulations bear a certain resemblance to the laws governing temple guilds in the Ptolemaic period, but find a more solid origin in the rulebook of the Roman army. Coptic literature shows a particular talent for observing even the smallest details of the natural environment, from the ants on the ground to the figs of the sycamore tree, and this can be traced back into Pharaonic religious metaphor such as the scarab beetle, but seems more a general characteristic of life in the Nile Valley than a specific inheritance from the pagan past.

Art presents one area of possible continuity. Most often modern commentators cite the example of Isis and Horus as a precursor to the image of Madonna and Child in Christian art. At first glance the form of Mary and the infant Jesus on her lap can appear directly modelled on the ancient Egyptian bronzes and faience figurines of the goddess Isis with the child Horus in human form on her lap, and their calcite antecedent more than one and a half thousand years earlier of the queen regent and her infant Pepy II. Yet that very antecedent should warn us of the dangers of seeing direct links between the same universal image at different periods. It seems highly unlikely that many statuettes of king and mother were produced,

The obelisk at Istanbul must be one of the last to have been moved from Egypt by the Roman emperors, following a tradition that brought no fewer than thirteen to Rome itself. By the time that Constantine had founded his city, and the obelisk arrived in its hippodrome, ancient Egypt had been eclipsed by late Roman customs. The new city marks a new era in which Christianity received official status as the imperial creed, and the formal dismantling of the pagan world began.

On the fifth-century base for the obelisk (*below*), the emperor Theodosius appears with the imperial family on a balcony, receiving homage.

and less likely still that the artists of the seventh century BC workshops knew of the statuette of Pepy II from the twenty-third century BC. At the later end of the story, we would need to establish that early Christian artists producing the motif of Madonna and Child had ever seen a bronze or faience Isis and Horus. Connections need more than a similarity, or apparent similarity to the outsider, they need a direct overlap between the two worlds to be connected.

If the first creator of an image of Madonna and Child had seen and been influenced by a figure of Isis and Horus, it would not be a Twenty-sixth Dynasty or even Ptolemaic bronze or faience figurine. The objects circulating in the late Roman period would more likely be terracottas in Hellenistic style. Some of these represent the divine child Horus, already absorbing Greek, Persian and Syrian attributes, others the divine mother Isis, but their pairing would not instantly suggest early Christian models for the Christian divine mother and child. When modern research addresses the question of a link between old and new, it must open itself to the multitude of old worlds, and with that openness examine works of art which shared or at least overlapped in their lifespan. Otherwise we end with no more than a superficial connection between Egyptian Late Period bronze and European Romanesque stone statue, or, for that matter, between Old Kingdom stone statue and Late Period bronze. The image of mother and child deserves better.

We may find ourselves on safer ground when we turn to continuous traditions within Egypt, above all the textile and stone workshops. The motif of a man with hands raised in worship runs through from Pharaonic monuments to the late Roman stelae found in the Western Delta cemeteries at Kom Abu Billo, one of the richest sources for the last phase before Christian conversion. From those monuments for eternal life the traditional pose moves uninterrupted into the new faith. As with the mother and child, a suspicion remains that this position occurs so commonly among religions that it does not prove a direct link between the early Coptic world and its pagan predecessor, but at least in this instance the record in art seems continuous. At the other end of the country, in the vicinity of Edfu in southern Upper Egypt, the stone workshops produced stelae for local citizens of standing, bridging the pagan to Christian conversion. Strikingly we cannot always determine from the motifs alone whether the person for whom the stone was carved belonged to the old or the new religion. Imperceptibly, yet before our eyes, the falcon-god Horus changes into a new and indistinct form, evoking the Christian dove of peace, classical eagle of sovereign power, or even the Asiatic phoenix of resurrection.

Most obvious of Coptic debts to its detested past, the Cross itself receives the shape of the hieroglyph *ankh* 'life'. A Copt would not feel the meaning *ankh* 'life', would not hear that word at the sight of the sign, as

An early Christian tombstone from Upper Egypt expresses the motif of the Cross through the hieroglyph *ankh* 'life', surrounded by the vine of eternal life. The latter is not an ancient Egyptian symbol, nor is the inclusion of a face within the *ankh*, but the *ankh* cross clearly illustrates the union of different traditions.

would a literate ancient Egyptian. Yet the same meaning has survived as an unspoken symbol, the eternal life granted to those who believe in Jesus who died on the Cross. When we consider the debt, in turn, of European to Coptic Christianity, the *ankh*-cross provides both clues and limits to the interchange. The Book of Kells, most celebrated product of early Christian civilisation on the north European islands, preserves occasional intruding signs in the body of its Biblical text, including the *ankh*, a sign of some connection, however tenuous. Yet this exceptional instance merely reminds us that the Cross in European art does not take the form of the ancient Egyptian hieroglyph. The life of the Pharaohs and their subjects went forgotten. Throughout medieval, Renaissance and Baroque painting, depictions of the ancient court of Pharaoh, for the Biblical stories of Joseph or Moses, reproduced contemporary European and Turkish luxury.

In 1798 a revolutionary army of the young French Republic under the command of Napoleon Bonaparte disembarked on the shores of Egypt. It faced eventual military defeat, but its stay shook Ottoman Egypt from medieval recession, and the carefully amassed records and material yielded a vast harvest for European scholarship. A generation later, partly on the basis of the Rosetta Stone, the Ptolemaic stela discovered by the French, Jean-François Champollion accomplished the decisive steps in the decipherment of the hieroglyphs, a script not read since the conversion to Christianity one and a half thousand years earlier. The texts could be read again, and the art seen on its own, not European, terms. Another way of looking at, and perpetuating, the world could be restored to human memory.

Author's Note

This book has grown from an original concept by Werner Forman, whose photographs provide the focus and inspiration for the text. I am grateful to him for the opportunity to provide the accompanying text, and would like to acknowledge in addition the unstinting support of colleagues in other museums, especially Dr Dorothea Arnold of the Metropolitan Museum of Art, New York, Dr Mohamed Saleh of the Egyptian Museum, Cairo, Dr Eleni Vassilika and Dr Penelope Wilson of the Fitzwilliam Museum, Cambridge, Dr Rosalie David of the Manchester Museum, and the Egyptian department of the Louvre. I am particularly indebted to Dr Jaromír Málek for his advice and suggestions on the text. Responsibility for any errors remains of course my own.

London
September 1995   Stephen Quirke

Glossary of Names and Terms

NAMES OF GODS AND GODDESSES

Aker deity expressing the guardian power of the earth, depicted in the Pyramid Texts as a strip of land ending at each end in human heads, later as a double-headed sphinx. Aker marks the doors of the earth, and is found primarily in funerary texts providing the blessed dead with access to a perfect afterlife, and guarding the body of the creator.

Amemet female monster with crocodile head, lion forepart and hippopotamus rear, whose name is interpreted in some manuscripts as 'swallower', in others as 'swallower of the dead'. She appears only at the scene of the weighing of the heart, when the dead person was judged by the heart being weighed against an emblem of Right (Maat); if the heart contained evil, it was swallowed by Amemet, a figurative expression of damnation.

Amun a god first attested in the Old Kingdom as one of the forces before creation, the name meaning 'hiddenness'; from the 11th Dynasty Amun becomes a patron of the Theban province and its governors in their bid to become kings of Egypt. The principal shrine of Amun at Karnak became the largest religious complex in the two thousand years of expansion and embellishment from the 11th Dynasty to the Roman Period. In iconography Amun is depicted either as a male figure with long divine beard and double plume on a modius, or as a male figure with mummiform body and erect penis, identifying him as incarnation of male fertility. In the second role Amun had a separate temple at Luxor, connected with Karnak by avenues of sphinxes from the reign of Amenhotep III.

Anubis god embodying the protection of the cemeteries, and the task of embalming the dead. He is depicted as a jackal or jackal-headed man, in order to ally with the dead the animals most likely to destroy the corpse.

Aten Egyptian word meaning 'sun-disk', separated from the more abstract Ra 'sun' to focus worship on the physical icon of the sun as it crosses the sky. Aten is attested as a separate god in the 13th Dynasty, but only becomes prominent in the reign of Amenhotep III, to be adopted by his son Akhenaten as the sole godhead appropriate to royal worship; in the art of Akhenaten, the Aten is depicted as a concave disk with rays extending as arms, ending in hands which offer the king the hieroglyph *ankh* 'life'. The Aten was given two cartouches, on the model of the two cartouches for throne name and birth name of a king; unlike royal cartouches the names of the Aten enclose a consecutive text 'Ra-Horakhty (or 'the sun, Horus of the horizon'), who rejoices in the horizon, in his name as Shu who (or 'the light which') is in the Aten (or 'sun-disk')'. These names were defaced after the reign of Akhenaten when his exclusive royal sun-cult and unusual depiction of the human form were considered inappropriate to sacred contexts.

Atum god whose name means 'the All', denoting all matter before it fissioned at the moment of creation. Atum is the supreme instance of creator, and can be considered the mythically original form of Ra, the sun-god and central creator-god of Egyptian religion.

Bes god with dwarflike physiognomy and leonine face, a form first found in the Middle Kingdom with the name Aha 'the Fighter', but from the New Kingdom regularly named Bes. The grotesque features were intended to protect mother and child from the evil forces threatening their survival. Bes is present at the birth of kings and ordinary mortals alike; a female form Beset is also attested.

Geb god of the earth, in myth expressed as the son, or more concrete form, of the dry air, Shu, and as father of Osiris, Isis, Seth and Nephthys.

Hathor goddess embodying the feminine principle of creation, necessary complement to the male sun-god Ra. Hathor is goddess of sensual desire and enjoyment, embracing female beauty, music and dance. Her cult centres are more numerous than those of any goddess until the rise of the cult of Isis after the Late Period; her temples include Dendera, Cusae in Middle Egypt, Memphis, where she was Lady of the Southern Sycamore, and Iunu (Heliopolis).

Heka Egyptian word for the creative power of the sun-god, and depicted as a male figure with the long divine beard, together with two other principles of supreme godhead, Sia 'farsightedness' and Hu 'creative pronouncement'. Heka is often translated 'magic' by Egyptologists, but is central to the belief in a creator, not a marginalised social practice like European 'magic'.

Horakhty literally 'the Horus of the horizon', this is a common form of expressing the identity of Ra the sun-god, as the divine power manifest at sunrise on the horizon. The compound form Ra-Horakhty is depicted as a falcon-headed man, and the name is included in the cartouches of the Aten.

Horus god attested from the early dynastic to the Roman Period, embodiment of sovereign power and thus of kingship. As a celestial power, Horus, like Ra, is depicted as a falcon or falcon-headed man, because the falcon is the most powerful and visible of keen sighted birds. Horus is called the *ka* or sustaining spirit of each king; each king thoughout Egyptian history had as first name a Horus name written in a rectangle marking a palace enclosure, with the Horus falcon above.

Hu Egyptian word for the power of the sun-god to create by pronouncing a word and thus bringing it into being. Hu is depicted as a male figure with the long divine beard, together with two other principles of supreme godhead, Sia 'farsightedness' and Heka 'creative power'.

Isis goddess of healing power; in myth, one of the children of Geb and wife of her brother Osiris; after his murder by their other brother Seth, Isis revived Osiris by her healing powers, and conceived the child Horus; Osiris withdrew to the underworld to become king of the dead, while Isis protected Horus until he was old enough to claim the kingship from Seth. Isis is depicted as a woman wearing on her head a throne, the hieroglyphic writing of her name. Isis was considered consort of the god Min at Coptos temple, but a separate cult centre for the goddess is not known before the Ramesside Period when she was worshipped in a temple at Behbeit in the Delta; from the fourth century BC her main cult centres were the Behbeit temple and its pendant at Philae in Nubia.

Khnum god of creation in its most material aspect, depicted as a ram or ram-headed man, and sometimes described or shown fashioning the human body on a potter's wheel as a potter would form a vase out of clay. His principal cult centres were at Elephantine and Esna in Upper Egypt, Herwer near Beni Hasan in Middle Egypt, and Shenakhen near Tarkhan between the Fayum and Memphis. Khnum is attested from the Early Dynastic Period, and was one of the principal patrons of kingship in earlier times, as seen in the full name of Khufu, Khufuikhnum 'Khnum protects me'.

Maat Egyptian word for 'what is right', personified as a goddess and called 'daughter of Ra'; she is depicted as a woman with an ostrich plume upright from her headband. In the Coffin Texts she is equated with Tefnet the daughter of Ra. Maat 'Right' includes the ideas of truth, in opposition to falsehood, and divine order, in opposition to evil chaos. At the judgment of the dead, the heart of the deceased individual is weighed against a figure of Maat 'Right' or her emblem, the feather, in the 'Hall of the two goddesses Maat' (the dual expressing universality in Egypt).

Min ithyphallic god expressing the sphere of male fertility. His iconography was shared after c.2000 BC with Amun. The Min festival marked the beginning of harvest in the first month of summer. His principal cult centre was Coptos, at the Nile valley end of the desert road to the Red Sea in Upper Egypt, and he is invoked as lord of the eastern deserts.

Mut goddess depicted as a woman wearing the Double Crown, first attested in late Middle Kingdom names, and regarded from the New Kingdom onwards as the consort of Amun at Thebes. Her temple at Karnak grew into one of the largest in that complex, and, though now much destroyed, was a major focus of cult and festival in the first millennium BC. Like other goddesses, she could be considered daughter of Ra, his furious eye that was sent out to destroy rebels and needed to be pacified in cult.

Neit goddess depicted as a woman wearing a crown of the same form as the Red Crown worn by the king; her principal cult centres in later times were Sais in the Delta and Esna in Upper Egypt, and she seems to have been considered as an androgynous primeval force. Her emblem is a pair of crossed arrows, attested from the Early Dynastic Period.

Nephthys goddess depicted as a woman wearing on her head a rectangular enclosure and basket, the hieroglyphic writing of her name, in Egyptian *nebet-hut*. As sister of Osiris, Isis and Seth, and wife of Seth, she assisted Isis in mourning for, and thereby reviving, Osiris after his murder by Seth. She was therefore important in funerary texts, but there were no temples dedicated to her.

Nun the anti-matter or non-existence outside the spatial and temporal bounds of creation, expressed in text as a watery void out of which the creator emerged.

Nut goddess of the sky, in myth expressed as the daughter, or more concrete form, of moist air, Tefnet, and mother of Osiris, Isis, Seth and Nephthys. In funerary texts and on coffins Nut is depicted as a naked woman with arms outstretched in protection over the deceased like the embrace of the coffin itself.

Osiris god depicted as a man with mummiform body, wearing a White Crown with ostrich plume on each side (the *atef* crown); one of the children of Geb and Nut, murdered by his brother Seth and revived by his sister-wife Isis; their son Horus avenged his father by winning the kingship from Seth in a series of physical and legal contests. The principal cult centres of Osiris were at Abydos in Upper Egypt, and Busiris in the Delta. From the Middle Kingdom onwards the deceased man or woman was identified with Osiris in order to gain eternal life as one of the blessed dead; the judgment of the dead took place in front of Osiris.

Ptah god of creation in its physical aspect of craft, depicted as a man with mummiform body wearing a blue skull-cap; he is attested as main deity of Memphis, centre of royal craftshops, from the Early Dynastic Period to the Roman Period. There his consort was from the New Kingdom Sekhmet, and their divine child was Nefertem. As patron of craft Ptah is a principal deity at Deir el-Medina, the community of craftsmen working on the royal tomb in the Valley of the Kings in the Ramesside Period.

Ra Egyptian word meaning 'sun', identified as the principal god of creation, and depicted as a falcon or falcon-headed god wearing the solar disk. Ra produced from himself the dry and moist air, Shu and Tefnet, and withdrew from direct rule of the world after a rebellion by mankind; according to the New Kingdom myth, he first sent his eye as a furious daughter to destroy the rebels, but then had her pacified to prevent her from annihilating mankind altogether. The king acted as deputy of the sun-god on earth, was considered consubstantial with him, and merged with the sun-disk again after death.

Ruty name of a deity perhaps to be interpreted as 'the god of the two lions', and understood as a designation of the creator-god in his form as Atum immediately prior to creation, with Shu and Tefnet as the two lions or divine forces awakening within him.

Sekhmet goddess whose name means 'the mighty one', depicted as a woman with the head of a maned lioness. As the most common expression for the destructive power that could emerge from the sun-god, his 'eye', Sekhmet is the goddess of plague, in constant need of being pacified; at Memphis she is considered consort of Ptah at least from the New Kingdom.

Seshat Egyptian word for 'writing', personified as a divine force and depicted as a woman wearing on her head the horns and star with which the word is written in hieroglyphs.

Seth god in form of a fantastic animal, with forked tail, blunt curving snout, straight-topped ears, and attested from the Early Dynastic Period, when he is named Ash and Sha (perhaps variant writings of the same word). From the later Old Kingdom he appears as one of the children of Geb and Nut, murderer of his brother Osiris and assailant of the child Horus; after the triumph of Horus, Seth is appointed to defend the boat of the sun-god against the forces of evil. The central characteristic of the god is anarchy or disorder, rather than utter evil in the model of the forces ranged against divine order.

Shu Egyptian word for 'dry', used as the name of the first male emanation of the creator, the light and air filling the space between the sun-god and his creation. As god of air, Shu is as necessary to human life as a sense of what is right, and his emblem is accordingly, like Maat 'Right', the ostrich plume in which the breath of air can be seen.

Sia Egyptian word for 'farsightedness', one of three faculties needed for creation by the sun-god, the others being Hu 'pronouncement' of the creative word and Heka 'creative power'. Sia is depicted as a male figure with the long divine beard.

Sobek god depicted as a crocodile or crocodile-headed man, embodying the voraciousness and worshipped especially at dangerous points of the river where crocodiles were most prominent, such as Kom Ombo and Rizeiqat in Upper Egypt, and throughout the Fayum and northwestern Delta marshes.

Taweret goddess protecting mother and child, and depicted as a pregnant hippopotamus with leonine face and paws, and crocodile or crocodile tail down her back. Her name means 'the great one', and she may be the same goddess as Usret 'the powerful one' in the Middle Kingdom. The three animals in her form embody voraciousness as well as protective power, and another name for her is Reret 'the sow', a violently voracious omnivore capable of devouring its piglets. Yet another name for the hippopotamus goddess is Ipy, perhaps the *ipet* 'private chambers' where women and young children lived within great houses; there is a temple to the goddess as Ipy at Karnak.

Tefnet Egyptian word for 'corrosion', used to name the first female emanation of the creator, complementing Shu 'dry air'. As daughter of the creator sun-god, she is identified also as his furious eye, and as Maat 'Right'.

Thoth god of knowledge, perhaps originally god of the moon, used in calculating time; depicted either as ibis or ibis-headed man, or as a baboon. His cult centre was Khemenu (Ashmunein, Greek Hermopolis) in Middle Egypt. Although Thoth is not attested securely before the 4th Dynasty, he may be present in the Early Dynastic record where we find the ibis on a standard as a divine emblem.

Wepwawet god depicted as a jackal on a standard with an unidentified protuberance, possibly originally connected with the placenta at the birth of the king; his name means 'opener of the ways', and his emblem precedes the king, and from the Middle Kingdom Osiris, in procession from the palace or temple.

Werethekau Egyptian name meaning 'great of *heka*-power', applied to the uraeus and crowns of the king, to goddesses such as Isis, and to ritual instruments used in the Opening of the Mouth. As a separate divine form Werethekau is found in New Kingdom temple reliefs protecting the king, as an extension from the protective power of the uraeus on his brow.

EGYPTIAN AND EGYPTOLOGICAL TERMS

akh Egyptian word for '(to be) light', and by extension for the transfigured 'blessed dead' in contrast to the living and to the damned. Whereas the *ba* and *ka* may be considered different aspects of the blessed dead, *akh* denotes the various features combined as one person.

ba spirit of mobility, an aspect of both gods and the blessed dead; the *ba* of the dead is depicted from the New Kingdom as a bird with human head, the body expressing the attribute of mobility, the head expressing the human identity.

Coptic European word most probably derived from Greek Aiguptios 'Egyptian' and applied to the Christian population of Egypt, their Church, script and language (the latest phase of the ancient Egyptian language), and to the distinctive material culture and art of Christian Egypt from the fourth to ninth centuries AD.

Day Bark boat in which the sun-god crosses the sky by day.

demotic cursive script for handwriting used from c.700 BC until the fifth century AD; it is also used for stone inscriptions from the third century BC, including in trilingual decrees such as the famous Rosetta Stone, now at the British Museum.

false door solid stone panel in the shape of a door, with a central hanging rolled up to form a rounded lintel; these are set into, or form part of, the offering chapel at the point where offerings were laid on the ground for the deceased, and the door shape expresses the idea that the spirit could move from the burial chamber below through the stone wall to receive the funerary offerings.

Fields of Hetep and **Fields of Reeds** names used in the funerary texts in reference to cultivated areas in the underworld where the deceased could harvest grain and flax for his or her eternal sustenance and clothing. A diagrammatic map of the Field of Hetep occurs inside Middle Kingdom coffins, and is given again in the Book of the Dead with a text known in the modern numbering as 'chapter 110'.

hieratic cursive script derived from hieroglyphs and used for handwriting in Egypt from the Early Dynastic Period; in the Second Intermediate Period and again after c.1000 BC hieratic was used for sacred texts such as the Book of the Dead. The Greek word *hieratikos* means 'sacred', reflecting the use of the script at the time that Greeks visited Egypt in the later first millennium BC.

hieroglyphic the first and central script of Egypt from c.3100 BC until the fourth century AD, used for inscriptions on monuments, preeminently in stone, intended to outlast eternity. The two settings for such inscriptions are the temple and the tomb. Hieroglyph derives from the Greek words *hieros* 'sacred' and *gluphos* 'carved sign'.

Horus stela form of stela or standing stone attested from the Third Intermediate Period to the Ptolemaic Period, consisting of a slab of wood or stone carved with the figure of Horus as a naked child standing on crocodiles and grasping dangerous or desert animals such as the oryx and serpent. The remainder of the surface is inscribed in hieroglyphs giving incantations to secure good health. Water poured over stone examples could be collected in a basin and drunk by a patient. The image of Horus on the stelae derives from New Kingdom images on small wooden plaques inscribed with the child in profile, holding noxious creatures and named in hieroglyphs as Shed 'the saviour'.

ka spirit of sustenance, written in hieroglyphs as two outstretched arms; each dead person had a *ka*, and the ka of kingship was Horus. Each king had a 'Horus name' identifying him as incarnation of the god Horus in the palace, and in formal art this is written between the arms of the *ka*-hieroglyph upon the head of a male figure with the long divine beard, personification of the king's *ka*.

Night Bark boat in which the sun-god crosses the sky by night.

sakhu Egyptian word meaning 'texts, rituals to transform a person into an *akh*'; these 'glorifications' or transfiguration texts form a special category within the funerary literature, but the word effectively captures the central purpose of all funerary texts, to secure the status of the blessed dead for the deceased.

stela Greek word meaning a standing stone, used in Egyptology for any single stone freestanding or set into a wall with inscriptions and/or images of its own.

uraeus   image of the divine force protecting the king in the form of a rearing cobra upon the brow of the king.

NAMES OF EGYPTIAN TEXTS

Amduat   Third Intermediate Period name for manuscripts placed along with a Book of the Dead in the burial; meaning 'what is in the Underworld', it derives from the fuller 18th Dynasty title 'book of the secret chamber which is in the underworld', applied to the texts written around the walls of the burial chamber of the king. These describe and depict in three registers the journey of the sun-god through the twelve hours of night. First attested in the reign of Hatshepsut, this is the earliest of the New Kingdom royal Underworld Books.

Book of Breathing: see **Documents of Breathing**

Book of Caverns   modern name for a funerary text reserved in the New Kingdom for the king. It describes the journey of the sun-god across six sections of the night, with three parallel registers, the centre one reserved for the sun-god, the lower one describing the punishment of the damned, The text first appears in the corridor to the cenotaph of Sety I at Abydos, decorated in the reign of Merenptah; it then recurs in later New Kingdom tombs in the Valley of the Kings, with a complete version in the tomb of Ramses VI. After the New Kingdom it is found in non-royal burials on papyri and coffins.

Book of Day   modern name for an illustration of the daytime journey of the sun-god across the sky, with short texts relating to the hourly ritual recited by the king to ensure the continuing safe journey of the sun; found in the tomb of Ramses VI.

Book of the Dead   modern name for manuscripts with texts drawn from a repertoire of about 175 individual 'chapters', named by the Egyptians the 'chapters for coming forth by day'. The corpus derives from the Middle Kingdom Coffin Texts, and appears first on coffins and shrouds of the royal family in the 17th Dynasty; from the

reign of Hatshepsut until the Roman Period the Book of the Dead was included in numerous elite burials, written on papyrus rolls; in the 26th Dynasty the sequence of chapters was standardised into a series of over 150 'chapters', most with their own vignette. Individual chapters occur on other funerary equipment, such as the *shabti*, headrest amulets, heart scarab, and also on the coffins, sarcophagi and walls of burial chambers and offering chapels.

Book of Gates   modern name for a funerary text inscribed on the walls of the royal tomb from the reign of Horemheb; like the Amduat it describes the journey of the sun-god through the twelve hours of the night, but the number of names has been reduced, and a scene of judgment before Osiris added, together with a concluding scene of solar rebirth. In the 20th Dynasty the final scene appears on non-royal papyri, and after the New Kingdom this and the judgment scene are found on non-royal coffins and papyri. One of the fullest finest versions is inscribed on the sarcophagus of king Sety I.

Book of Night   modern name for an illustration of the night journey of the sun-god through the body of the sky-goddess Nut, first attested in the cenotaph of Sety I at Abydos.

Book of the Hidden Chamber see **Amduat**

Book of Outlasting Eternity   modern designation, following a reference within the text to itself, for one of the funerary compositions of the late Ptolemaic and early Roman Periods, in which earlier funerary literature is condensed and reworked to secure for the deceased safe passage through the afterlife.

Book of Two Ways   modern name for the map and accompanying texts of the passage past the obstacles of the afterlife, found principally on the floors of coffins of the early Middle Kingdom from Bersha, the cemetery of Khemenu (Ashmunein); included within the Egyptological designation 'Coffin Texts'.

Coffin Texts   modern name for funerary texts of the Middle Kingdom found preeminently on the interior walls of coffins and burial chambers; the corpus derives in part

from the Pyramid texts, and includes numerous texts included in the later corpus of funerary literature the Book of the Dead.

Documents of Breathing   ancient name for funerary compositions of the late Ptolemaic and early Roman Periods, in which earlier funerary literature is condensed and reworked to secure for the deceased safe passage through the afterlife.

Litany of Ra   modern name for a composition anciently entitled 'Book of the Adoration of Ra', with seventy-five forms of the sun-god addressed and pictured; most of these are mummiform with a wide variety of heads, and the names of the forms includes well-attested deities as well as otherwise unknown designations. The text occurs first in the tomb of Useramun, vizier of Hatshepsut, and after her reign is exclusive to the tomb of the king until the end of the New Kingdom. In the Third Intermediate Period the mummiform figures of the great god become the dominant motif of the second papyrus included in Theban burials, with the title 'Amduat', to be succeeded in the later 21st Dynasty by 'Amduat' papyri containing motifs from the other main royal funerary composition of the 18th Dynasty, the 'book of the hidden chamber which is in the underworld'.

Opening the Mouth   ancient name, originally 'Opening the Mouth and Eyes', denoting a ritual performed on statues in the Old Kingdom whereby the mouth and eyes of the finished statue was anointed and touched with special instruments to enable it to receive the spirit of the deceased at moments of offering. After the Old Kingdom it was also performed on coffins; in New Kingdom tomb-chapels, on the coffin of Butehamun of the early 21st Dynasty, and on early Roman Period papyri from Saqqara, the ritual was used as a funerary text to ensure the revival of the deceased. At Akhmim an early Roman Period demotic composition called the Book of Opening the Mouth for Breathing combined the two principal concerns of that period into a single funerary text.

Pyramid Texts   modern name for the corpus of texts inscribed in the inner chambers of late Old Kingdom pyramids; the earliest example is the pyramid of Unas. In later periods some of these texts continued to be used in ritual, and sometimes copied as funerary texts.

Bibliography

Translations in the text are by the author from the Egyptian; for literary texts see also M. Lichtheim, *Ancient Egyptian Literature* (3 vols, University of California Press, Berkeley 1973–80), and for funerary texts R. Faulkner, *The Ancient Egyptian Pyramid Texts* (Clarendon Press, Oxford 1969); id, *The Ancient Egyptian Coffin Texts* (3 vols, Aris & Phillips, Warminster 1973–78); id, *The Ancient Egyptian Book of the Dead* (ed. by C. Andrews, British Museum Publications, London 1985). No English translation is available for all royal New Kingdom underworld books, but for a general introduction see E. Hornung, *The Valley of the Kings: horizon of eternity* (transl. D. Warburton, Timken, New York 1990), and for German translations his *Ägyptische Unterweltsbücher* (Artemis, Zurich & Munich 1972).

In the following list these abbreviations are used:
LÄ – *Lexikon der Ägyptologie* (7 vols, ed. by W. Westendorf & W. Helck, Harrassowitz, Wiesbaden 1972–92)
BD – Book of the Dead, OK – Old Kingdom, MK – Middle Kingdom, NK – New Kingdom, LP – Late Period

Chapter One
sakhu: J. Assmann, in *LÄ* V, 998–1006
creation texts: J. Allen, *Genesis in Egypt, The philosophy of ancient Egyptian creation accounts* (Yale Egyptological Studies 2, New Haven 1988)
Egyptian encyclopaedic wordlists: A. H. Gardiner, *Ancient Egyptian Onomastica* (3 vols, Oxford University Press, 1947) in the light of M. Foucault, *Les mots et les choses, une archéologie des sciences humaines* (Gallimard, Paris 1966)
antecedents of hieroglyphs: W. S. Arnett, *The predynastic origin of Egyptian hieroglyphs* (University Press of America, Washington 1982)
earliest hieroglyphs: paper by G. Dreyer at British Museum 1993 colloquium on predynastic and early dynastic Egypt, publication forthcoming
Egyptian scripts: W. V. Davies, *Egyptian Hieroglyphs* (British Museum Publications, London 1987)
literacy: A. Bowman and G. Woolf (eds.), *Literacy and Power in the ancient world* (Cambridge University Press, 1994)
writing equipment: W. J. Tait, 'Rush and reed: the pens of Egyptian and Greek scribes', in *Proceedings of the 17th International Congress of Papyrology*, vol. II (Athens 1988), 477–81
Amenhotep son of Hapu statue: L. Berman, in A. Kozloff *et al.*, *Egypt's Dazzling Sun. Amenhotep III and his world* (Cleveland Museum of Art, 1992), 252–52
Egyptian formal art: G. Robins, *Proportion and Style in Ancient Egyptian Art* (Thames and Hudson, London 1994)
heka: R. Ritner, *The Mechanics of Ancient Egyptian Magical Practice* (Studies in Ancient Oriental Civilizations 54, Chicago 1993)
Werethekau/Tutankhamun pendant: M. Eaton-Krauss and E. Graefe, *The Small Golden Shrine from the tomb of Tutankhamun* (Griffith Institute, Oxford 1985), 6–7, pl. 6–7; N. Reeves, *The Complete Tutankhamun* (Thames & Hudson, London 1990), 140–41
Djedher statue: E. Jelinkova-Reymond, *Les inscriptions de la statue guerrisseuse de Djed-Her-le-sauveur* (Institut Français d'Archéologie Orientale du Caire, Bibliothèque d'Etude 23, Cairo 1956)
Auibra Hor statue: J. de Morgan, *Fouilles à Dahchour mars-juin 1894* (Adolphe Holzhausen, Vienna 1895), 91–3, pl. 33–5
ka: P. Kaplony, *LÄ* III, 275–82
ba: L. Žabkar, *A study of the ba concept in ancient Egyptian texts* (Studies in Ancient Oriental Civilization 34, Chicago 1968)

Opening the Mouth: E. Otto, *Das ägyptische Mundöffnungsritual* (2 vols, Ägyptologische Abhandlungen 3, Harrassowitz, Wiesbaden 1960)

Chapter Two
cult of the dead and tomb-chapels: A. J. Spencer, *Death in Ancient Egypt* (Penguin, Harmondsworth 1982)
pyramid development: A. J. Spencer, *Early Egypt* (British Museum Press, London 1993)
Huni and Sneferu: paper by S. Seidlmayer at British Museum 1993 colloquium on predynastic and early dynastic Egypt, publication forthcoming
OK pyramid estates: H. Jacquet-Gordon, *Les noms des domaines funéraires sous l'Ancien Empire égyptien* (Institut Français d'Archéologie Orientale du Caire, Bibliothèque d'Etude 34, Cairo 1962)
Abusir papyri: P. Posener-Kriéger and J-L. de Cenival, *Hieratic Papyri in the British Museum. Fifth series. The Abu Sir Papyri* (Oxford University Press for the British Museum, London 1968)
Pyramid Text sequence: J. Osing, 'Zur Disposition der Pyramidentexte des Unas', in *Mitteilungen des Deutschen Archäologischen Instituts Abteilung Kairo* 42 (1986), 131–44
Medunefer shroud: M. Valloggia, *Balat I. Le mastaba de Medou-nefer* (Fouilles de l'Institut Français d'Archéologie Orientale du Caire 31, Cairo 1986), 74–8
Ankhenmeryra PT on Berlin 7730: *Aegyptische Inschriften aus den königlichen Museen zu Berlin* I (J. C. Hinrichs, Leipzig 1913), 3 late OK coffins and tomb-chambers: G. Lapp, *Typologie der Särge und Sargkammern von der 6. bis 13. Dynastie* (Studien zur Archäologie und Geschichte Altägyptens 7, Heidelberger Orientverlag, Heidelberg 1993)
late OK wish to reach sky, non-royal monument: Saqqara burial chamber of Khabaukhnum, published G. Jéquier, *Fouilles à Saqqarah. Le monument funéraire de Pepi II* III (Institut Français d'Archéologie Orientale du Caire, Cairo 1940), 64

Chapter Three
Meketra models: H. Winlock, *Models of Daily Life in Ancient Egypt from the tomb of Meket-Re at Thebes* (Metropolitan Museum of Art, New York 1955)
early MK coffins: H. Willems, *Chests of Life* (Ex Oriente Lux, Leiden 1988)
Lisht coffins and mayor Amenemhat coffin: respective papers of J. Allen and J. Assmann at the Leiden 1993 Coffin Texts colloquium, publication forthcoming
general coffin typology: J. Taylor, *Egyptian Coffins* (Shire Publications, Aylesbury 1989)
pyramidion text: H. Willems, *Chests of Life* (Ex Oriente Lux, Leiden 1988), 168–69
Book of Two Ways: text, Lesko, *The Ancient Egyptian Book of Two Ways* (University of California Press, Berkeley 1977); vignettes, E. Hermsen, *Die zwei Wege des Jenseits. Das altägyptische Zweiwegebuch und seine Topographie* (Orbis Biblicus et Orientalis 112, Universitätsverlag Freiburg and Vandenhoeck & Ruprecht, Göttingen 1991)
early shabtis: H. Schneider, *Shabtis* (3 vols., Rijksmuseum van Oudheden, Leiden 1977) I, 32–68
end of great provincial governor tomb-chapels: D. Franke, 'The career of Khnumhotep III of Beni Hasan and the so-called "decline of the monarchs"', in S. Quirke (ed.), *Middle Kingdom Studies* (SIA, New Malden 1991), 51–67
Elkab tomb-chapel scene of nurses: photograph in D. Wildung,

Sesostris und Amenemhet. Ägypten im Mittleren Reich (Hirmer, Munich 1984) 95

Haraga tomb 72 with three fish pendants: R. Engelbach, *Harageh* (British School of Archaeology in Egypt, London 1923), 14–15

late MK burials: J. Bourriau, 'Patterns of change in burial customs during the Middle Kingdom', in S. Quirke (ed.), *Middle Kingdom Studies* (SIA, New Malden 1991), 3–20

Lahun mask: W. M. F. Petrie, *Kahun, Gurob and Hawara* (Kegan Paul, Trench, Trübner, and Co., London 1890) 30, pl. 8

late MK papyri from beneath the Ramesseum: tomb and objects, J. Quibell, *The Ramesseum* (Bernard Quaritch, London 1898), 3 and pl. III; papyri, A. H. Gardiner, *The Ramesseum Papyri* (Griffith Institute, Oxford 1955)

Chapter Four

NK BD: I. Munro, *Untersuchungen zu den Totenbuch-Papyri der 18. Dynastie* (Kegan Paul International, London 1988)

general introduction to BD: J-L. de Cenival, *Le livre pour sortir le jour. Le livre des morts des anciens égyptiens* (Musée d'Aquitaine & Réunion des Musées Nationaux 1992)

17th and early 18th Dynasty royal family BD texts: R. Parkinson and S. Quirke, 'The coffin of prince Herunefer and the early history of the *Book of the Dead*', in A. Lloyd (ed.), *Studies in Egyptian Society presented to J. Gwyn-Griffiths* (Egypt Exploration Society, London 1993), 37–51

Hatshepsut: G. Robins, *Women in Ancient Egypt* (British Museum Press, London 1993), 45–52; A. Roberts, *Hathor Rising* (Northgate Publishers, Totnes 1995), 118–28

Senenmut tombs: P. Dorman, *The Tombs of Senenmut. The architecture and decoration of Tombs 71 and 353* (Metropolitan Museum of Art Egyptian Expedition, New York 1991)

Amun, Ra and Aten: J. Assmann, *Egyptian Solar Religion in the New Kingdom. Re, Amun and the crisis of polytheism* (transl. A. Alcock, Kegan Paul International, London and New York 1995)

tomb of Akhenaten: G. T. Martin, *The Royal Tomb at El 'Amarna* I (Egypt Exploration Society, London 1974), II (Egypt Exploration Society, London 1989)

text of Amenhotep II papyrus: A. Piankoff, *The Wandering of the Soul* (Bollingen Series XL.6, Princeton University Press, 1974), 40–114

NK royal sarcophagi: W. Hayes, *Royal sarcophagi of the XVIII Dynasty* (Princeton University Press, 1933)

Tjanefer texts: K. Seele, *The Tomb of Tjanefer at Thebes* (University of Chicago Oriental Institute Publications 86, Chicago 1959), pl. 31–8

Chapter Five

end of NK: K. Jansen-Winkeln, 'Das Ende des Neuen Reiches', in *Zeitschrift für Ägyptische Sprache und Altertumskunde* 119 (1992) 22–37

royal mummies caches: K. Jansen-Winkeln, 'Die Plünderung der Königsgräber des Neuen Reiches', in *Zeitschrift für Ägyptische Sprache und Altertumskunde* 122 (1995) 62–78, and C. N. Reeves, *Valley of the Kings. The decline of a royal necropolis* (Kegan Paul International, London 1990)

Third Intermediate Period funerary manuscripts: A. Niwiński, *Studies on the illustrated Theban funerary papyri of the 11th and 10th centuries B.C.* (Orbis Biblicus et Orientalis 86, Universitätsverlag Freiburg and Vandenhoeck & Ruprecht, Göttingen 1989)

Shaq cylinders: published J. Ray, 'Two objects in the Fitzwilliam Museum. B. An oracular amuletic decree case', in *Journal of Egyptian Archaeology* 58 (1972) 251–53, pl. 43.2, and J. Ray and J. Bourriau, 'Two further decree-cases of Shaq', in *Journal of Egyptian Archaeology* 61 (1975) 257–8, pl. 29

Twenty-second Dynasty royal funerary texts: kings, P. Montet, *La Nécropole Royale de Tanis* I (Paris 1947), pl. 24–45 (Osorkon II), III (Paris 1960), pl. 29–42 (Sheshonq III); princely Memphite high priest, A. Badawi 'Das Grab des Kronprinzen Scheschonk, Sohnes Osorkon's II. und Hohenpriester von Memphis', in *Annales du Service des Antiquités de l'Egypte* 54 (1956–7) 153–177 with 16 pl.

mid-Twenty-second Dynasty civil war: R. Caminos, *The Chronicle of Prince Osorkon* (Analecta Orientalia 37, Pontificium Institutum Biblicum, Rome 1958)

earliest coffins with LP BD: H. Gauthier, *Catalogue Général des Antiquités Egyptiennes du musée du Caire. Nos. 41042–41072. Cercueils anthropoïdes des prêtres de Montou. I* (Institut Français d'Archéologie Orientale du Caire, Cairo 1913), e.g. 95 (CG 41046, Wennefer), early seventh century

god's wife of Amun: G. Robins, *Women in Ancient Egypt* (British Museum Press, London 1993), 149–56

stone Harwa shabtis: H. Schneider, *Shabtis* (3 vols., Rijksmuseum van Oudheden, Leiden 1977) I, 225–26, 234

LP temple-tombs: Eigner, *Die monumentalen Grabbauten der Spätzeit in der thebanischen Nekropole* (Österreichische Akademie der Wissenschaften, Vienna 1984)

Padiamenipet texts: A. Piankoff, 'Les grandes compositions religieuses dans la tombe de Pédéménope', in *Bulletin de l'Institut Français d'Archéologie Orientale du Caire* 46 (1947) 73–92

stela of Nitiqret: R. Caminos, 'The Nitocris adoption stela', in *Journal of Egyptian Archaeology* 50 (1964) 71–101, pl. 7

Tanis discovery of BD 162–165: J. Yoyotte, 'Contribution à l'histoire du chapitre 162 du Livre des Morts', in *RdE* 29 (1977), 194–202

LP BD sequence: P. Barguet, *Le Livre des Morts des anciens égyptiens* (Editions du Cerf, Paris 1967)

D26 BD papyri: U. Verhoeven, *Das Saitische Totenbuch der Iahtesnacht P.Colon.Aeg.10207* (Dr Rudolf Habert GMBH, Bonn 1993) I, 41–2

earliest LP BD vignettes: coffins Cairo CG 41004 (Ankhefenkhons), 41009 (Tabetjet) of mid-7th century, published A. Moret, *Catalogue Général des Antiquités Egyptiennes du musée du Caire. Nos. 41001–41041. Sarcophages de l'Epoque Bubastite à l'Epoque Saïte* (Institut Français d'Archéologie Orientale du Caire, Cairo 1913), pl. 12 and 17

LP Saqqara tombs: E. Bresciani *et al.*, *Tomba di Bakenrenef (L.24). Attività del Cantiere Scuola 1985–1987* (Giardini, Pisa 1988); E. Bresciani *et al.*, *La Tomba di Ciennehebu, capo della flotta del Re* (Giardini, Pisa 1977)

Persian Period inscriptions: G. Posener, *La Première Domination Perse en Egypte. Recueil d'inscriptions hiéroglyphiques* (Institut Français d'Archéologie Orientale du Caire, Bibliothèque d'Etude 11, Cairo 1936)

fourth to third century BC burials: in Saqqara tomb of Bakenrenef, E. Bresciani *et al.*, *Saqqara I. Tomba di Boccori. La Galleria di Padineit, visir di Nectanebo I* (Giardini, Pisa 1980); in Theban tomb of Ankhhor, M. Bietak and E. Reiser-Haslauer, *Das Grab des 'Anch-Hor, Obersthofmeister der Gottesgemahlin Nitokris* II (Österreichische Akademie der Wissenschaften, Vienna 1982)

Osiris library texts: J. Assmann, Egyptian mortuary liturgies', in S. Groll (ed.), *Studies in Egyptology presented to Miriam Lichtheim* (Magnes Press, Jerusalem 1990), I, 1–45

Ptolemaic Egypt: A. Bowman, *Egypt after the Pharaohs 332 BC–AD 642: from Alexander to the Arab conquest* (British Museum Publications, London 1986)

trilingual decrees: C. Andrews and S. Quirke, *The Rosetta Stone facsimile drawing* (British Museum Publications, London 1988)

Chapter Six

Memphite area papyrus with Opening the Mouth: W. Golénischeff, *Catalogue Général des Antiquités Egyptiennes du musée du Caire. Nos. 58001–58036. Papyrus hiératiques. I* (Institut Français d'Archéologie Orientale du Caire, Cairo 1927), 231–68, pl. 36–9 (CG 58036, from Abusir el-Meleq)

latest funerary texts: J-C. Goyon, *Rituels funéraires de l'ancienne*

Egypte (Editions du Cerf, Paris 1972); F-R. Herbin, *Le livre de parcourir l'éternité* (Orientalia Lovaniensia Analecta 58, Leuven 1994)

pigment change: E. Delange *et al.*, 'Apparition de l'encre métallo-gallique en Egypte à partir de la collection de papyrus du Louvre', in *Revue d'Egyptologie* 41 (1990) 213–17

Soter family burial: L. Kákosy, 'The Soter tomb in Thebes', in S. Vleeming (ed.), *Hundred-Gated Thebes* (E. J. Brill, Leiden 1995), 61–7

Akhmim papyri: M. Smith, *Catalogue of Demotic Papyri in the British Museum* III *The Mortuary Texts of Papyrus BM 10507* (British Museum Publications, London 1987); *id., The Liturgy of Opening the Mouth for Breathing* (Griffith Institute, Oxford 1993)

range of Tebtynis papyri: W. J. Tait, *Papyri from Tebtunis in Egyptian and Greek* (Egypt Exploration Society, London 1977)

Tanis papyri: house of Ashaikhet, W. M. F. Petrie, *Tanis* I (Egypt Exploration Fund, London 1885), 41–50; the papyri, F. Ll. Griffith and W. M. F. Petrie, *Two Hieroglyphical Papyri from Tanis* (Egypt Exploration Fund, London 1889)

Diocletian at Luxor: 19th century copy of fresco (now mainly destroyed), in A. Bowman, *Egypt after the Pharaohs 332 BC–AD 642: from Alexander to the Arab conquest* (British Museum Publications, London 1986) 54–55

last hieroglyphic text: D. Devauchelle, '24 aout 394–24 aout 1994, 1600 ans', in *Bulletin de la Société Française d'Egyptologie* 131 (October 1994) 16–8

Philae and Blemmyes: E. Winter, in *LÄ* IV, 1026 with n.28 on 1027

Meroe: J. Taylor, *Egypt and Nubia* (British Museum Press, London 1991); S. Wenig, in *LÄ* IV, 98–101

early monasticism: A. Guillaumont, in A. Atiya (ed.), *The Coptic Encyclopaedia* 5 (Macmillan, New York 1991), 1661–4

Coptic script: R. Kasser, 'Alphabets, Coptic', in A. Atiya (ed.), *The Coptic Encyclopaedia* Appendix (Macmillan, New York 1991), 32–41

Kom Abu Billo stelae: F. Hooper, *Funerary Stelae from Kom Abou Billou* (Kelsey Museum of Archaeology Studies 1, Ann Arbor 1961)

Acknowledgments

Acknowledgment is made to the following institutions and individuals for permission to reproduce illustrations on the pages indicated:

Ägyptisches Museum, Berlin 17, 100, 102T

Ashmolean Museum, Oxford 12, 14

British Museum 15, 68, 104L

Brooklyn Museum, New York 126

Christies, London 1, 65, 109, 169–171, 173

Egyptian Museum, Cairo 8, 13B, 16, 18, 22, 25, 29, 32, 37, 43, 47–9, 52, 53, 59, 73, 90, 94, 98, 127, 139, 159–164

Fitzwilliam Museum, Cambridge 107

L'Ibis, New York 166, 168

John Kluge Collection, Virginia 150, 151

Luxor Museum 125, 129

Manchester Museum 106, 108

Metropolitan Museum of Art, New York 10, 20, 33, 36, 66, 71, 76–87, 93, 96, 97, 101, 103T, 112, 124, 130, 131, 136, 141–4, 155, 157R, 179

Musée du Louvre, Paris 2, 26, 28, 102B, 119, 122, 123

Museo Egizio, Turin 9, 147

McAlpine Collection, London 19, 103B

Ny Carlsberg Glyptotek, Copenhagen 42, 89

Collection of George Ortiz, Vandoeuvres 74, 75, 88

Otago Museum, Dunedin, New Zealand 13T

Royal Museum of Scotland, Edinburgh 104R

Norbert Schimmel Collection, New York 148, 149

Schultz Collection, New York 6

Sir John Soane's Museum, London 132, 133

Chronological Table

including names of kings mentioned in the text

PREDYNASTIC
c.4500–3100 BC

EARLY DYNASTIC
First Dynasty
c.3100–2890 BC
Second Dynasty
c.2890–2686 BC
Third Dynasty
c.2686–2613 BC
Netjerkhet (Djoser)
Sekhemkhet

OLD KINGDOM
Fourth Dynasty
c.2613–2494 BC
Huni
Sneferu
Khufu
Radjedef
Khafra
Menkaura
Fifth Dynasty
c.2494–2345 BC
Sahura
Neferirkara
Niuserra
Isesi
Unas
Sixth Dynasty
c.2345–2181 BC
Teti
Userkara (?)
Meryra Pepy I
Merenra
Neferkara Pepy II
Seventh Dynasty
'seventy kings in seventy days'
(later historiographical device
to mark the end of the Old
Kingdom)
Eighth Dynasty
c.2181–2125 BC
Ibi

FIRST INTERMEDIATE
PERIOD
c.2125–2025 BC
Ninth *and* **Tenth**
Dynasties *in northern Egypt,*
Eleventh Dynasty *in*
southern Egypt

MIDDLE KINGDOM
Eleventh Dynasty *(all*
Egypt) c.2025–1985 BC
Nebhepetra Mentuhotep
    2055–2004
Twelfth Dynasty
c.1985–1795 BC
Amenemhat I   1985–1955
Senusret I   1965–1920
Amenemhat II   1922–1878
Senusret II   1880–1874
Senusret III   1874–1855
Amenemhat III   1855–1808
Amenemhat IV   1808–1799
Sobekneferu   1799–1795
Thirteenth Dynasty
(all Egypt) c.1795–1700 BC
Auibra Hor   c.1775

SECOND INTER-
MEDIATE PERIOD
c.1700–1550 BC
early phase   c.1700–1650
Thirteenth Dynasty *over*
all Egypt except **Fourteenth**
Dynasty *in eastern Delta*
late phase   c.1650–1550
Fifteenth *and* **Sixteenth**
Dynasties *in northern Egypt,*
Seventeenth Dynasty *in*
southern Egypt
Sobekemsaf II   c.1600
Seqenenra Taa   c.1560
Kames   c.1555–50

NEW KINGDOM
Eighteenth Dynasty
c.1550–1295 BC
Ahmes   1550–1526
Amenhotep I   1526–1506
Thutmose I   1506–1493
Thutmose II   1493–1479
Thutmose III   1479–1425
Hatshepsut   1478–1458
Amenhotep II   1425–1401
Thutmose IV   1401–1390
Amenhotep III   1390–1352
Amenhotep IV   1352–1348
= Akhenaten   1348–1338
Tutankhamun   1336–1327
Ay   1327–1323
Horemheb   1323–1295

Nineteenth Dynasty
c.1295–1186 BC
Ramses   1295–1294
Sety I   1294–1279
Ramses II   1279–1212
Merenptah   1212–1202
Tausret   1196–1188
Twentieth Dynasty
c.1186–1069 BC
Ramses III   1184–1154
Ramses IV   1154–1148
Ramses VI   1144–1136
Ramses IX   1125–1107
Ramses XI   1098–1069

THIRD INTER-
MEDIATE PERIOD
Twenty-first Dynasty
c.1069–945 BC
kings at Tanis
Nesbanebdjed (Smendes)
    1069–1043
Amunemipet   1043–1039
Pasebakhenniut
(Psusennes) I   1039–993
generals and high priests of
Amun at Thebes
Heryhor   c.1069
Menkheperra   1045–992
Twenty-second Dynasty
c.945–715 BC
Sheshonq I   945–924
Osorkon I   924–889
Osorkon II   874–850
Sheshonq III   825–773
Twenty-third Dynasty
c.818–715 BC
Twenty-fourth Dynasty
c.727–715 BC
Tefnakht   727–715

LATE PERIOD
c.715–332 BC
Twenty-fifth Dynasty
c.715–664 BC
kings of Kush ruling Egypt
Shabako   715–702
Shabatko   702–690
Taharqo   690–664
Tanutamani   664–656

Twenty-sixth Dynasty
664–525 BC
Psamtek I   664–610
Psamtek III   526–525
Twenty-seventh Dynasty
525–404 BC
Egypt part of Persian empire
Cambyses   525–522
Darius I   522–486
Xerxes I   486–465
Twenty-eighth Dynasty
404–399 BC
Amyrtaios   404–399
Twenty-ninth Dynasty
399–380 BC
Thirtieth Dynasty
380–343 BC
Nakhtnebef
    (Nectanebo I)   380–362
Nakhthorhebyt
    (Nectanebo II)   360–343
Second Persian
Occupation
343–332 BC

GREEK ADMINISTRA-
TION OF EGYPT
(Hellenistic and Roman
Periods)
Macedonian Period
332–305 BC
Alexander the Great 332–323
Ptolemaic Period
305–30 BC
Ptolemy I   305–282
Ptolemy IV   222–205
Ptolemy V   205–180
Cleopatra VII   51–30
Roman Period
30 BC–AD 330
Byzantine Period
AD 330–641

ISLAMIC PERIOD
after AD 641

The **Coptic Period** covers
the fourth to eighth
centuries AD when early
Christian art has its own
distinctive form in Egypt

Map of Ancient Egypt

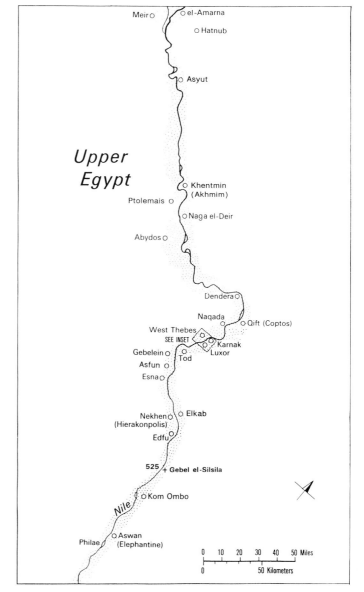

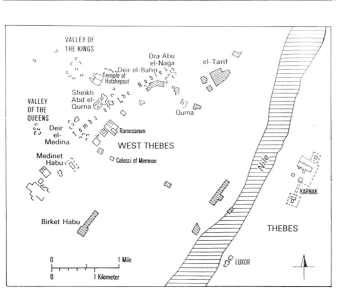

Index